Bernard Shaw and Totalitarianism

Bernard Shaw and Totalitarianism
Longing for Utopia

Matthew Yde

© Matthew Yde 2013

All rights reserved. No reproduction, copy or transmission of this publication may be made without written permission.

No portion of this publication may be reproduced, copied or transmitted save with written permission or in accordance with the provisions of the Copyright, Designs and Patents Act 1988, or under the terms of any licence permitting limited copying issued by the Copyright Licensing Agency, Saffron House, 6–10 Kirby Street, London EC1N 8TS.

Any person who does any unauthorized act in relation to this publication may be liable to criminal prosecution and civil claims for damages.

The author has asserted his right to be identified as the author of this work in accordance with the Copyright, Designs and Patents Act 1988.

First published 2013 by
PALGRAVE MACMILLAN

Palgrave Macmillan in the UK is an imprint of Macmillan Publishers Limited, registered in England, company number 785998, of Houndmills, Basingstoke, Hampshire RG21 6XS.

Palgrave Macmillan in the US is a division of St Martin's Press LLC, 175 Fifth Avenue, New York, NY 10010.

Palgrave Macmillan is the global academic imprint of the above companies and has companies and representatives throughout the world.

Palgrave® and Macmillan® are registered trademarks in the United States, the United Kingdom, Europe and other countries.

ISBN 978–1–137–330192

This book is printed on paper suitable for recycling and made from fully managed and sustained forest sources. Logging, pulping and manufacturing processes are expected to conform to the environmental regulations of the country of origin.

A catalogue record for this book is available from the British Library.

A catalog record for this book is available from the Library of Congress.

Dedicated to Jacqulyn Yde
1935–2009

"Blessed *are* they which do hunger and thirst after righteousness: for they shall be filled"

Contents

Acknowledgments	viii
Introduction: George Bernard Shaw: Revolutionary Playwright	1
1 Previsions of the Superman in the Coming Age of Will: *The Quintessence of Ibsenism*	25
2 Utopia in Flames: Shaw and Wagner's *Ring: The Perfect Wagnerite*	46
3 From Hell to Heaven: Creative Evolution and the Drive toward the Military-Industrial-Religious Complex: *Man and Superman, John Bull's Other Island, Major Barbara*	66
4 Shaw's Modern Utopia: *Back to Methuselah*	111
5 Shaw's Totalitarian Drama of the Thirties; or, Shaw and the Dictators: *Geneva, The Millionairess, The Simpleton of the Unexpected Isles*	143
6 George Bernard Shaw 1856–1950, Utopian to the End: *Farfetched Fables*	185
Epilogue	201
Notes	208
Bibliography	228
Index	236

Acknowledgments

Parts of this book were presented, in modified form, as papers at various conferences and symposia around the world, and I would like to thank the organizers and participants for allowing me to present my work and for generously sharing their insightful comments. Particular thanks must be extended to Penny Farfan and Julia Walker for organizing a seminar on "Troubling Modernism" at the American Society for Theatre Research conference in Seattle. Both Penny and Julia have been great friends and mentors since I first met them at The Ohio State University Department of Theatre's symposium on Sophie Treadwell, where they were keynote speakers. An expression of gratitude is also due to Tony Stafford, who never failed to invite me to present my work at the Comparative Drama Conference. I would also like to thank Lawrence Switzky for organizing a Modern Language Association session on Shaw's later plays. Larry has been very encouraging ever since I met him in Washington DC at my very first Shaw conference.

I am especially grateful to all the members of the International Shaw Society (ISS) for their continued support and friendship. The ISS has been most generous, allowing me to travel and present my work at their conferences and symposia; without their assistance I would simply not have been able to attend the many wonderful scholarly events that they have organized. I have met many gifted scholars at these events whom I now consider friends. The kindness and largess of Jay Tunney and Charles and Roelina Berst is most humbly acknowledged. Among the ISS, I would be remiss if I did not single out Leonard Conolly for his gracious encouragement and assistance over the years, Brad Kent for his enlightened mentorship, Ellen Dolgin and Charles Del Dotto for their friendship and unflagging enthusiasm for my work, and Richard Dietrich for his indefatigable leadership within the ISS.

I owe a big debt of gratitude to Lesley Ferris, Richard Dutton, and Beth Kattelman: their sensitive reading, valuable suggestions, and continued encouragement and support are greatly appreciated. I also want to thank Thomas Postlewait and Simon Williams for reading my prospectus and recommending me for a Presidential Fellowship; without that generous award I cannot imagine how I would have finished this daunting project as expeditiously as I did. Tom has been a continual source of encouragement and support, and for that I am very grateful. A big thank you is also due to Sebastian Knowles, who took time away from his very busy schedule to read a very long chapter; his support and excellent suggestions are greatly appreciated. Likewise, Leo Cabranes-Grant read a chapter and sent me very thoughtful, detailed suggestions. Thank you, Leo. A debt of gratitude is also owed to Tracy Davis, who assuaged any lingering doubts I had about writing a book on such a towering and canonical figure as Shaw. My vacillating was immediately dissolved when she confirmed what I already suspected, declaring emphatically that Shaw's relationship to totalitarianism was an "under researched" topic.

There are too many Ohio State students and colleagues to thank individually, but it has been my privilege to be ensconced within an encouraging and intellectually stimulating environment. But a special thank you is due to Pamela Decker, who read an early version of the manuscript. Her insightful comments, and her many instances of generosity, assistance, and support along the way, are greatly appreciated. Jennifer Schlueter also deserves thanks for her kindness in patiently answering my many queries. I want also to pay tribute to The Ohio State University Graduate School for awarding me the Presidential Fellowship and The Ohio State University College of Arts and Sciences for awarding me a Post-Prospectus Fellowship. Both awards made the research and writing of this book possible, and for that I am truly grateful. The Ohio State University Theatre Department also provided valuable financial assistance: thanks to the munificence of the department I was able to attend a great many conferences and symposia, and I am especially grateful for the generous grant that enabled me to attend the International Federation for Theatre Research conference in Munich, Germany.

I also wish to acknowledge the University of Toronto Press. A section of Chapter 5 first appeared in a slightly different form as "Bernard Shaw's Stalinist Allegory: *The Simpleton of the Unexpected Isles*" in *Modern Drama*. The article is reprinted with permission from University of Toronto Press (© 2013 University of Toronto). I wish to thank especially *Modern Drama*'s editor Alan Ackerman and his excellent copy-editor Rosemary Clark-Beattie. Alan is a superb editor and an encouraging critic, and Rosemary is appreciated not only for her superlative copy-editing but also for the very kind words she shared with me about the article. I would likewise like to acknowledge the Penn State University Press for allowing me to reprint my article, "Building the New City of God: Shaw's Provisional Supermen," which originally appeared in *SHAW: The*

Annual of Bernard Shaw Studies. This article also appears, in modified form, in Chapter 5. A particular thank you must be extended to Michel Pharand, editor of the *SHAW*, and Desmond Harding, special editor of *SHAW 32*. Michel has been very encouraging over the years that I have known him and Desmond did a fantastic job editing that special issue. I also wish to thank Palgrave Macmillan's stalwart editor Paula Kennedy and her able assistant Sacha Lake and in fact everyone at Palgrave Macmillan who worked on this book; and I am especially grateful to the insightful criticism and encouragement I received from the anonymous reader at Palgrave Macmillan. His/her excellent suggestions did much to improve the book. I am also beholden to Devasena Vedamurthi at Integra Software for her great patience, and for the meticulous care she took typesetting the book.

I would be terribly remiss if I did not thank my dad, who has been a bulwark of support throughout my life. Lastly, the writing of this book began a little over two months after my mom passed away; that loss, but also her inspiration, was deeply felt always, and to her the work is dedicated.

Introduction

George Bernard Shaw: Revolutionary Playwright

In July 1931 George Bernard Shaw embarked on his first and only trip to the Soviet Union. He had been a champion of this new experiment in political and economic organization from the outset, but had refrained from visiting because he wanted to give the experiment time to develop before he offered his first-hand observations. By 1931 Lenin's New Economic Policy had been succeeded by Stalin's First Five Year Plan of crash industrialization and agricultural collectivization, and Shaw felt that the time was finally right to make a visit. Soon after their arrival in Russia, Shaw and Lady Astor, one of his traveling companions (and like Shaw something of a celebrity), received cablegrams from an exiled Russian professor of civil engineering at Yale University, Dmitry Krynin. Worried for his family, the exiled scholar implored the two eminent visitors "in the name of humanitarian principles, please help my wife in Moscow." Shaw remained silent, but Lady Astor went down on her knees importuning her host Maxim Litvinov to come to the aid of this man and his destitute family. The obviously embarrassed Litvinov simply remarked that he was unable to help, and walked away. But Lady Astor would not let the matter rest, and was soon at the central office of the GPU or Soviet secret police, Shaw and Viscount Astor in tow, pleading with them to help the distressed family. After the visitors had returned to England it was discovered that Mrs. Krynin's apartment was "occupied by a new tenant. The Krynin family had 'disappeared.'"[1]

I begin my introduction with this brief anecdote because it gives a picture of Shaw, the "revolutionary writer," in his own words (vol. 1, 336),[2] in the country where his utopian aspirations were finally being pursued, and shows him face to face with the reality of utopian political formation and its central humanitarian problem, the "disappearance" of invidious social elements—that is, human beings not appropriately conforming to the standards set by the state. Although Shaw was surely proud of his dramatic talent and of his achievements as a famous playwright, he viewed himself principally as a political revolutionary and considered his art to be in the service of his political goals. The totalitarian regimes that sprouted up in the 1920s and 1930s, especially in the Soviet Union, seemed to him to decisively signal the end of the anarchical, wasteful, and disorderly capitalist system that so appalled him, and to whose eradication he had dedicated his life. Shaw came of age during the British Socialist Revival of the 1880s, when many artists and intellectuals believed that socialism would soon put an end to the poverty and squalor that was the apparent by-product of industrial capitalism. Shaw was a part of this movement, and it gave meaning and purpose to his life.

His chaotic early years predisposed him to hope for the eventual formation of a centrally organized, hierarchical political system ruled by benevolent philosopher-statesmen. Shaw's father was dipsomaniacal and of infirm will, and "Sonny," as George was called, was never disciplined as a child. As it turned out Shaw was able to discipline himself, but he recognized that most people lacked this ability. He admired forceful, pitiless rulers who raised themselves up from nothing to become leaders of their countries, individuals who could shape reality according to the dictates of their will, and believed that such persons were direct expressions of the Life Force, the means by which evolution did its work.

In *Bernard Shaw and Totalitarianism* I take Shaw's view of himself as a revolutionary writer seriously, and am not inclined to dismiss things he said simply because of their seeming outrageousness, which was actually integral to Shaw's technique of disseminating ideas that he knew his audience was not yet prepared for. He wanted those ideas to take root in the mind and bear fruit through the will later on; it was part of his Lamarckian evolutionary vision. Shaw believed his own artistic and political work to be a part of that same evolutionary process, but they were also a concerted effort on his part to restore totality to his fragmented world, to impose order on a deep sense of chaos, which stemmed ultimately from his unhappy childhood.

Shaw retained a deep hatred for his early life and most everything associated with it, and this animus was channeled into a desire to explode the world and remake it. A year before he died, when he was ninety-three years old and had learned that a plaque was to be erected in front of his childhood home, he remarked that he would rather "see it blown to smithereens"; and at about the same time he said that writing a play was for him "my way of building a house."[3] Shaw desperately needed to restore order through imagining utopian perfection, to overcome a sense of powerlessness by maintaining rigid control over his own life and by identifying with the powerful; and he frequently shocked his friends with his approval of cruel acts that, he argued, served a positive social end. Shaw's career as a playwright as well as his overtly political activity served the same ends, as is apparent from the very beginning of his career; there is a sense of continuity in Shaw's work, even if the totalitarian aspect was not fully formed and expressed until later when totalitarianism itself came of age. By that time Shaw had lost all patience with utopia's delay and was delighted to see many of the ideas he had championed for years put into practice by forceful leaders who had, like himself, risen by sheer force of will to a significant place in the world.

Shaw hated disorder, and he wanted to see society managed efficiently by a small caste of technocratic experts who were at the same time, in Karl Popper's memorable phrase, "utopian social engineers."[4] He had very little confidence in the average man and woman, who "could not work mentally at the same speed" as the Fabian executive committee, his ideal of what a ruling caste would look like.[5] Shaw's ideal society, what I am calling his utopian vision, resembles Plato's ideal city or Comte's Religion of Humanity more than any society that has presumably ever existed on earth. This need for absolute order and control found many means of expression in both his life and his work, and was intricately bound up with his longing for perfection.

The body makes constant demands and is subject to decay, and is therefore imperfect. Shaw sought to deny the body's claims as much as was humanly possible, was anemic at one time at least, and quite possibly remained celibate throughout the last forty-five years of his life.[6] In his last completed play a race of bodiless supermen have evolved who no longer ingest food, but instead subsist on air. Shaw found the body's very instincts to be rebels in need of extermination. His lifelong advocacy of eugenics was based on this need to eliminate the disorderly, the inefficient, the merely human, which he wanted to see superseded by the superhuman. In this way we can see that his lauded dictators were simply doing on a larger scale what the superior individual does on a smaller scale when he exercises his will against the unruly instincts.

While I have thought it important to mention some of the facts of Shaw's childhood and how they may have been factors in his later development, I am positioning Shaw within the context of an emerging new phenomenon in politics, the rise of totalitarianism; and while not discounting psychological motivations, I believe Shaw's political goals and their expression in his plays and essays are important in themselves, regardless of the exact nature of their cause. Speaking of Plato in terms that apply equally to Shaw, Karl Popper observes that when the "artist-politician" is intent on full scale "canvas-cleaning" he "must eradicate the existing institutions and traditions. He must purify, purge, expel, banish, and kill. ('Liquidate' is the terrible modern term for it.)...The view that society should be beautiful like a work of art leads only too easily to violent measures."[7] Shaw is usually viewed as a peace-loving social reformer and artist, but he was all too willing to shed blood in his longing for utopia—as will become all too clear in the following pages—and uncompromising in his view that those who do not conform to the standard the new society demands must be exterminated if they cannot be reconditioned.

George Orwell remarked in a 1944 essay that "no one has ever pointed out the sadistic element in Bernard Shaw's work, still less that this probably has some connection with Shaw's admiration for dictators."[8] In 1982, Arnold Silver took up Orwell's suggestion and wrote *Bernard Shaw: The Darker Side*. Silver's book is extensively researched and very suggestive, and one of the only books dedicated to exploring some of the issues I am raising. However, his thesis is too reductive: he sees a sadistic streak in Shaw that he claims was the result of three sexually frustrating relationships. Nonetheless, this is an important book and his argument for Shaw's sadism is not to be too readily dismissed. Shaw clearly had an "impulse toward omnipotence, toward *total* control of his environment," and this has been linked to sadism, as psychiatrist Robert Jay Lifton asserts in his book on the medical profession in Nazi Germany.[9] Shaw contends that Creative Evolution is leading to human omniscience and omnipotence, to more or less total control over the material environment, and he has devoted a number of the plays we will be looking at to this thesis. Shaw himself sought control wherever possible, was obsessed with state power over life and death, and in "moments of exaltation...felt not merely that he was godlike, but actually that he was God."[10] But while it is requisite that we occasionally consider Shaw's idiosyncratic psychological make-up, for the most part I leave final psychoanalytic judgments to the psychologists, or to those so inclined to make them. I look at more of the plays than Silver does, and believe I uncover a more complex and multi-dimensional personality than he, although my intention throughout is to view the plays in the light of Shaw's vexing relation to totalitarianism and its leaders.

While Shaw was psychologically predisposed to imagine a well-ordered utopian future and expended a great deal of his extraordinary energy attempting to make that vision a reality—and failing that, identifying with leaders and regimes that he felt were more successful—the environment around him became more chaotic. Population in London and elsewhere exploded, and Victorian morality, which he had done much to relax in his early years, seemed to dissolve completely, while freedom and liberty had apparently come to mean the unleashing of the appetitive and undisciplined self. It was a terrifying vision; evolution seemed to be favoring the worst elements. Shaw's response under these conditions was a more forced optimism, at least in the plays we will be considering, as well as an exuberant response to the totalitarian regimes that so forcefully expunged these frightening chaotic elements. His utopianism, present from the beginning, found more wild and fantastic expression in his most utopian plays, such as *Back to Methuselah* (1921), *The Simpleton of the Unexpected Isles* (1934), and his last completed play, *Farfetched Fables* (1950). Yet Shaw's dramaturgical utopianism, and its relation to his political and eugenic utopianism, has found meager expression in the critical literature, and this book is an attempt to redress that shortcoming.

While we will look at all manner of Shaw writings, my principal purpose is to explore a number of Shaw's plays for evidence of this utopian desire. Dramatically Shaw found his utopian voice in his first play of the new century, *Man and Superman* (1903), ten years after his first play, *Widowers' Houses*, was produced by Jacob Grein's Independent Theatre Society. But Shaw wrote two very important essays in the 1890s, *The Quintessence of Ibsenism* (1891) and *The Perfect Wagnerite* (1898), which I will argue show clear and unmistakable intimations of his later more fully articulated totalitarian vision. These essays were explorations of two pioneering social reformers (in Shaw's view, anyway), who happened also to be great dramatists, like Shaw himself, and are quite different from the criticism and Fabian essays that Shaw had written prior to the composition of the essays. They are both imaginative explorations of creative men with whom he strongly identified. It was in the realm of imagination that the Fabian executive committee member was able to let himself go, freed from doctrinal considerations.

In Shaw's first plays it is clear that he was trying very hard to conform to Fabian standards, and bring the content of the bluebooks the Fabians so assiduously studied onto the stage for consideration. As his career developed and he gained more independence he moved further and further from this early stance, and more toward the construction of a utopian or totalitarian worldview, usually ushered in by or composed of Nietzschean supermen. It should be noted that Shaw's adulation of the superman preceded his first readings of Nietzsche, and if anyone served as a model for his worship of the heroic individual it was Carlyle; Nietzsche simply confirmed a worldview already held, just as Bergson would later confirm another aspect of Shaw's worldview in his book *Creative Evolution* (1907, first English version 1911), although Shaw originally modeled his "philosophy" on the work of Samuel Butler.

Shaw was not inclined to violent acts himself, but greatly admired the bold and assertive men of action who had embarked on political careers with the presumed intention of remaking the world for the better; these were provisional supermen, men who by their ruthless action could compel order and efficiency, mold an unruly and recalcitrant population into a disciplined social body, and therefore clear the ground for the true supermen who would evolve biologically in the distant future. Some have argued that this side of Shaw developed only after the First World War, when it became especially apparent that parliamentary liberalism would be unable to achieve a more stable and egalitarian world;[11] but Beatrice Webb, who knew Shaw as well as anyone, remarked that Shaw's "naïve faith in the Superman, before whose energy and genius all must bow down, is not a new feature in Shaw's mentality."[12] This was in response to Shaw's passionate support of Mussolini, and was written in Webb's diary in 1927.

Shaw still remains one of the most puzzling figures in literary history; revered by some, his totalitarianism is seldom explored or even mentioned by Shaw scholars.[13] But while there has been little written on this aspect of Shaw over the last several decades, it did not go unnoticed during his lifetime or in the years just after his death. Generally speaking, books written in the 1930s through the 1960s tend to be more candid about Shaw's totalitarianism than the more recent criticism; Shaw admirers such as Maurice Colbourne, C.E.M. Joad, Hesketh Pearson, Allan Chappelow, R.F. Rattray, and Shaw's secretary Blanche Patch are quite open about Shaw's totalitarian inclinations, usually considering them a perplexing and unfortunate quirk but in no way diminishing his greatness. Joad takes it a little harder, stating that what he found "hard to forgive was the welcome he [Shaw] accorded to the Fascist dictators," and goes on to say that it seemed to him that Shaw had simply ignored egregious acts of wrongdoing that "had shocked the imagination of civilized mankind. Facts which thousands far less acute than himself had apprehended, outrages which thousands far less sensitive than himself were revolted, seemed to escape his notice."[14] Shaw was a perspicacious critic of political life, and of course the outrages that Joad alludes to did not escape his notice; he simply viewed them as necessary to the forging of the new world order that he longed for so passionately.

Shaw was an obsessive "world betterer," as he called himself, and it was precisely this unrelenting pursuit of a better world that led him to support Italian Fascism, National Socialism, and Soviet Communism—utopian political structures and civic religions hostile to political liberalism; and the latter two, at least, sought to replace or transform Judeo-Christian religious traditions with an ideology altogether new, and were fervently believed in and practiced by many ordinary and well-intentioned people. It is my contention that the need for absolute control, when exercised by the state, leads to totalitarianism, and that all utopias of this controlling sort in real life turn out to be dystopias. Russell Jacoby makes a distinction between what he calls "blueprint utopias" and "iconoclastic utopias."[15] The blueprint kind seeks to determine and control all facets of society, while the iconoclastic variety merely longs for and works toward a better world without making too rigid demands on how it should appear. Jacoby's opposition is essentially the same as Popper's, who argues that utopian social engineering focused on achieving "ultimate good" excuses the gravest of human rights abuses in pursuit of its future-directed aim whereas piecemeal engineering focuses on remedying the greatest social evils as it discovers them.[16] Shaw, never reticent about evils in the democratic countries, failed to decry the much worse abuses in the totalitarian countries because he believed in their future-directed aims.

To be clear: Shaw was a creative artist who sometimes wrote in the utopian genre, but whose works even when not in that genre frequently express utopian longing. At the same time, he was a political agitator who expressed his delight with the totalitarian governments that came to power after the First World War. These two sides of Shaw should not be separated, although they invariably are. This book will show that Shaw's utopian longing was fully present thirty years or so before the totalitarian regimes came to power, and that some of his earlier works contain elements later found in those movements; at the same time his utopian plays, plays that idealized certain types of societies, whether in the far future or on a fictitious island, contain all the elements of totalitarianism. I am referring to *Back to Methuselah*, *Farfetched Fables*, and *The Simpleton of the Unexpected Isles*, the former two depicting the process of Creative Evolution and whose later parts take place far in the future, and the latter modeled on Soviet Russia and taking place on a remote island.

Utopian literature has a long and fruitful history, going back well over two thousand years to Plato's *Republic*, which occupied a central place in Shaw's imagination. The genre takes its name from Thomas

More's *Utopia* (1516), another work that Shaw very much admired. Significantly, the word means "no place," but its homophone, *eutopia*, means "good place." Utopian literature and utopian political thinking were prevalent in the late nineteenth century, and both linked up in Shaw's powerful imagination. He was a friend and great admirer of William Morris, founder of the Socialist League and author of the utopian romance *News from Nowhere* (1892), while H.G. Wells, author of *A Modern Utopia* (1905) and other utopian romances, was a much admired colleague. Edward Bellamy's *Looking Backward*, which was published in 1888, became the most popular novel of its time and was probably almost as important in Shaw's thinking as Plato's *Republic*. Harold Bloom has famously written about the anxiety that writers experience while creating their works in the shadow of their predecessors; when we go back and read the earlier works we sometimes have a strange sense that we are reading the later writer or that the later writer impossibly influenced the former. Something like that happens when we read *Looking Backward* in the light of our knowledge of Soviet Russia. In fact Edward Rothstein has said: "Look closely at Edward Bellamy's vision of the American future, published in 1888, and it seems like an ideological glorification of the Soviet Union in the 1930s."[17] Indeed it may be doubted that political formation is absolutely independent from the world of literary creation, as historians and philosophers such as Modris Eksteins, Steven Sage, and Karl Popper have suggested.

Shaw is not usually considered a utopian writer like Bellamy, Morris, and Wells, probably because his belief in Creative Evolution is antithetical to the idea of a static society. For Shaw, utopia is a process and cannot properly begin until capitalism has been replaced by socialism and the idle are compelled to work. Although utopian longing is present from the beginning of Shaw's career, a number of works conform specifically to the conventions of utopian literature, particularly the last plays of Shaw's magnum opus *Back to Methuselah*. But for Shaw utopia was more than just a literary genre; he wanted to see a meticulously ordered hierarchical society established in his lifetime, an environment conducive to Creative Evolution, and he believed that heroic benevolent individuals, subject to no external law, were the ones who would initiate this project and maintain it once it arrived. I have found only one scholar who treats Shaw as a utopian writer, Fredric Jameson (in *Archaeologies of the Future: The Desire Called Utopia and Other Science Fictions*), but Jameson only looks at *Back to Methuselah*. In all other cases, Shaw is omitted from the canon of utopian writers. This book seeks to redress that omission.

One of the barriers to a more complete understanding of Shaw is the desire to retain the vision of Shaw as great hero and humanitarian. I believe we do ourselves, and Shaw the iconoclast, a disservice when we allow our admiration of him to deter us from a more thorough exploration of the totalitarian side of his work and personality, which was so integral to his whole being. Shaw also wrote some of the most brilliant polemical prose of the modern period, and his essays and articles attacking the dark side of capitalism remain unequaled even now in their passion for justice and the incisiveness of their critique. This writing rightly inspires admiration, and for this reason it can be difficult to accept how far Shaw was willing to go to derail the catastrophe he believed was inevitable if capitalism was allowed to continue on its present course.

Another obstacle to the recognition of Shaw as utopian, as just mentioned, is his advocacy of Creative Evolution, which presupposes a dynamic ever-moving biological Life Force. Shaw's vision of utopia was not of an unchanging and static entity, as in more traditional utopias. However, in the post-Darwinian age the very idea of utopia had changed, while its allure was undiminished—in the chaos of the industrial age it may even have been a more potent force than ever before, as we see from the horrific results of its attempted implementation in the twentieth century. The modern utopia is dynamic and dispenses with all traditional barriers to its free expression.

Shaw was adamant about this in his first major critical essay, *The Quintessence of Ibsenism*, where the "realist," as he denominates his first delineation of the superman, is unhampered by all laws and covenants, true only to his own will, which, it is believed, is an expression of the "world will." All of the totalitarian movements which became full-fledged political systems believed precisely this. The leader (like Shaw's realist) is uniquely qualified to bring in the millennial age and eschews all formal legal apparatuses. Like Creative Evolution itself, totalitarian movements, according to Hannah Arendt, "can have only a direction, and... any form of legal or governmental structure can be only a handicap to a movement which is being propelled with increasing speed in a certain direction."[18] Shaw wanted to control evolution; to substitute, if possible, planned selection for natural selection, which is the essence not only of National Socialism but of Soviet Communism as well. What is remarkable is how uncanny Shaw's anticipation of the totalitarian age was; in *The Quintessence of Ibsenism* he calls the glorious new age about to dawn the age of will, and alludes significantly to the incipient millennial age of the Third Empire (following the Pagan and the Christian) in Ibsen's great play *Emperor and Galilean* (1873).

In his wise and perceptive book looking back on the twentieth century, Tzvetan Todorov claims that three "preexisting strands" had to coalesce before totalitarianism could emerge: "revolutionary ardor, implying the use of force; the millenarian dream of building an earthly paradise here and now; and the pseudoscientific doctrine asserting that complete knowledge of the human species was about to become available. The moment of this meeting marks the birth of totalitarian ideology."[19] What we see in Shaw again and again is precisely these three factors: the millenarian streak, what I am calling his utopianism, is there from the beginning and remained to the end of his life; the necessity of using force to bring in the new age, despite his Fabianism, is there as well, as is scientism, despite his frequent lament that science was now, like religion formerly, the unquestioned infallible institution in credulous minds. This latter was more a critique of the incessant credulity of human beings than of science itself. In *Bernard Shaw and Totalitarianism* we will see just how prevalent these factors are in Shaw's work, present from the very beginning and especially pronounced in his overtly utopian plays.

Central to Shaw's utopian vision was the biological improvement of the species—that is, the eradication of the "unfit" or "unworthy"; and just as important was the scientific management of work. Both are connected. Those unwilling to work should be compelled, and if still unwilling should be exterminated. Shaw was appalled by what seemed to him the central fact of the capitalist economy: those holding the wealth made others do the necessary work of society for them. Shaw's statements about sending the idle rich to the gas chamber—or, as he put it, the "lethal chamber"—were not merely rhetorical pronouncements, as is often assumed; and although the parasitic capitalist class was a frequent target of his invective, he was clear about the need to exterminate (or "liquidate") all of those who would not engage in productive activity, regardless of class.

He believed that "the most sacred obligation of the individual is to pay his way" and that idleness was "*the* Sin against the Holy Ghost."[20] Ideally the ratio of production to consumption would be scientifically determined. Part of managing work would be the inculcation of a work ethic by the state. In drafting notes for a speech he was planning to give in 1921 he wrote that the essential moral basis of socialism was the "Ruthless extirpation of Parasitic Idleness," and "Compulsory Labour on Pain of Death." On the note card, which is reproduced in Alan Chappelow's book, *Shaw—"The Chucker-Out,"* we see the numeral one followed by the word "Killing" and the numeral two followed by the words "Inculcating the State Morality in Schools"; he believed that this was the basis for "A New Morality" and "A New Religion."[21] This was written during the sanguinary days of the Russian Revolution and the Bolshevik regime's bloody power grab, but such comments appear frequently throughout Shaw's career, although with greater frequency and greater vehemence after the dawn of the revolutionary era in 1917.

In 1898, in the first edition of *The Perfect Wagnerite*, Shaw urges statesmen to recognize that

> their business is not the devising of laws and institutions to prop up the weaknesses of mobs and secure the survival of the unfittest...The majority of men at present in Europe have no business to be alive; and no serious progress will be made until we address ourselves earnestly and scientifically to the task of producing trustworthy human material for society.[22]

And two years later Shaw remarked in a letter that he would like to see "each citizen appear before a Board once in seven years, and defend his claim to live. If he could not, then he should be put into a lethal chamber."[23] As these actual policies of extermination came to fruition in the 1930s Shaw became even more vocal, devoting much of *The Rationalization of Russia* and the prefaces to his plays *On the Rocks* and *The Simpleton of the Unexpected Isles* to the advocacy of a policy of exterminating recalcitrant, unproductive citizens: "if we desire a certain type of civilization and culture we must exterminate the sort of people who do not fit into it" (vol. 5, 482). Yet this important aspect of Shaw's thinking is rarely mentioned in contemporary Shavian scholarship; in recent biographies of Shaw it is not mentioned at all.[24] As mentioned earlier, this was not always the case.

Perhaps it was Eric Bentley's 1947 book *Bernard Shaw* that began the move away from seriously dealing with the more unpleasant facts of Shaw's utopian vision. Bentley's book, often very perceptive, is marred by his admiration for the man and his work and his eagerness to defend Shaw from himself. Shaw was a poet of the theater, not a philosopher or political scientist, Bentley claims, and so his persona as a political philosopher is better given little heed, especially as his ambivalence toward the British often inclined him to play the devil's advocate. This is powerfully argued, but as this study will show Shaw's support of Oswald Mosley, Mussolini, Hitler, and especially Stalin cannot be dismissed as

Shaw's simply taunting the hypocritical Brits. Bentley wrote the book, so he said, to undo the "myths" surrounding Shaw, but he has simply created a new myth and led us further from the truth.[25] It seems the far more credible witnesses would be the people who knew Shaw, such as Hesketh Pearson, Allan Chappelow, and Blanche Patch, who served as his secretary for thirty years. According to Patch, Shaw

> was perfectly sincere when he startled a group of simple Lancashire chapel-goers with his remedy for idlers.
>
> "I would like to take everyone before a tribunal" he said, "and if it were found that they were not doing as much for the community as the community was doing for them, I would give them a few days to make their peace and then put them in the lethal chamber. I would have no Weary Willies and Tired Tims."[26]

Unfortunately, Bentley's great admiration for Shaw led him to gloss over or deceive himself regarding the more unpleasant truths of Shaw's totalitarianism, and being one of the greatest scholars of the modern drama his lead has been followed by many critics.

Some critics maintain that Shaw's recommendations for the "euthanasia" of the socially maladjusted were merely exercises in Swiftian hyperbole, piquant satire in the fashion of *A Modest Proposal* (1729).[27] Yet as we have seen already, and will see throughout this book, Shaw made such recommendations far too frequently over the course of fifty years—both privately and publicly—and was in fact obsessed with the idea, and in deadly earnest in his defense of Stalin's liquidation policies. Some critics seem irked by the very idea of talking about it, as if it were a non-issue and distracted from an "objective" critical examination of the work. This is the impression I received from reading Margery Morgan's otherwise astute and interesting book, *The Shavian Playground*; she devotes an entire section to *The Simpleton of the Unexpected Isles*, but never even mentions what the play is, as seems obvious to me, clearly about: the elimination of the socially and economically unproductive. The central event of the play is the appearance of an exterminating angel who very matter-of-factly makes these undesirables "disappear." Morgan analyzes the play as an eighteenth-century Oriental Fable in the manner of Voltaire. While this is surely the case, she does not mention that this form is in the service of a theme that most people would rightly find morally abhorrent.[28]

Shaw was caught in the web of a utopian ideology that demanded blood sacrifice. He was not alone of course in embracing this seductive ideology, but he was one of its most tireless promoters, much of his art and especially his essays devoted to the dissemination of this ethos that actually became reality in countries he naturally identified with psychologically. I do not imagine that Shaw had anything directly to do with this coincidence, and I can only attribute it to the "Zeitgeist," but it was a coincidence that did much to reinforce his belief in Creative Evolution. The totalitarian ideology that bore such deadly fruit in Russia and Germany viewed human beings as functional parts within a totalized yet dynamic socio-political machine. For all his claims to be a mystic and religious philosopher, the truth is that Shaw fell into the trap of technocratic thinking, seeking to remedy the world's ills by engaging in a dangerous "spirit of abstraction," as the philosopher Gabriel Marcel would say, by an excessive focus on human beings as a technical or scientific *problem*.[29] Shaw denied that human beings had any inherent sacred dimension, a political opinion that, once accepted, opens up a world of potential trouble. Of course Nazism had a pseudo-mystical as well as a highly technocratic (or bureaucratic) dimension, and I want to briefly compare Shaw's eugenic and technocratic utopianism with the reality of medical killing in Germany in the late 1930s.

Germany's "Final Solution of the Jewish Problem" grew directly and *organically* out of its earlier euthanasia program, and the ideological atmosphere that pervaded Germany destroyed many men and women who might have been good people in another environment. This does not excuse them, of course, as individual moral responsibility can never be abrogated, but it is important to keep in mind. What is unnerving is how similar Shaw's program was to the Nazis'. Shaw advocated the "humane killing" of all people deemed by the state to be "unworthy of life." In his essay on prisons he puts it this way:

> We may now begin to arrange our problem comprehensively. The people who have to be dealt with specially by the government because for one reason or another they cannot deal satisfactorily with themselves may be roughly divided into three sections. First, the small number of dangerous or incorrigibly mischievous human animals. With them should be associated all hopeless defectives, from the idiot children who lie like stranded jellyfish on asylum floors, and have to be artificially fed, to the worst homicidal maniacs.[30]

Shaw goes on to list the other two types: those who need constant discipline and tutelage, but who are otherwise useful; and those who commit minor crimes. Shaw wanted to see prisons abolished, and here he states that with the first group you can either kill or cage, but the waste of manpower involved in their maintenance offends him and he clearly believes they should be "humanely killed." It might be said that Shaw favored what Robert Jay Lifton calls a "biocracy," where the model "is a theocracy, a system of rule by priests of a sacred order under the claim of a divine prerogative. In the case of the Nazi biocracy, the divine prerogative was that of a cure through purification and revitalization of the Aryan race."[31] Shaw's biocratic vision, as we will see especially in our analysis of *Back to Methuselah* and *Farfetched Fables*, his most utopian plays, is not as crude as the Nazi, principally because Shaw's vision is idealized in dramaturgical form.

Nonetheless, they both have in common the intention to eliminate all life deemed unworthy of life: *lebensunwertes Leben*. Himmler and Shaw used the same metaphor to describe this process: "weeding the garden," excising the biologically and morally inferior from the larger body politic. Nazi biocracy and Shavian bio-religion are surprisingly commensurate regarding much of what kind of life they regarded as unworthy of life—congenital "idiots," the "work shy," for example—but Shaw strenuously opposed the inclusion of Jews as unworthy, which he claimed was an absurd delusion since the "races" were so mixed anyway. But *in principle* Shaw and the Nazis were in complete agreement, Shaw even writing to Beatrice Webb that they should "admit the right" of the Nazis as well as all other states to "make eugenic experiments by weeding out all strains that they think undesirable, but insisting that they should do it as humanely as they can afford to."[32] This letter was written in 1938 as the Nazis were implementing their program of medical killing, "mercy killings" or "euthanasia," the first child killed in late 1938 or early 1939.[33] Even the language, "humane killing," is found in both; Shaw repeatedly claimed that extermination of the unfit should be "humane," that is, it should be quick and painless with the victim, if possible, not aware of its coming.

Again it must be borne in mind how insidious and pervasive is the power of ideology, how it is capable of seducing even those who might otherwise have been good. The head of the Nazi child euthanasia program T4, Karl Brandt, was by all accounts a "decent" man but was caught up in what Lifton calls the "Nazi Biomedical Vision," the idea of healing through killing, and was motivated "not by brutality, but by a certain idealism... inherent in his conception of life."[34] He was initially hesitant about the employment of carbon monoxide (the precursor of Zyklon B or hydrogen cyanide, the gas used at Auschwitz and the other death camps), because as a doctor it did not conform to his medical preconceptions as a pharmacological substance would have. Nonetheless he eventually decided that gas "would be the most humane form of death." Even Hitler inquired, according to Brandt, "Which is the most humane way?"[35] Of course the big difference is that Hitler put these ideas into practice while Shaw's utopian ideas remained frustrated by Britain's refusal to relinquish its liberal tradition. But it has to be remembered that in Germany "mercy killing" started as a relatively small operation and grew by the power of its own logic. Shaw did not believe the reports of the scale of Nazi killing and would never have endorsed racially based murder on such a massive scale, yet according to Alan Chappelow, who knew Shaw and was a great admirer, he "frequently expressed himself in sympathy with what he termed 'the liquidation of undesirables', and actually claimed that Hitler should have given him the credit for first putting forward the idea of gas chambers."[36]

Brandt believed he was participating in the revitalization of the social body, but he was also mesmerized by Hitler's powerful presence. Shaw was mesmerized by power also. He longed literally for omnipotence and admired men who had approximated that position; the omnipotent, immortal supermen that we see in *Back to Methuselah* and *Farfetched Fables* are a dramatization or fantasy of that same longing. We see this desire quite clearly early on in *The Quintessence of Ibsenism* and in *The Perfect Wagnerite*. And Shaw's preoccupation with killing, with the rights of the powerful to weed "out all strains that they think undesirable," as he wrote to Webb, is not only a manifestation of his desire for order and perfection but also an impulse toward omnipotence. Until Hitler broke the pact he had made with Stalin and began his disastrous march eastward Shaw was very much behind almost everything he did, writing in a speech intended for broadcast on the BBC in 1940 that

> nine-tenths of what Mr. Hitler says is true... I was a National Socialist before Mr. Hitler was born. I hope we shall emulate his great achievements in that direction. I have no prejudice against him personally: much that he has written and spoken echoes what I myself have written and said. He has adopted even my diet.[37]

Shaw could also be very insensitive toward his Jewish friend and German translator Siegfried Trebitsch, writing to "congratulate" him on Hitler's "glorious achievement" of annexing Austria. The day before Shaw had applauded the move publicly in an article titled "And so—Heil Hitler," published in the *Evening Standard*.[38]

But power that was not efficiently wielded could produce no admiration in Shaw, and it was Hitler's program as well as Stalin's that he so admired. These two regimes are often seen as polar opposites, the Nazis being on the "right" and the Soviets on the "left," but such differences in ideology were merely superficial. Shaw was a perceptive political observer and realized that the two states were structurally the same. In another letter to Trebitsch, Shaw applauds Hitler's "two great steps" of compulsory labor and nationalizing the trade unions; the first he says is "pure Bernard Shawism" and the second is "borrowed from Russia."[39] Both totalitarian regimes had forced labor camps and projects, were composed of one ruling party that tolerated no opposition, violently expunging any form of debate or democracy, stressed the health of the state over the rights of individuals, viewed themselves as grafted to the "world will," beyond good and evil, ruthlessly sweeping away any perceived mess (or preventing them from appearing in the first place)—they were in fact just what Shaw desired a government to be, "absolute, automatic, and totalitarian," in his own words, "in fact, a Church."[40] Shaw hoped to see a politically established modern religion, and he believed Germany and Russia had achieved just that. Russia was ruthlessly stamping out any remnant of Orthodox Christianity, converting the churches into prisons and torture chambers and melting down the church bells. And growing as it did out of Judaism, Christianity was despised by the Nazis. The National Socialists abhorred the Christian virtue of compassion, considering it a dangerous weakness, and "conscience, that Jewish disease,"[41] in the words of Hitler, was an ailment that must be violently excised. The prototype in Germany for the superman was the SS officer, not at all dissimilar, in fact, to Shaw's supermen Siegfried and Undershaft.

Both Russia and Germany sought absolute control over the social environment, and this was most important to Shaw, as he believed that "it is no exaggeration to say that civilization is perishing from Anarchism."[42] When in *Geneva* the Judge recommends a surveillance society, saying that due to a technological advance "there are no longer any secret places where evil things can be done and wicked conspiracies discussed," and therefore we can hope for "a great improvement in morals," we feel sure that this is Shaw's view as well (vol. 5, 716). Shaw hoped that absolute external control would amend the chaos he feared, and he longed for *"complete State regulation of...lives and thoughts."*[43] This quote is taken from an article Shaw wrote in 1941, and it is often assumed that wild statements of this sort were a product of his old age and began to develop only after the First World War. Of course it was only after the war that he was able to observe totalitarian political systems; but he had intimated his desire for such political organization before the war.

In the 1915 preface to *Androcles and the Lion* (1912), for instance, a play we will not otherwise be looking at, he says that people "without self-control enough for social purposes may be killed, or may be kept in asylums with a view to studying their condition and ascertaining whether it is curable" (vol. 5, 385). Shaw imagined a world of total control: no poverty, no prisons, and equal income for everybody. This certainly does sound utopian, yet it was the foundation of his political philosophy, and driven by deep psychological needs. Prisons are a waste of resources; they degrade the inmates and waste the lives of those employed in the industry, and therefore Shaw felt that it would be much better to painlessly liquidate all seemingly incorrigible offenders. Regarding one such imprisoned offender, he says again in the preface to *Androcles*: "It would have been far easier to kill him as kindly as possible" (vol. 5, 386). The Soviets and the Nazis seemed to agree that it was more efficient to kill offenders than leave them languish in jail, but even so prisons were in no way abolished.

If we are unable to change this evil system, Shaw said to Hilaire Belloc the same year he wrote *Androcles*, then we might as well "go and cut our throats, though I am not sure that we might not do a little more good by beginning to cut other people's throats. I am prepared to go that length if the existing system could be put an end to."[44] So we see that Shaw before the war often espoused violence, and was quite inclined to embrace the totalitarian regimes once they came on the scene. Certain bellicose Shaw heroes that appeared before the war bear a remarkable resemblance to the SS, Soviet, and Fascist elite that would appear later on. Shaw greatly admired Soviet commissar Felix Dzerzhinsky, "that man without humor whom infamy will remember as the inventor of the police state,"[45] and even kept a picture of him on the wall of his office; he was fond of telling how this dedicated man, this "true believer, the sanctified fanatic of absolute state power,"[46] in the words of Stephen Koch, in an effort to improve efficiency and set an example for others, murdered a lazy railroad employee. Dzerzhinsky, who told his men to be "determined comrades—solid, hard men without pity,"[47] was the quintessential Shavian revolutionary hero, as were Mussolini, Hitler, Lenin, Stalin, and Britain's own Oswald Mosley, who was in turn a great admirer of Shaw.

It must be remembered that Shaw did not simply admire hardness and cruelty; he believed they served the ends of Creative Evolution, as in a similar way Karl Brandt believed he was serving the species biologically in his role as a leading doctor of Germany's euthanasia program. Beatrice Webb recalls Charlotte, Shaw's wife, saying that she and Shaw "looked forward to a new world with a new race of men—or supermen."

She adds in her diary by way of comment: "What with no political or personal freedom, with compulsory equality and compulsory work, it is a weird utopia. We are utterly baffled. There seems neither poetry nor reason nor common sense in GBS's state of mind."[48] Beatrice wrote this in 1927, but she may have remembered a similar bafflement that her husband experienced when he first heard Shaw read aloud what was later published as *The Quintessence of Ibsenism*.

The genesis and organization of this book

It was Shaw's adulation of the untrammeled individual will that alarmed Sidney Webb, and this was my own reaction when I re-read *The Quintessence* about six years ago. At that time I knew little of Shaw's totalitarianism, but as I re-read the book I felt his longing for an age of will with its heroes who were to exist above the law was a very frightening predilection, prescient of the totalitarian age that would dawn a few decades later, and I wanted to know more. As I began to do research I learned that Shaw had indeed given support to Mussolini and Hitler, as well as to Stalin, and this seemed to confirm my perception of the text's implicit dangers. Yet while I found a prodigious quantity of primary source material to reinforce this impression, there was very little secondary source material, and so I set about to write a dissertation on the topic and now this book.

This investigation of Shaw's utopianism will cover approximately sixty years, beginning with *The Quintessence of Ibsenism,* first read aloud to an audience of Fabians in a restaurant in 1890, and will end with his last completed play in 1950, *Farfetched Fables*. In between we will look closely at one other essay and eight plays, but will frequently turn our attention briefly to articles, speeches, one of the novels, letters, and other plays when appropriate. We will see that while Shaw may have changed a lot over those sixty years, in his utopianism he changed very little, except that it became more elaborately conceived and more entrenched. What will be made clear is that Shaw was predisposed to accept and promote just the type of ruler and totalitarian system of government that came to dominate Europe after the First World War, and in fact while this support was perhaps not inevitable, it would seem to have been at least likely.

Shaw's belief in the incipient coming of a superman to clear the ground for a new utopian era can be found in inchoate form in two of the three *Major Critical Essays* he wrote in the 1890s. So it is appropriate that we begin our study with the first of these essays, *The Quintessence of Ibsenism*, my own initiation into the topic and, I believe, the best place to begin the inquiry. Shaw here extols a rare being he calls "the realist" and pits him against the idealists and philistines, much more common and a major impediment to the advance of the species. In fact Shaw exhibits a kind of Manichaean thinking that we will see frequently in the course of this study. For instance, in *The Perfect Wagnerite* Shaw delineates the realist figure from *The Quintessence* in the figure of Wagner's Siegfried, a pugnacious revolutionary whose only law is his own will. He has no conscience to deter him from his goal, and is a perfect Manichean, demonstrating that the only course is for the good to annihilate the bad. Terror is his primary, in fact his only, weapon.

Todorov writes of a "grammar of totalitarianism" which recognizes only two types of persons: Us and Them. Those aligned against the "good" must be converted, destroyed or enslaved. The other choice available to us is a "grammar of humanism," which rejects this binary thinking; instead of Us and Them, as in the grammar of totalitarianism, this grammar consists of I and Thou, as in the title of Martin Buber's great book, and it embraces all of humanity, even those whom we might find reprehensible, whom we are exhorted to try to understand. Despite his reputation as a great humanitarian, Shaw frequently employs this totalitarian grammar, as we see in *The Perfect Wagnerite* where the hero must enslave or else ruthlessly destroy the gods, giants, and dwarves (the idealists and philistines, in the language of *The Quintessence*) if the new age is to dawn.[49] *The Quintessence of Ibsenism* is the subject of Chapter 1, and *The Perfect Wagnerite* is the subject of Chapter 2.

During the 1890s, when these essays were written, Shaw was still finding his way as a dramatist, but he had a major breakthrough with *Man and Superman* just after the turn of the century. In Chapter 3 we will turn our attention to this play and two others, *John Bull's Other Island* and *Major Barbara*, viewing them as a trilogy that together work toward greater unity, until by the end of *Major Barbara* we have, essentially, utopia in miniature. In *Man and Superman* Shaw extends considerably the idea of Creative Evolution, which is presented in much less distinct and perhaps unconscious form in the earlier essays.

After the war Shaw wrote *Back to Methuselah: A Metabiological Pentateuch*, the subject of the fourth chapter. This five-play cycle depicts the history of humankind from Adam and Eve to the year 31,920. In this massive work, which Shaw hoped would form part of a "Bible of Creative Evolution," he dramatizes his vision of the race of supermen as they evolve toward bodiless omnipotence. In the fourth part we see them on the verge of destroying the unfortunate race of ordinary men and women, a ruthless Siegfried-like decision that prepares the way for the exclusive presence of the divine beings of the last play in the cycle.

In Chapter 5 we reach the period of totalitarianism proper and look at two plays, *The Millionairess* and *Geneva*, the former as an allegory of fascist power and the latter as a satire that reveals a great deal of Shaw's view of leadership and government: fascist, communist, and democratic. In this chapter we will also look at a third play, *The Simpleton of the Unexpected Isles*, analyzing it as an allegory of the Soviet Union.

And lastly in Chapter 6 we will explore *Farfetched Fables*, Shaw's last completed play and an attempt to recapitulate on a smaller scale *Back to Methuselah*. Shaw was ninety-three years old when he wrote this play, apparently unfazed by or perhaps in some way unable to grasp the degree of evil manifest in the recently expunged Third Reich, but still very enthusiastic about Stalin and the Soviet experiment.

Shaw was still quite lucid in his last year. The play is not without merit, and in his preface he describes the totalitarian dynamic in terms that recall Arendt's description that was cited earlier:

> [O]ur British parliamentary system is far too slow for twentieth century social organization. The Soviet system in Russia outstrips it because, being faster, it is more immediately responsive to the continual need for reforms and adaptations to changing circumstances... Incidentally it gives Stalin the best right of any living statesman to the vacant Nobel peace prize, and our diplomatists the worst. This will shock our ignoramuses as a stupendous heresy and a mad paradox. Let us see.
>
> (vol. 6, 476)

Let us see indeed! Remarkably, this last play of Shaw's, one of his most utopian—the superman has finally shed his body entirely (which is difficult to dramatize, but Shaw manages)—ends with an intimation of totalitarian militarist regimentation. The play concludes with the stage direction "*A jubilant march is heard,*" and the teacher saying to her pupils as the bell rings for lunch: "March. [*Beating time*] Left-right, left-right, left-right. *They tramp out rhythmically*" (vol. 6, 521). What we see is the great freedom Shaw demanded for his heroes—whose wills were not to be bound by any tablet of laws or previously made covenant with an imaginary deity—exercised in the onerous task of regimenting their inferiors.

And finally, a short epilogue looks very briefly at Shaw in the context of some of his contemporaries who also gave their support, at least for a time, to one or another of the totalitarian regimes.

It will have been noted that one of Shaw's greatest plays, and most successful depictions of the Shavian superman, is not included in the list of plays covered in this book. I am referring to Shaw's great 1913 romance, *Pygmalion*, and its god-like central character Henry Higgins. Although I decided not to include a chapter or section on this play, I think we would profit by a brief look at this fascinating incarnation of the Shavian superman. Of Shaw's heroes, Higgins most resembles the whirlwind that dominates his play *The Millionairess*, Epifania Ognisanti di Pererga. Both characters are depicted as forces of nature, and although Shaw is not uncritical of his creations, he ultimately views them as existing in a realm beyond good and evil, as superior beings the Life Force has lodged within to an uncommon degree; they are drivers of Creative Evolution.

While Higgins is often faulted for his insensitive treatment of Eliza, it is not so often noted that her unceasing demand for his attention and approval exemplify the behavior of the slave. When she says to him, "Dont sneer at me. It's mean to sneer at me," he shoots back that he was not sneering; he was expressing his "righteous contempt for Commercialism. I dont and wont trade in affection" (vol. 1, 276). Eliza may grow out of her slavery by the end of the play, and at that moment earn Higgins' respect, but throughout most of the play she remains a slave. She is exceptional in that she is able, with the help of a master builder, to rise above her station. In Plato's ideal city it occasionally happens that a gold-stamped child is born into the bronze-based class, and when noticed removed by the guardians to the higher class and educated as a future guardian. Something like that happens with Eliza. Both characters are necessary to the scheme of the play, but Higgins is Shaw's representation of the great creator—part scientist, part artist, part god—and he lives in a realm above that inhabited by mere mortals. This makes him socially difficult, like Epifania, but he is the driving engine of the race. It is no accident that Higgins' area of reform is the English language, as Shaw was preoccupied with phonetics his entire life and desperately wanted to see the English alphabet reformed; and this intense desire was part of the same impulse for control in social as well as political matters.

Higgins is a hard, cold man, obsessed with his work and frequently cruel. Shaw believed that the supermen of the future would be cold and yet possessed of a mesmeric power. The supermen, then as now, are always destroyers as well as creators. Higgins must destroy the old Eliza if the new is to be born, and he is relentless in his task. For Shaw the supreme quality is the ability to improve the world, to make something better of it. Higgins has nothing but contempt for Freddy, and when Eliza threatens to marry him replies, "Can he make anything of you? Thats the point" (vol. 1, 278). Eliza is initially *"not at all an attractive person"*: she is dirty, dressed in threadbare shoddy clothes, her hair is in tangles, and as *"she needs the services of a dentist"* no doubt exudes a foul odor—she is in fact repulsive (vol. 1, 198–99). Her speech and primitive noises are disgusting as well, and Higgins tells her that a "woman who utters such depressing and disgusting sounds has no right to be anywhere—no right to live" (vol. 1, 206). While it is easy to pass over such remarks, their prevalence in Shaw's work should make us take note. Obviously he wants to see exterminated the conditions that produce such foul persons, and he would like to see as many Cinderella-like transformations as are humanly possible. But what is a eugenically responsible society to do with those who are incapable of transformation and resistant to management?

When Eliza continues to demand kindness and attention from Higgins, he says to her, "If you cant stand the coldness of my sort of life, and the strain of it, go back to the gutter...You find me cold, unfeeling, selfish, dont you? Very well: be off with you to the sort of people you like" (vol. 1, 278–79). Shaw believed the super race of the future would be by our standards cold, passionless, remote, just as the people of the "gutter" feel about cultured people now, according to Higgins. When Eliza accuses him of not caring for her he tells her that, on the contrary, "I care for life, for humanity; and you are a part of it" (vol. 1, 276). It is the collective, the organic whole that matters, and not each selfishly preoccupied individual. When Eliza is perplexed about why he has taken so much trouble over her, he replies "[*heartily*] Why, because it was my job," and significantly queries: "Would the world ever have been made if its maker had been afraid of making trouble? Making life means making trouble" (vol. 1, 276). Perhaps we get a hint here of how much trouble Shaw personally would have been willing to take over each individual before giving him or her up as a hopeless job, because he adds that there is "only one way of escaping trouble; and thats killing things. Cowards, you notice, are always shrieking to have troublesome people killed" (vol. 1, 276). Colbourne and Chappelow both admit that Shaw wanted to see socially troublesome people killed, but believed he would likely have undergone a great deal of trouble to improve them before signing their death warrants.[50]

Higgins is a force of nature. Always *"thundering"* and *"storming,"* he is a *"hurricane"* (vol. 1, 213, 215, 216), a peremptory creature born to command, and who frequently threatens violence against his refractory pupil, and once almost loses his self-control and attacks her (vol. 1,

280); and although he lacks his creator's god-like poise, he must possess an inordinate capacity for self-control not only to have mastered his science but to have accomplished the superhuman transformation of Eliza. Higgins, Shaw believes, should not be judged by the same moral code that lesser mortals must abide by, for he is a creature of another sort. Shaw puts it this way in the preface to *Farfetched Fables*:

> The Life Force, when it gives some needed extraordinary quality to some individual, does not bother about his or her morals... Apparently its aim is always the attainment of power over circumstances and matter through science, and is to this extent benevolent; but outside this bias it is quite unscrupulous, and lets its agents be equally so.

It is the "simple credulous souls [who] are models of integrity and piety, high in the calendar of saints" (vol. 6, 458–59). In fact Higgins and Shaw seem to bear more in common than their passion for phonetic reform and social engineering; Higgins says that he is at heart shy and diffident, has "never been able to feel really grown-up and tremendous, like other chaps" (vol. 1, 224). And we know that one of Shaw's greatest accomplishments—among so many—was his ability to overcome an almost paralyzing shyness and become perhaps the greatest public speaker in England. But we must still wonder if he was ever able to feel "quite grown-up and tremendous, like other chaps" and if this might explain some of his admiration for unscrupulous men of action.

Shaw wanted to see a race of supermen, and claimed that until

> there is an England in which every man is a Cromwell, a France in which every man is a Napoleon, a Rome in which every man is a Caesar, a Germany in which every man is a Luther plus a Goethe, the world will be no more improved by its heroes than a Brixton villa is improved by the pyramid of Cheops.
>
> (vol. 3, 701)

He hoped that "the brute force of the strong-minded Bismarckian man of action, impatient of humbug, will combine with the subtlety and spiritual energy of the man of thought whom shams cannot illude or interest" (vol. 3, xlv). And though we must account for a certain amount of rhetoric in statements like the following—"I would hold it good statesmanship to blow every cathedral in the world to pieces with dynamite, organ and all, without the least heed to the screams of the art critics and cultured voluptuaries" (vol. 3, xliv)—such statements taken with his later support of such violent real-life supermen attest to a certain level of sincerity. He once said of Hitler that he was "a very remarkable, very able man. There is one thing about Hitler which recommended him to me from the very first, and that is his face—it has an expression of intense resentment. That is the expression that every statesman in the world ought to have."[51] These two last statements are separated by more than thirty years, and yet are remarkable for their similarity; a good statesman should have "an expression of intense resentment" and it would be "good statesmanship to blow every cathedral in the world to pieces." And when the resentful statesmen appeared and started blowing up cathedrals and much else, Shaw gave his approbation.

Margery Morgan once claimed that violence in Shaw's plays is "always symbolic or metaphorical,"[52] yet I believe that Shaw's political utopianism and his dramaturgical utopianism cannot be separated; at least not without doing violence to our understanding of the man and the plays. Shaw the political revolutionary and Shaw the revolutionary playwright are one and the same person. Had he never backed such brutal dictators or given his support to murderous regimes, but instead vigorously protested as he should have when human rights were so ruthlessly trampled on, I probably would never have felt compelled to scrutinize his work so carefully for those totalitarian elements that I believe the following chapters uncover.

John Stuart Mill famously said in his most acclaimed essay, *On Liberty* (1859), that circulating versions of the truth are only partial truths, half-truths, and that it was necessary to listen to other often suppressed versions of the truth to gain a more complete understanding of any given complex issue. This version of Shaw that I am presenting should be understood in just that way. It does not claim to be the whole truth about Shaw, but only a partial truth that has been for too long unconsidered and unexplored. By no means would I expect or want this neglected version to become the dominant version, and other views ignored. No one scholar can expose the full truth of any complex artist, but it is my hope that I have made some contribution to a richer and more complete understanding of that most driven utopian, Bernard Shaw.

1
Previsions of the Superman in the Coming Age of Will: *The Quintessence of Ibsenism**

> He who had to all appearance mocked at the faiths in the forgotten past discovered a new god in the unimaginable future. He who had laid all the blame on ideals set up the most impossible of all ideals, the ideal of a new creature.
>
> G.K. Chesterton[1]

I

In the preface to *The Quintessence of Ibsenism* Shaw remarks that during the spring of 1890 he and his fellow Fabians were at a loss for a topic to which to devote a series of lectures for that coming summer. Finally, they were "compelled to make shift with a series of papers put forward under the general heading 'Socialism in Contemporary Literature' " (vii). Such are the humble beginnings of what has turned out to be one of Shaw's most fascinating essays. Shaw delivered the lecture at St. James's restaurant on the evening of 18 July 1890. It was not long after this that Ibsen took London by storm, and Shaw thought it an opportune time to revise and expand his original essay and add it to the many discordant voices just then arguing over the relative merits or demerits of the Norwegian playwright. It was first published in the summer of 1891.

---

*This chapter will be focusing on the 1891 first edition of *The Quintessence of Ibsenism*. Page numbers will follow quotes in the body of the text. George Bernard Shaw, *The Quintessence of Ibsenism* (New York: Dover, 1994). Unless otherwise noted, all quotes from Shaw's plays and prefaces will be from the edition, *Bernard Shaw: Complete Plays and Prefaces*, six volumes (New York: Dodd, Mead & Company, 1963) and also cited within the body of the essay. Shaw's spelling and use of apostrophes is often idiosyncratic.

Since then the essay has usually been understood as a good indicator of Shaw's own thinking, rather than a reliable guide to understanding Ibsen's dramaturgical strategy and philosophy of life: the quintessence of Shavianism rather than the quintessence of Ibsenism.

Shaw wrote *The Quintessence* shortly before completing his first play, *Widowers' Houses* (1892), and prior to its publication he had been known mostly as a talented music critic and powerful orator and propagandist for socialism. It is hard to know what exactly Shaw's intentions were when he moved from Dublin to London in 1876, but clearly they involved a literary career, as between 1879 and 1883 he wrote five ambitious novels. The last one, *An Unsocial Socialist*, reflected his conversion to socialism in 1882, which was instantaneous after hearing the American economist Henry George deliver a lecture on land nationalization. After *An Unsocial Socialist* he exchanged novel writing for progressive politics and was a familiar presence within the Socialist Revival, appearing frequently at the many socialist organizations and delivering speeches. In 1884, he joined the Fabian Society, a newly formed organization of moderate, middle-class socialists. Although he began a career as a book reviewer at the *Pall Mall Gazette* in 1885, his primary preoccupation at this time was intense study of economics, helping to formulate Fabian policy as a member of its executive committee, and indefatigably promoting the virtues of socialism in both print and speech. Consequently his short book of 1891, *The Quintessence of Ibsenism*, was something of a departure for him.

More than anything else, the essay is an account of Shaw's faith in the autonomous will of human beings, his philosophy of history, and his view that his age marked a turning point toward a radically new age. Major changes in the way humankind views its place in the world, which eventually manifest in a restructuring of institutions, are initiated by rare individuals—pioneers, Shaw calls them—who have the courage to see reality unadorned with illusions. One such individual is Ibsen. Pioneers are of two types: one sees certain activities normally regarded as ethical as being wrong; the other sees an activity normally regarded as wrong as being acceptable. Shelley was a pioneer of both types, according to Shaw, and Ibsen of the second variety—which is evident, Shaw says, by the frequency of scurrilous attacks against him in the daily newspapers. Shaw shows that progress depends on individuals who strike against convention, thereby scandalizing their contemporaries, by reminding his readers that many of their heroes were formerly denounced: "Luther as an apostate, Cromwell as a traitor, Mary Wollstonecraft as an unwomanly virago, Shelley as a libertine, and

Ibsen as all the things enumerated in the *Daily Telegraph*" (4). Of course Shaw has been proved right by Ibsen's subsequent status as a classic of Western literature.

It should be remembered that Shaw initially presented his essay as a speech to the Fabian Society, and that it was supposed to be directly concerned with the issue of socialism. But while socialism is rarely mentioned or alluded to, the essay does concern itself with a future society of re-made institutions brought about by a revolution in thinking about ethics and the individual's relation to the world, society, and his or her own self. In other words, *The Quintessence* does relate to Shaw's lifelong passion for "world-bettering," for fashioning a new society, precisely what the Fabians were devoted to; but Shaw looks at the problem from the angle of the single individual, an angle he had never publicly presented before and which only indirectly, in the most implicit way, deals with the economic reordering of society. Shaw sees history as passing through various stages; having passed through an age of faith, Shaw sees his own period as being in the last throes of the age of reason, where the utilitarian ethic of Bentham dominates and "acting logically with the object of securing the greatest good of the greatest number" (5) is the dominant ethos; but he sees this as passing, or at least he hopes that it is, and Ibsen, he believes, is one of the pioneers signaling the advent of the next age, which will be an age of will, an age where "happiness consists in the fulfilment of the will" (69).

It is not that the individual no longer uses the faculty of reason, but that reason is now to be understood as the servant of the will. Charles Carpenter has written that Shaw's doctrine is tripartite, that it "consists of three basic elements. The human will, man's link with a cosmic force, channels the evolutionary impulse; the intellect, a distinctively human faculty, looks for the most efficient way to fulfill the will; and ideas... the alternative paths that the intellect considers in its search."[2] All ages involve a different orientation and a different conception of duty: in the age of faith the orientation was "to God, with the priest as assessor. That was repudiated; and then came Man's duty to his neighbor, with Society as the assessor. Will this too be repudiated, and be succeeded by Man's duty to himself, assessed by himself?" (8). This, Shaw contends, is the prophetic message of Ibsen's plays, and Shaw himself clearly believes such a new orientation is imminent.

Shaw lived in a period of great social change, and intellectuals were busy trying to figure out and influence the course of the future, oscillating from despair at God's seeming abdication to overwhelming joy at the possibilities of building a new world with new men and women independent of God and his burdensome claims. Shaw's optimism and utopian mindset might very well have overlaid a deeper sense of panic at living in this brave new world. In May of 1887, he had reviewed Samuel Butler's *Luck or Cunning?* for the *Pall Mall Gazette*. Butler's book was an attack against the Darwinian idea that mere chance was the guiding force in the evolutionary development of humankind, where "mind is banished from the universe."[3] The book had a profound impact on Shaw, and its ideas form the background to his major philosophic plays, *Man and Superman* (1903) and *Back to Methuselah* (1921). Besides Butler's positive philosophy, Shaw had recently been influenced by Schopenhauer's *The World as Will and Representation* (1818), although he converted Schopenhauer's pessimistic philosophy of will into a philosophy of will that was much more optimistic.[4] Shaw did not believe in evil as a force in the human personality, only in the evil of institutions that had outlived their time, such as capitalism in the late nineteenth century. Such a view explains why Shaw did not think of Hitler, Mussolini, or Stalin as evil, but rather applauded them for, as he believed, attempting to dismantle a moribund capitalism.

Whether or not Shaw's optimism regarding the future of humankind was a cover for darker forebodings, the fact remains that the 1891 *Quintessence* intimates the dawning of a new era, where the human being will live first and foremost for his or her own self, and since "social progress takes effect through the replacement of old institutions by new ones" (4) this new era will result in the formation of new social institutions. And while the idea that the human being will live to satisfy his or her own will might sound like an endorsement of selfishness or solipsism—subjectivism—Shaw says that the will of human beings will be in conformity to a larger will, Schopenhauer's "world will," which will later be renamed the Life Force and become the cornerstone of his philosophy. But this element is barely mentioned in *The Quintessence*; in fact it is so underemphasized that Sidney Webb, a key member of the Fabians, wrote his future wife after hearing the initial paper, saying, "It's very clever... But his glorification of the Individual Will distresses me."[5] Webb was not the only one concerned with Shaw's glorification of the individual will; Shaw republished the book in 1913 with additions meant to make it "clear that he is enshrining individual will only when it works in harmony with the world-will."[6] This begs the question: how does one know—and perhaps more importantly, how are others to be assured—that one's will is in harmony with the "world's will" or Life Force? The Nazis claimed to be in harmony with the world's will, working according to the laws of evolution and preparing the way for a superior race to lead us into the Promised Land; and the Soviets also believed they were in harmony with the Law of Historical Change, leading the way to a classless society.

Shaw believed that those he called in *The Quintessence* philistines and idealists were the greatest impediment to the arrival of the golden age he hoped for; with the decline of religious belief, they would need to be inculcated with a new faith that would guarantee their cooperation. Positive change required strong highly intelligent and motivated leaders with benevolent intentions and a docile population ready to follow their lead. This point of view would develop over the years, not receiving clear and detailed articulation until he was able to view and consider the totalitarian regimes that achieved so much success while his Fabians achieved, so he thought, so little. His religion of the Life Force, which was much more to him than simply a convenient replacement for a lost Judeo-Christian worldview, was developed fully some time after the writing of *The Quintessence*, and is first announced in *Man and Superman* at the beginning of the twentieth century.

We can see the Shavian religion in inchoate form in this essay. His very first sentence, if we exclude his brief preface, announces such a point of view. After the chapter heading, "The Two Pioneers," we read: "THAT IS, PIONEERS of the march to the plains of heaven (so to speak)" (1). This is significant not only because it alludes to Shaw's ultimately religious intentions, but also because it signifies, by his parenthetical "so to speak," that for Shaw religion was a matter of this world, with nothing otherworldly about it. After boasting in his boyhood that he was an atheist, he later claimed to be a mystic; but his teleological view was oriented in the concrete world of human beings and institutions; this world was literally to become, through the efforts of pioneers like Ibsen and himself and Sidney Webb (and later of such ruthless political animals as Lenin and Stalin), a heaven on earth. And this "religious" intention is clear already in *The Quintessence*, where he announces in a footnote that "the will is our old friend the soul or spirit of man" (6).

There is a sense of inevitability about the golden age that men like Ibsen are heralding. If Shaw had any doubts about a world governed by individual will supposedly in harmony with a larger world will, they are not announced in this essay. Certainly the kind of future that might be imminent in a world unmoored from its theological base does not seem to trouble him, at least not in this essay, as it did Nietzsche, who according to Camus in *The Rebel* was terrified of such a future and worked incessantly to eliminate its possibility:

> Nietzsche never thought except in terms of an apocalypse to come, not in order to extol it, for he guessed the sordid and calculating aspect that this apocalypse would finally assume, but in order to avoid it and to transform it into a renaissance. He recognized nihilism for what it was and examined it like a clinical fact.[7]

Nietzsche of course also lauded the individual of superior will, but in 1891 Shaw had not yet read Nietzsche, and later claimed he arrived at his ideas independently. Shaw attempts to subvert the subjectivism that pervades the ethos of his book by alluding to a larger spiritual reality; he mentions the "soul or spirit of man" in the footnote just mentioned, and briefly references the importance of the individual will being in harmony with the larger world will, but the prevailing message of the book is the supremacy of the ungoverned individual will, which should have to answer to no one but itself.

In *The Rebel*, Camus—writing with a backward glance at the Holocaust and two world wars with untold millions slaughtered, as well as Stalin's purges and the development and dropping of the atomic bomb—was able to see more clearly what Shaw could or would not, but interestingly his outline of history is almost identical to Shaw's. For Camus, the killing of Louis XVI was more than just the murder of another king; it was the death of an idea—the divine right of kings—and the beginning of our modern era. By killing one of God's anointed, the regicides were in fact killing God, and in his place they substituted reason or the idea of secular justice. In this sense Camus and Shaw are in agreement, the age of reason and secular justice does indeed follow upon the age of faith; and for Camus, too, the age of reason is succeeded by an age of will, but with a horrifying aspect that Shaw was unable or unwilling to envisage: "the will to power came to take the place of the will to justice, pretending at first to be identified with it and then relegating it to a place somewhere at the end of history."[8] Camus goes on to say that "the revolutionary movement of our times is primarily a violent denunciation of the formal hypocrisy that presides over bourgeois society" and that all "that they have preserved is the vision of a history without any kind of transcendence."[9] Shaw was of course a revolutionary engaged in a "violent denunciation of the formal hypocrisy that presides over bourgeois society"; and I would argue as well that Shaw's revolutionary outlook is consonant with Camus' recognition that the revolutionary movement of his time is "the vision of a history without any kind of transcendence." Shaw's Life Force may theoretically be transcendent as well as immanent, but his concern is purely with an immanent force and its manifestation in individuals, in human society and its institutions. And as will be found out in the 1920s and 1930s, he will cling to this ideal vision of the future and condone almost any atrocity if he feels it necessary for bringing forth a new world order. Justice will indeed be relegated to the end of history—that is, to the final triumph of utopia; until then, anything goes.

II

While we can see Shaw's philosophy of the Life Force and the triumph of a future utopia ruled by heroic men and women implicit in *The Quintessence*, nonetheless he makes certain ethical pronouncements that his commitment to his ideal will later force him to abandon. For instance, in condemning men for treating women as objects with which to fulfill their desires he propounds the following maxim: "to treat a person as a means instead of an end is to deny that person's right to live" (19). In his analysis of *The Wild Duck* Shaw makes the very sensible observation that it is not possible to compel a person to a higher plane of being if they are not yet inwardly prepared to rise to it: "It is useless to make claims on him which he is not yet prepared to meet" (51). And speaking of Ibsen, Shaw says that he "protests against the ordinary assumption that there are certain supreme ends which justify all means used to attain them; and insists that every end shall be challenged to show that it justifies the means" (67). But while this might be true of Ibsen, and perhaps true of Shaw in 1891, later in his career Shaw will contradict these words with statements such as the following:

> How is it then that the leaders of the Russian revolution have been able to do what I cannot do: that is, to set up an effective inquisition to enforce to the death the dogma that forsytism—parasitism—is the sin against the Holy Ghost.
> (*The Rationalization of Russia*, 94)

> Now comes the question, is there such a thing as a class which ought to be exterminated?... Our question is not to kill or not to kill, but how to select the right people to kill.
> (*The Rationalization of Russia*, 111–12)

> [W]e need a greatly increased intolerance of socially injurious conduct... together with a sufficient school inculcation of social responsibility to make every citizen conscious that if his life costs more than it is worth to the community the community may painlessly extinguish it.
>
> (Preface to *The Simpleton of the Unexpected Isles*, "Preface on Days of Judgment," vol. 6, 539)

> [W]hat we are confronted with now is a growing perception that if we desire a certain type of civilization and culture we must exterminate the sort of people who do not fit into it.
>
> (Preface to *On the Rocks*, vol. 5, 482)

> The notion that persons should be safe from extermination as long as they do not commit willful murder, or levy war against the Crown, or kidnap, or throw vitriol, is not only to limit social responsibility unnecessarily, and to privilege the large range of intolerable misconduct that lies outside them, but to divert attention from the essential justification for extermination, which is always incorrigible social incompatibility and nothing else.
>
> (Preface to *On the Rocks*, vol. 5, 492–93)

> The only country which has yet awakened to this extension of social responsibility is Russia... For example, when the Russian railways were communized, some of the local stationmasters interpreted the change as meaning that they might now be as lazy and careless as they pleased... The unfortunate Commissar who was Minister of Transport found himself obliged to put a pistol in his pocket and with his own hand shoot stationmasters who had thrown his telegrams into the dustbin instead of attending to them, so that he might the more impressively ask the rest of the staff whether they yet grasped the fact that orders are meant to be executed.
>
> (Preface to *On the Rocks*, vol. 5, 493–94)

These could be multiplied many times over. It should be noted here that the type of behavior exemplified by the "unfortunate Commissar" is exactly consonant with Shaw's definition of the individual of superior will in *The Quintessence*, "the realist." Therefore we should keep this in mind as we analyze the essay in greater detail. I believe that we will find the germ—notwithstanding the ethical pronouncements enumerated above—for the type of thinking that will later manifest itself so disconcertingly to those who had always trusted in Shaw's humanity.

Previsions of the Superman: The Quintessence of Ibsenism 33

The original 1891 version of *The Quintessence of Ibsenism* contains five chapters: the first three—"The Two Pioneers," "Ideals and Idealists," and "The Womanly Woman"—outline Shaw's philosophy, while the fourth and longest chapter, "The Plays," takes us through Ibsen's major plays up to 1891, and the fifth chapter, "The Moral of the Plays," sums up the book. (There is also a very interesting appendix, but its content does not concern us here.) Chapter 1, "The Two Pioneers," we have already briefly discussed. We learned that the pioneer of social progress will, at the cost of vehement denunciation and outcry, lead society, despite its resistance, to the golden future that it is destined for. Shaw outlines the course of recent history, spending most of the chapter attempting to allay any fears his readers may have regarding the supersession of an age where duty to God or reason and secular justice is binding by an age that exalts only the individual will:

> [T]o both theologist and rationalist progress at last appears alarming, threatening, hideous, because it seems to tend toward chaos. The deists Voltaire and Tom Paine were, to the divines of their day, predestined devils, tempting mankind hellward. To deists and divines alike Ferdinand LaSalle, the godless self-worshipper and man-worshipper would have been a monster. Yet many who to-day echo LaSalle's demand that economic and political institutions should be adapted to the poor man's will to eat and drink his fill out of the product of his own labor, are revolted by Ibsen's acceptance of the impulse toward greater freedom as sufficient ground for the repudiation of any customary duty, however sacred, that conflicts with it. Society—were it even as free as LaSalle's Social-Democratic republic—*must*, it seems to them, go to pieces when conduct is no longer regulated by inviolable covenants. (8)

We are embarking on a new age, where the repudiation of all covenants and customary duties, however sacred, are to be replaced by an ethos that exalts the freedom of the individual will. He even seems to drop the word "duty" as it was used earlier in relation to the self; at first we had a duty to God, then we had a duty to society, then a duty to ourselves; but in the age of "self-worship" the idea of duty, which is seen as simply tyrannous, is dropped altogether:

> this [self-worshipping] is the last step in the evolution of the conception of duty... [I]n due course of the further growth of his spirit or will, a sense at last arises in him of his duty to himself. And when

this sense is fully grown, which it hardly is yet, the tyranny of duty is broken; for now the man's God is himself; and he, self-satisfied at last, ceases to be selfish. The evangelist of this last step must therefore preach the repudiation of duty. (8–9)

There is no cause for alarm because in the age of self-worship man is "self-satisfied" and has "ceased to be selfish." Since this is the last step in the evolution of the conception of duty, we have, or will have in due course, reached Camus' infamous end of history.[10] Shaw never dropped this vision of utopia, and was later forced into the most appalling violence against his own sense of reality. He became a victim of what he most warned against in this very essay, the idealist who by his slavery to his ideal is guilty of the most egregious self-deception.

In Chapter 2, "Ideals and Idealists," Shaw divides society into three categories, and uses the institution of marriage as his case study. He asks us to imagine a society of 1000 persons modeled on the Britain of his day, where 700 will be philistines, 299 idealists, and the remaining individual he denominates a realist. The philistines are entirely content with things as they are and desire no restructuring of society. The idealists are secretly discontent, but all the more vociferously do they clamor about the sanctity of marriage and monogamy; the realist sees that the institution is flawed and says so, much to the horror of the idealists. Shaw admits that the term "ideal" with its derivative "idealist" is problematic, since it can refer both to the mask which covers over the sordid reality and to what we would desire to have in its place. In point of fact, it would be better to call the realist an idealist since he longs to create a better world than the mendacious one that currently exists, and to call the idealists conventionalists. But the nomenclature has been determined by Ibsen, who frequently uses the term "idealist" in the sense of one who gilds over corrupt institutions with a false veneer. Looked at in this way we can see that Shaw himself was an idealist in the more positive sense at this point in his career, and later in life when he defended Stalin, Mussolini, and Hitler he was an idealist in the negative sense that he is criticizing so forcefully in this essay.

In Shaw's scheme the idealists are higher on the evolutionary scale than the philistines, but the realist is highest of all. In fact these idealists are the cultured of society, the ones who worry most that without God or reason as guide the realist will lapse into a life of crime:

> The man who has risen above the danger and fear that his acquisitiveness will lead him to theft, his temper to murder, and his affection to

debauchery: this is he who is denounced as an arch-scoundrel and libertine, and thus confounded with the lowest because he is the highest. And it is not the ignorant and stupid who maintain this error, but the literate and cultured. (14)

Despite Shaw's prodigious intellect, he rarely recognized the seduction of power itself, the intoxicating effect of increasing individual lawlessness and power for its own sake.[11]

Shaw's tripartite division with one of the parts labeled philistine inevitably brings to mind Mathew Arnold's *Culture and Anarchy* (1869), where society is divided into three classes, the barbarians, the philistines, and the populace. Written about two decades before *The Quintessence*, Arnold's essay deals with many of the same issues. Indeed, it could be argued that Shaw has written a book lauding anarchy while Arnold was imploring his countrymen to forestall what he sensed was an incipient age of anarchy by the cultivation of what he termed culture. Anarchy, in Arnold's view, proceeds from willfulness unregulated by clarity of thought and a disinterested regard for what he called the intelligible law of things or right reason; he wanted all three classes to engage more in "reading, observing, or thinking, to come as near as we can to the firm intelligible law of things, and thus to get a basis for a less confused action and a more complete perfection than we have at present."[12] If Shaw admired resolute action, Arnold was wary of it, believing "the Englishman's impulse to do as he likes" and his estimation of "this impulse as something primary and sacred to be the bane of the nation."[13] (Ironically, this will later become Shaw's view as well.)

Arnold would agree with Shaw on the importance of the human will acting in unison with the world will—God's will, he calls it—which would indeed be acting in accordance with the firm intelligible law of things and right reason, but he would never say with Shaw that "for now the man's God is himself," for he would be horrified at such an expression. And where Shaw gives scant attention to this larger supposedly divine will, and no mention at all to how one comes to understand this will and its demands, Arnold's essay repeatedly emphasizes the importance of thinking, reading, and observing, of maintaining a vigilant regard for the good of the community and humanity in general, and of prioritizing the demands of the higher self over the demands of the ordinary self:

> We have found that at the bottom of our present unsettled state, so full of the seeds of trouble, lies the notion of its being the prime right

and happiness, for each of us, to affirm himself, and his ordinary self; to be doing, and to be doing freely and as he likes. We have found at the bottom of it the disbelief in right reason as a lawful authority.[14]

Arnold wanted to maintain Christianity, but he wanted to see the coarse "Hebraism" of industrial England rectified by more enlightened thinking. For all their differences, both Shaw and Arnold believed in the importance of the state, Arnold believing that the state, for all its present limitations, simply needed to increase its culture—its cultivation of inwardness and reflection rather than its readiness for prompt unreflective action—but should not be agitated against, and Shaw believing that the state needed to convert as expeditiously as possible to socialism. Temperamentally the two men could not have been more different, but both wanted to see, ultimately, a strong state ruled by Plato's philosopher kings.

When Arnold speaks of barbarians, philistines, and populace he means the aristocracy, the middle class, and the working class, and their characteristic ways of thinking and acting; Shaw is less concerned with class, but just as intent as Arnold on delineating mental attitudes. For Shaw the philistine majority, we can presume, would be found mostly in both the working and the middle class, while the idealists would be the more cultured members of the middle class and aristocracy. Technically the realist may be found in any class, although Shaw usually draws his heroes from the upper classes. In *The Quintessence* Shaw more or less ignores the philistines and puts the emphasis on the idealists and the realist. For society to move forward ideals must be discarded, for "these ideals are only swaddling-clothes which man has outgrown, and which insufferably impede his movements" (15). Shaw is impatient with the entire structure of society, its codes and commandments, its standards and rules, its laws, ideals, and canons. The institution he concentrates on in the essay is marriage, which he believes will in time, after certain modifications, proceed "finally to its disuse and disappearance as the responsibility for the maintenance and education of the rising generation is shifted from the parent to the community" (18). Shaw's utopian vision is, even at this point in his career, not far from Plato's *Republic*, and it is fitting that his understanding of the word "realist" should not be associated with "Zola and Maupassant, but with Plato" (14). I mentioned earlier that Shaw's essay could possibly be read as an endorsement of anarchy, but at the same time I have said he is Platonic in his utopian thinking, wishing for a strong state ruled by philosopher kings. This contradiction needs clarification.

Previsions of the Superman: The Quintessence of Ibsenism 37

An anarchist is one who believes human beings can govern themselves, and have no need for external codes or governments to provide them with structure in their lives. For the realists that Shaw describes in *The Quintessence* this is certainly true. But Shaw's incipient utopia, at least in its initial stages, would still contain its fair share of philistines and idealists; Shaw believed in gradual change (although he often shows a propensity for violent apocalypticism and quantum evolutionary transformation). Shaw knew that the society he was describing as the age of will, in its beginning phase at least, would not apply to everybody; or rather, everybody would benefit, but only an elite group of extraordinary men and women would be strong enough to operate without external codes. And it was these strong-willed, benevolent, and intellectually astute individuals who would necessarily usher in and provide the leadership of the socialist state.

In 1888, Shaw may have praised the ideals of communist anarchism, as James T. Hulse has remarked in his book *Revolutionists in London*, but was too much of a "Hobbesian" to believe human beings would spontaneously do the necessary toil of society if totally free: "Communism cannot be entirely anarchistic; men must be compelled, at least in the foreseeable future, to do their share of the essential labour."[15] Consequently, we can extrapolate from his imaginary society that the realists will plan and rule, the idealists and philistines forming the bureaucracy and laboring contingent of society. In other words, *The Quintessence* can in some ways be seen as a generalized sketch of the broad political structure of the coming socialist utopia of Shaw's imagination. In fact, in *The Rationalization of Russia* he also uses a tripartite model of human society, with thinkers doing the "higher brain work," bosses or "peremptory people who could convey these instructions and see that they were obeyed," and workers "who could and would work when somebody told them what to do."[16] Shaw was an enthusiastic admirer of Lenin from the very beginning, and to the end of his life was an enthusiastic supporter of Stalin and his commissars. These were strong individuals who did as their will dictated, "realists" in other words, unbothered by religious scruples or moral codes. In *Seeds of Evil: Lenin and the Origin of Bolshevik Elitism* Robin Blick remarks that Shaw "had grasped, in his own idiosyncratic fashion, the core of Leninist theory: namely, that socialism only could be realized under the leadership of a self-selecting elite."[17]

Although Shaw's view in *The Quintessence* is pretty straightforward and unambiguous, foretelling a day when illusions will be a thing of the past, all codes and commandments unnecessary, it must be understood that this is Shaw giving way to his exuberant vision of utopia and jumping over the less pleasant steps on this march to a new social reality. Just five years after publishing *The Quintessence* he published another essay that explores idealist thinking, "The Illusions of Socialism," a brilliant work that accurately anatomizes the millenarian streak in Marxist thought. Shaw upbraids his fellow socialists for thinking a socialist utopia will happen overnight once the proletariat has the wherewithal to shake off its chains. This was the illusion of socialism. And indeed, the Fabian Society came into existence in part because its highly educated middle-class members never believed for a minute that the proletariat was capable of leading or even assisting in a revolutionary movement: "socialist consciousness must be introduced into the working class 'from without' by bourgeois intellectuals."[18] And Shaw would write many years later in "Sixty Years of Fabianism" that "cultural segregation is essential in research, and indiscriminate fraternization fatal."[19]

Shaw wanted to warn his readers that to engage in this kind of utopian thinking was to be setting oneself up for a big letdown; bringing forth a new and better world was a long hard job requiring experts, and was necessarily going to proceed slowly, even after the first big transition to socialism. He was afraid that socialists expecting an immediate transition to a totally reformed golden age would lose heart and give up the cause, and that is why he wrote the book. But he also recognized that illusions—ideals—were necessary to infuse faith into a person, energizing him or her for the work at hand. He called these kinds of illusions "necessary illusions" and distinguished them from "flattering illusions," which "nerve us to strive for things we do not know how to value in their naked reality and reconcile us to the discomfort of our lot or to inevitable actions which are against our consciences."[20] Necessary illusions are "the guise in which reality must be presented before it can rouse a man's interest or hold his attention, or even be consciously apprehended by him at all."[21] The "Illusions of Socialism," with its more complex examination of illusions or ideals, was written, according to Alfred Turco, because by 1896 Shaw was becoming disillusioned with Fabianism. Turco believes that it was about this time that Shaw began to develop his theory of the superman, who will initiate the new era through the force of his will. But as we have seen already, the superman figure is implicit in the realist as delineated in *The Quintessence*.

Before moving on to an examination of Shaw's longest chapter, and his examination of the plays of Ibsen, I think we should look a little further into Shaw's microcosmic society of 1000 persons. Shaw has us imagine a unit of 700 self-satisfied and ignorant philistines, 299 cultured idealists, and one heroic individual, a realist. Yet the tone of Shaw's essay is one of unbridled optimism that a new dawn for humanity is arising, a time when the individual will be free of all external constraints: his duty to God and his duty to society discarded, and no longer a slave to codes and commandments, the newly made human being will be a sort of God himself. In his book *The Revolt of the Masses*, first published in 1930, Jose Ortega y Gasset cites an interesting statistic: "From the time European history begins in the VIth century up to the year 1800... Europe does not succeed in reaching a total population greater than 180 million inhabitants. Now, from 1800 to 1914... the population of Europe mounts from 180 to 460 millions!"[22] The twentieth century was not the century of the superman, the extraordinary individual, it was the century of the masses, and Ortega blames the nineteenth century—the most successful century in the history of the world from the standpoint of material, social, and political progress—for not foreseeing and planning for this contingency. This is not the place to go over all of Ortega's concerns, but I bring it up as a contrast to Shaw's focus on the superior individual and his neglect of an examination of the masses, the philistines who in terms of pure numbers totally dominate the social sphere. After all, *The Quintessence* was originally an address to the Fabian Society, a socialist organization, and was supposed to be concerned with the issue of socialism in contemporary literature; and socialism is supposedly concerned with the collectivization of society. Shaw later came to believe that the overwhelming numbers of incorrigibly recalcitrant citizens should be scientifically exterminated, as the Soviet Union had begun to do:

> the planners of the Soviet State have no time to bother about moribund questions; for they are confronted with the new and overwhelming necessity for exterminating the peasants, who still exist in formidable numbers. The notion that a civilized state can be made out of any sort of human material is one of our old Radical delusions.
>
> (vol. 5, 498)

But in 1891 Shaw was too excited by the coming of the realist, the man of will, and gave little heed to the masses of philistines who would soon overwhelm the earth. That would come later.

III

In the fourth and longest chapter of *The Quintessence*, "The Plays," Shaw finally gets into his analysis of Ibsen's dramatic work. Actually, it would be fairer to say that he analyzes some of the plays while providing simple plot outlines of others, hoping that this will be enough to prove his point that Ibsen is an exponent of Ibsenism. By far the most time is spent on Ibsen's great two-part epic play *Emperor and Galilean* (1873), and this we will look into shortly, as it has a lot to say about Shaw's utopian thinking as well as offering us an opportunity to better see if perhaps Ibsen himself does not share in Shaw's vision. In 1882, Ibsen completed writing what Michael Meyer has claimed is "the most Shavian of Ibsen's plays," *An Enemy of the People*.[23] The play is still one of the most powerful articulations of the moral corruption inherent in a society ruled by the economic imperative. The play takes aim at the public, the press, and party politics and portrays the character of Dr. Stockmann as a lone hero exercising formidable will power in standing against the entire community. His attempt to expose a lie which has been transmuted into official "truth" by the corrupt forces of power and their influence over the majority costs him dearly; he endures threats and vilification and material losses that few people could tolerate without capitulation. A close friend of Ibsen's, Lorentz Dietrichson, remarked that the "ideas which are expressed in *An Enemy of the People*...were aired in almost every conversation we had at that time."[24] Thomas Stockmann is a heroic figure, his energy and moral commitment are awe-inspiring, yet he has a salient flaw that in the post-fascist age cannot be ignored. In the turbulent fourth act Stockmann finally manages to address the mindless mob that has so abused him:

> What does the destruction of a community matter, if it lives on lies! It ought to be razed to the ground, I tell you! All who live by lies ought to be exterminated like vermin! You will end by infecting the whole country; you will bring about such a state of things that the whole country will deserve to be ruined. And if things come to that pass, I shall say from the bottom of my heart: Let the whole country perish, let all these people be exterminated![25]

For all his tenacity, moral conviction and heroism, Stockmann has the traits of the fanatic. He even imagines himself a kind of modern-day Christ, at the end of the play exhorting his children to find him twelve boys that he can educate as his disciples. In a remarkable book, *Ibsen and*

Hitler: The Playwright, the Plagiarist, and the Plot for the Third Reich, the historian Steven F. Sage has convincingly documented how this speech was paraphrased by Hitler in some of his political speeches, with the Jews of course being the vermin that must be exterminated. As Hitler realized the war was lost in 1945 he denounced Germany as cowardly and weak, worthy only of destruction, an obvious echo of Stockmann's similar curse against his morally craven countrymen.[26]

Ibsen has Stockmann espouse a policy of eugenics as a scientific solution to the problem of a nineteenth-century Europe overrun by the masses:

> The common people are nothing more than the raw material of which a People is made... Isn't there an enormous difference between a well-bred and an ill-bred strain of animals? Take, for instance, a common barn-door hen... [A]s soon as I extend the principle and apply it to two-legged animals, Mr. Hovstad stops short. He no longer dares to think independently, or to pursue his ideas to their logical conclusion.[27]

Eugenics was very much coming into vogue at the time among Europe's educated classes, and remained so well into the twentieth century; and we know that the idea *was* followed to its logical conclusion. Shaw was and remained a eugenicist throughout his life. Many years later Shaw would sound very much like Stockmann when he remarked in the preface to *On the Rocks*: "Sooner or later this situation [scientific extermination of the socially unfit] will have to be thoroughly studied and thought out to its logical conclusion in all civilized countries" (vol. 5, 496).

Shaw gives two pages to *An Enemy of the People*, but he devotes nine pages to *Emperor and Galilean*, more than twice the length devoted to any of the other plays, and uses the play for a more detailed description of his philosophy of historical development. Julian, the play's protagonist, is caught between two creeds: Christianity, which the Roman Empire had adopted as the official religion during the age of Constantine a few decades earlier, and the recently quitted paganism, which many citizens naturally still adhere to. Julian finds Christianity too demanding and longs to relinquish himself of its moral burden. The mystic Maximus guides Julian, trying to bring him to the realization that he requires no creed at all, that everything he needs is within him; he must simply access the necessary resolution and will. Maximus hopes that Julian will be the first to realize the "third kingdom."

The play is one of Ibsen's most Kierkegaardian in that he seems to be taking Kierkegaard's three stages of individual development and applying them to an image of historical evolution. The pagan period which is waning corresponds to the aesthetic stage, the Christian period which is just beginning corresponds to the ethical, and "the third kingdom" would correspond to the religious stage. For Kierkegaard, unlike for Ibsen and Shaw, there could be no higher phase of humanity that dispensed with the essence of the Christian message found in the gospels. The obvious corollary for Shaw in *The Quintessence* would be a philistine period followed by an idealistic and culminating in the third empire of the realist; however, in his section on *Empire and Galilean* he uses a different nomenclature. In *The Quintessence* Shaw expands on Ibsen's theme and incorporates it into his own philosophical system. The first empire, which Shaw calls "pagan sensualism," is clearly over, while the second empire, what Shaw calls "Christian or self-abnegatory idealism, is already rotten at heart. 'The third empire' is what he looks for—the empire of Man asserting the eternal validity of his own will" (32).

It is interesting that in *Brand* Shaw believes the destruction that Brand's actions cause result from his "idealism," even though it would be fair to judge Brand a Shavian realist breaking away from institutional religion in the manner of a Protestant rebel asserting the validity of his own will. In fact, in a Kierkegaardian analysis of *Brand* Halib C. Malik believes that Brand fails to achieve the religious stage because "in Brand's case this calling is not from God, as for Abraham, but from Brand's own will."[28] Ibsen was much more ambivalent than Shaw about the dawning of a new age, and could say at one moment that "every historical development has been but a lurch from one delusion to another"[29] and at another that "the historical theme [of *Emperor and Galilean*]... has a closer relation with our own time than people might suppose."[30] Meyer goes on to say that the "problem that baffled and finally destroyed Julian was one that was always at the back of Ibsen's mind, though he seldom if ever mentioned it; where to find a faith to replace the Christianity of his upbringing."[31]

Shaw had a similar concern, and went to great lengths to establish such a faith. Of course when Ibsen wrote his play the idea of a third kingdom or empire, a Third Reich, had not yet taken on the sinister connotation that we hear in the phrase today. In his research on the influence of Ibsen on Hitler, Sage has found three plays to be of significant influence: *An Enemy of the People*, as has already been remarked, *The Master Builder*, and *Emperor and Galilean*. I do not want to get into the details of Sage's research, but it is clear that the idea of a single individual leading humanity to its "final" destiny and establishing a Third Reich exercised a powerful spell on Hitler's imagination. The idea also cast its spell on Shaw, and he enthusiastically gave his support to such powerful individuals when they entered the historical stage, whether it was Lenin, Mussolini, Hitler, Stalin, or Oswald Mosley, leader of the British Union of Fascists (BUF), who was himself deeply influenced by Shaw. The twentieth century did indeed turn out to be the age of will, but it was will in the service of absolute naked power unencumbered by the social and moral strictures that had always been an intricate and fragile means of upholding human civilization. It was the century of utopias—actually, dystopias—such as Soviet Communism and the National Socialists in Germany, among others. What sustained these pernicious systems was the cult of the charismatic individual, the strong leader, "the realist," the superman leading society on to a perfect future. What is interesting to note—but Shaw's optimistic hope for a glorious future unmoored from the past failed to note—was that Julian's misunderstanding of Maximus entailed the doom of his reign, just as the many attempts at establishing a "third empire" throughout the tumultuous twentieth century spelled the destruction of the dictators who attempted to create them, as well as for the millions who were their innocent victims.

Shaw derives a systematic through-line in Ibsen's corpus of plays, which he claims was expressed unconsciously in the great early poetic plays *Brand* (1865) and *Peer Gynt* (1867) and subsequently discovered by Ibsen and given conscious dramaturgical expression. Ibsenism, according to Shaw, is a position articulated in the plays of Ibsen that says that "the real slavery of to-day is slavery to ideals of virtue" (63) and that

> there is no golden rule—that conduct must justify itself by its effect upon happiness and not by its conformity to any rule or ideal. And since happiness consists in the fulfilment of the will, which is constantly growing, and cannot be fulfilled to-day under the conditions which secured its fulfilment yesterday, he claims afresh the old Protestant right of private judgment in questions of conduct. (69)

Shaw later reverses this, relegating the desire for individual human happiness as subservient to the evolution of humankind as a biological species. And for this reason he substituted the term "life" for "happiness" in the 1913 re-issue of the book. But in 1891 this is his vision of the utopian future, not Ibsen's, who had actually moved away from his middle phase of social plays to examine the darker side of the human will: just the side that Shaw neglected to consider in *The*

Quintessence and actually continued to neglect throughout the extent of his long career.

Ibsen, who believed that "our whole being...is nothing but a fight against the dark forces within ourselves,"[32] seemed to have a sense of the darker side of the human will that would define the next phase of human history. He began exploring the manipulation of the will of others in such plays as *Hedda Gabler* and *The Master Builder*, partly, as Meyer notes, due to his interest in the new science of hypnotism, a topic that fascinated Strindberg as well. Certainly he was more ambivalent than Shaw about the future, did not participate in any social or political agitation, refrained from joining socialist groups or political societies of any kind, and merely wrote plays that expressed his mood of the moment. Shaw no doubt shocked some of his socialist friends, as we know he did Webb, with his strong advocacy of an individual will bound by nothing beyond its own subjectivity. He always admired the Protestant spirit, as is evident in his love for *Pilgrim's Progress* (1678) and his admiration for its non-conformist author, who spent many years of his adult life in jail. Shaw believed mythical representations were merely masks covering over naked reality, and that "now every mask requires a hero to tear it off" (10). The twentieth century would be defined by the loss of centuries-old values as well as an explosion of self-concocted utopian fantasies like the Third Reich, which *was* a mask covering over an unbridled will to power. Shaw may have believed that "every step of progress means a duty repudiated, and a scripture torn up" (4) or that a "whole basketful of ideals of the most sacred quality will be smashed"(22) on the road to utopia, but he later recognized that while this was fine for the few realists out there—the Lenins and the Stalins, whom he believed were forging the future in the service of the Life Force—it was not all right for everybody else; these supermen would bring order, Shaw thought, while the masses could only bring chaos.

Ortega tells the story of a gypsy who goes to confession; the priest asks him if "he knew the commandments of the law of God. To which the gypsy replies: 'Well, Father, it's this way: I *was* going to learn them, but I heard that they were going to do away with them.'"[33] For Ortega, the problem of our time, an unprecedented problem, was that of a growing population with nothing to believe in, nothing to guide them; he laments a Europe that has lost "definite standards" and exhorts that "[b]efore supplanting them, it is essential to produce others."[34] He also feels that economic stability, relative wealth, in itself is no guarantee of a higher moral life; on the contrary, those with money to spend, living in a society that values nothing higher than personal gratification, tend to be morally deformed.

Shaw ends his book by saying that the quintessence of Ibsenism is "that there is no formula" (69), yet one wonders if he might ever have been willing to reconsider for universal application that old formula so carelessly tossed away, "to love one's neighbor as oneself." A decade later he would write as one of the "Maxims for Revolutionists," appended to *Man and Superman,* that the "golden rule is that there are no golden rules" (vol. 3, 731). Shaw later recognized the necessity of ideals or illusions; but unfortunately he himself fell under the sway of one of the most tragic illusions of the century. The age of will would come to maturity not too long after Shaw wrote *The Quintessence,* but first he would write another utopian essay based on another "artist-philosopher," this time the megalomaniac and anti-Semite, Richard Wagner.

2
Utopia in Flames: Shaw and Wagner's *Ring: The Perfect Wagnerite*

Shortly after the first edition of *The Quintessence of Ibsenism* was published in 1891 Shaw began his own career as a playwright. Although he had started work on *Widowers' Houses* in 1885 in collaboration with and at the suggestion of William Archer, the text lay dormant and unfinished until 1892. The play was originally titled *Rhinegold*, after the first play in Wagner's *Ring* cycle. Shaw completed and re-named the play when he learned that the Dutch impresario Jacob Grein was looking for edgy and controversial plays for his new enterprise, the Independent Theatre Society, a small non-commercial theatre modeled on Andre Antoine's Theatre Libre. The Independent Theatre Society actually had its genesis when the Lord Chamberlain refused to issue a license for a production of Ibsen's *Ghosts*. So in more ways than one Ibsen seems to have initiated Shaw's career as a playwright.

Shaw's first three plays, published in 1898 as *Plays Unpleasant* (along with another volume titled *Plays Pleasant*, which included his next four plays), seemed to follow the model established by Ibsen's middle period of social problem plays. They deal with slum landlordism, marriage, and prostitution in a realistic vein; and except for two performances of *Widowers' Houses* privately produced at the Independent, they languished unperformed until the Victorian period was over. These plays were quite controversial in their time, like *Ghosts* and *A Doll's House*, and Shaw seemed intent on continuing his role as Fabian social reformer even as he expanded this role to dramatically permeate London society.

At about the time Shaw was seeing the two volumes through the press, he wrote another essay on a controversial nineteenth-century dramatist, this time Richard Wagner. Wagner was of course also a composer, one of the few to write the libretto as well as the music for his operas and music dramas. Both *The Quintessence of Ibsenism* and *The Perfect Wagnerite* were later brought together, along with *The Sanity of Art*,[1] and published in 1932 as Shaw's *Major Critical Essays*. It is revealing that Shaw chose these two artists to represent his own deepest feelings and hopes about the future. Both Ibsen and Wagner were outsiders who, like Shaw, lived in exile for many years; Shaw certainly viewed himself as an outsider—in 1898 he was an Irishman living in England just as he was earlier a member of the Protestant minority living in predominantly Catholic Ireland, and he was a member of the intelligentsia but never attended university (and this could be extended, as for example his family's relative poverty among their wealthier relatives).

All three were also apparently in some doubt about their "legitimacy," or at least had reason to feel some anxiety over whether their male parent was their biological father. In Wagner's case he had reason to believe his real father might have been Jewish.[2] In Ibsen's case "it was openly rumored that Henrik was not Knud Ibsen's son, but that of an old admirer of his mother named Tormod Knudesen."[3] And in Shaw's case there was the figure of his mother's music teacher and house-mate George Vandeleur Lee. Whether or not there is any truth to the rumors and conjectures that the three artists were the biological sons of men their mothers loved outside the sanctified boundaries of the traditional home is irrelevant; what is of significance are the possible psychological ramifications on the artists and the influence of these on their worldview and work. In any case, it is certainly an interesting coincidence. For despite the artistic achievements and formal innovations of Ibsen and Wagner, in both essays Shaw is most intent on elucidating a vision of the future which he descries in the works of both men. He sees both Ibsen and Wagner as prophets of a new dawn.

As mentioned in the previous chapter, of Ibsen's plays it is *Emperor and Galilean*, a work preoccupied with a coming age described as "the third empire," that Shaw gives the most attention to in *The Quintessence*; and in his essay on Wagner he is almost exclusively devoted to providing a socio-political analysis of Wagner's massive four-play cycle, *Der Ring des Nibelungen*, which Wagner worked on for a period of over twenty years (from approximately 1848 to 1874), and which was inspired by the events of the 1848–49 revolutions, particularly the Dresden uprising, in which Wagner played an active role. *The Perfect Wagnerite* can be read as an expansion and clarification of the themes presented in *The Quintessence* seven years earlier. Both essays provide a clearer and more forceful expression of Shaw's deeper political and religious imagination than he was able to present in his Fabian essays and other similar works; in explicating the work of these two iconoclastic creative artists Shaw is able to draw on his own power as a creative artist and body forth a vision of the world he hoped would soon appear, and to delineate the type of heroic individual he longed to see, and perhaps secretly wished himself to be.

At the same time Shaw's aggressive instincts and desire for domination find perfect satisfaction in Wagner's bellicose and amoral hero, Siegfried. For where in Ibsen's play Julian is unable to implement the third empire, as he is still hampered by doubts and looking outside himself for gods, Wagner presents in Siegfried an ideal image of the aggressive self-confidence of the hero to come; a being who corresponds to what in *The Quintessence* Shaw labeled the "realist" as well as any single character Ibsen himself created. Siegfried has no conscience, has totally extricated himself from that burden (or as a kind of genetic improvement is born without one), and lives by the law of his will only. And not only is Shaw able to expound on his vision of the realist-hero we first learned of in *The Quintessence*. Wagner's tetralogy appealed to him because it neatly divides humanity into a similar three-fold partition, such as we saw in his essay on Ibsen; he is able to use Wagner's allegory to expand on his vision of human society as composed of philistines and idealists, soon to be transcended or at least brought to order by the imminent appearance of the longed-for superman, a utopian visionary free of conscience, released from primal fear, and prepared to use his prodigious strength to strike down the old order.

Perhaps it will be a good idea to briefly recapitulate the outline of Wagner's allegory before going into a deeper analysis of Shaw's interpretation. In the first play, *Das Rheingold*, three Rhine maidens happily cavort by the river, enjoying the gold submerged in its water purely for the aesthetic pleasure it provides, with no desire to exploit it for any other purpose. A dwarf named Alberic comes along and is entranced by the beauty of the maidens, and wishes to be loved by one of them. But they find him hideous, and after teasing him for a while they reject him completely. According to the myth no one can remove the gold from the Rhine unless he first renounces love, which the maidens believe no one would ever do and so have no fear of its being stolen. When Alberic is rejected by the maidens he forswears love and steals the gold.

Alberic then enslaves his fellow dwarves who live under the earth in Nibelheim. They pile up the gold for him and also fashion for him a ring which enables him to rule the world. His brother Mime, a smith, forges for him a magic helmet, whereby he can change shape. In the meantime the king of the gods, Wotan, has hired two giants, the brothers Fasolt and Fafner, to build Valhalla for him, a mighty fortress. The price demanded by the giants, however, is Wotan's sister-in-law Freia, whose golden apples provide the gods with eternal life. Wotan does not want to pay the giants and Loki, the fire god, looks for a way out; but there is no way out and Wotan is forced to pay up. He promises the giants the Nibelung gold in place of Freia. The giants take Freia until he comes with the gold, and Wotan and Loki devise a plan to steal the gold from Alberic. After stealing the gold Wotan tries to withhold the ring, but to no avail. The giants now have the ring and the gold and proceed to argue over it, Fafner then killing his brother, after which he turns himself into a dragon with the aid of the helmet and stands guard over the gold.

This first play Wagner considered a prelude to the other three, mostly so he could announce his great cycle as a trilogy in the manner of the classic Greek tragedies which played the Dionysian Festival in Athens in the fifth century.

In the second play, *Die Walkure*, the action moves to the story of Wotan's illegitimate children Sieglinda and Siegmund. Sieglinda is unhappily married to Hunding, and her long lost brother Siegmund arrives at her place for aid. It turns out Hunding is his enemy, and the deeply bonded brother and sister escape together; but first Siegmund extracts from the Ash Tree the sword Nothung, which only a true hero can remove. Fricka, Wotan's wife, is upset about the incestuous and adulterous love between the siblings and forbids Wotan from interfering the next day when Hunding and Siegmund meet for battle. Wotan is forced to comply and he shatters Siegmund's sword Nothung during the battle; Siegmund is slain but Wotan's child and favorite Valkyrie Brunnhilde picks up the broken pieces of Nothung and rescues Sieglinda, who is pregnant with the future hero Siegfried. Wotan then punishes Brunnhilde for her disobedience by putting her into a deep sleep and surrounding her with fire; there she will remain until a hero brave enough to pass through the fire wakes her.

In the third play, *Siegfried*, we learn that Sieglinde has died giving birth to her son, but has instructed Alberic's brother Mime to raise the child, destined to be a great hero. She also gives him the broken pieces of Siegmund's sword, Nothung. Mime raises Siegfried in the hope that when he is old enough he will be able to wrest the ring from Fafner, in which case Mime would possess the ring and be ruler of the world. Despite Mime's talent as a smith he is unable to refashion Nothung, although the now grown-up Siegfried is able to succeed, despite his lack of experience, where his foster father could not. With the hope of learning what fear is, and not for any acquisitive motive, he takes Nothung and slays the dragon. Mime has created a potion to kill Siegfried after he destroys Fafner and obtains the ring. In combat Siegfried tastes some of the dragon's blood, which gives him the power to discern Mime's thoughts and also to understand the language of a bird, who tells him of Brunnhilde's existence; he kills Mime and goes in search of her. On the way to Brunnhilde he encounters Wotan and breaks his spear; he then finds and wakes the sleeping Brunnhilde.

This is where Shaw believes the *Ring* should have ended. With the destruction of Wotan's spear the hero has supplanted the power of the gods, and so the utopian era should in theory have begun. It is not even necessary for Siegfried to unite with Brunnhilde; in fact it spoils the allegory, for which reason Shaw detested the last scene, a love duet between Siegfried and Brunnhilde. According to Shaw, Wagner conceived the final play of the four-play cycle, *Gotterdammerung*, first; it was only after the cataclysmic events of 1848–49 that Wagner decided to go back to the earlier part of the medieval saga and create a cycle of music dramas. However, the music for *Gotterdammerung* was composed last and is, according to Shaw, in the style of grand opera and not, like the three preceding pieces, music drama. For this reason, I will forego an exposition of the final part of the cycle, in which Siegfried is treacherously stabbed in the back by Alberic's son Hagen.

Shaw was intrigued by the *Ring* because for him it allegorically prophesied the coming utopia he longed to see brought to fruition; it was not only Wagner's depiction of Siegfried as a superman figure free of law and conscience that appealed to Shaw, but also his depiction of the lower orders of humanity in the two groupings of dwarves and giants, who correspond to the philistines as presented in *The Quintessence*. Wagner has divided them according to disparate characteristics (but all found predominantly in the philistines as Shaw conceived them), the dwarves representing cunning opportunism and the giants dull stupidity and the brute force of labor, with both groups ignorant of their own best interests, possessed by greed and incapable of imagining a higher order of existence. Shaw sees Wagner's allegory as representing the evolutionary movement of society as it advances beyond its current deplorable state. It was Shaw's hope and belief that society would be transformed by a small group of superior biological beings who would dismantle the political and religious institutions as they then existed and usher in the age of heroic socialism. Siegfried and the other Volsungs represent a higher stage in biological evolution, and interestingly they are the offspring of Wotan, the idealist. As we remember from *The Quintessence*, the idealists (although equally held in contempt) are more evolved than the philistines.

In this major critical essay of 1898 Shaw's eugenic vision is formed and announced. As we saw in the last chapter, this vision is articulated by Dr. Stockmann, one of Shaw's favorite Ibsen heroes, in *An Enemy of the People*. In 1849, Wagner had written the essay "The Work of Art of the Future," the title of which alludes to both future aesthetic products and society itself as a work of art. In that essay Wagner states that the German *Volk* will be redeemed only when their enemies ceased to exist, by inducing "that which it does not want into that which has no right to exist" and is "only worthy to be destroyed."[4] Shaw says practically the same thing in *The Perfect Wagnerite*, where the idealist Wotan wills his own destruction because, unlike the philistines, he has the foresight to realize that a higher order of existence is possible and necessary. Shaw believes that the utopia he longs for and believes in is within reach, but that it will not begin to emerge until the real-life idealists make the same realization as Wotan and institute policies and procedures to ensure the eradication of philistines and the production of heroes (or realists), when

> they see that their business is not the devising of laws and institutions to prop up the weaknesses of mobs and secure the survival of the unfittest, but the breeding of men whose wills and intelligences may be depended on to produce spontaneously the social wellbeing our clumsy laws now aim at and miss. *The majority of men at present in Europe have no business to be alive*; and no serious progress will be made until we address ourselves earnestly and scientifically to the task of producing trustworthy human material for society. In short, it is necessary to breed a race of men in whom the life-giving impulses predominate, before the New Protestantism becomes politically practicable.
>
> (242, my italics)[5]

Shaw is known for his philosophical vitalism (soon to have dramatic expression in *Man and Superman*) and for his opposition to social Darwinism, but he is in many respects a quite typical representative of the dominant materialist thinking of his day. As L.D. Rather says in his book on the *Ring*, "Eugenic ideas of this kind drew new strength in the nineteenth century from Darwinism and its bastard offshoot, social Darwinism."[6] As Shaw states here, he believes human beings are "material" that can be shaped "scientifically," that society can be improved by selective breeding, by the legislative and scientific elimination of the undesirable. The majority—those 700 out of 1000 denominated as philistines in *The Quintessence*—apparently "have no business to be alive."

Although Shaw is critical of rationalism, he recognizes and approves of instrumental rationality, represented by Loki, when in service to the higher will—in this case Wotan, who is willing his own destruction as a precondition for the arrival of the reign of Siegfried. Likewise in this intermediate phase the philistines will continue to serve the larger organizational apparatus as ordered by the elite planners. Those who are unwilling or unable to perform their role will simply be eliminated. Shaw's position leads logically to the efficient extermination of the unfit or recalcitrant, which of course the Nazis and the Soviet Politburo put into rationally ordered practice with their trains and gas chambers, show trials, purges, and labor camps, and which regimes Shaw would later expend a great deal of energy defending. Shaw expressed this opinion both in public (for instance his prefaces to *On the Rocks* and *The Simpleton of the Unexpected Isles*) and in private (as for instance a 1938 letter to Beatrice Webb, where he urges her to admit "the right of States to make eugenic experiments by weeding out all strains that they think undesirable, but insisting that they should do it as humanely as they can afford to").[7] Shaw is famous for his "humanity," that which the second clause of the sentence supposedly alludes to; his inhumanity, his endorsement of the state's right to weed out the "strains that they think undesirable" is rarely ever mentioned. It is important to note that this position is clearly stated as early as 1898 in *The Perfect Wagnerite*.

In the previous chapter we learned that the supreme individual, in Shaw's view, has freed himself from the constraints and limitations of law and morality. In the *Ring* Wagner presents Wotan as having compromised himself in contract negotiations with lesser beings. His wife Fricka represents mechanical law, which Wotan is enslaved by. Brunnhilde represents Wotan's deeper will, what Shaw calls in *The Quintessence* "the world will," an idea he gained from his reading of Schopenhauer. It is Shaw's belief that the realist (in the terminology of *The Quintessence*) or the true hero, or what he will soon call the superman in *Man and Superman*, is free of the past yet somehow connected to the deeper will of the world, which at this time in history needed to break free of the accretions of tradition and start fresh. But Wagner's Siegfried hardly seems an evolutionary advancement. He is possessed chiefly of a vigorous brutality, a need to exercise his prodigious strength in acts of violence; he lacks any intellectual or moral development, and is purely a spontaneous creature of the woods. What sets him off from most of the other characters in the *Ring* is his freedom from any acquisitive motive and his inability to experience fear. Shaw describes Siegfried as possessing a "joyous, fearless, *conscienceless* heroism" (245, my italics), and indeed it is his lack of a human conscience that Shaw seems to estimate as his greatest advantage. When we first meet Siegfried at the top of the third play he has reached young adulthood and is abusing his foster father, Mime. As Shaw puts it:

> the son [Siegfried] knows no law but his own humor; detests the ugly dwarf who has nursed him; chafes furiously under his claims for some return for his tender care; and is, in short, a totally unmoral person, a born anarchist, the ideal of Bakoonin, an anticipation of the "overman" of Nietzsche. He is enormously strong, full of life and fun, dangerous and destructive to what he dislikes, and affectionate to what he likes; so that it is fortunate that his likes and dislikes are sane and healthy. Altogether an inspiriting young forester, a son of the morning, in whom the heroic race has come out into the sunshine from the clouds of his grandfather's majestic entanglements with law, and the night of his father's tragic struggle with it. (227–28)

Wotan became entangled in law, his son Siegmund struggled tragically against it, and Siegfried is free of it.

But his freedom from conscience and law expresses itself most frequently in acts of violence. While the major religions have taught that the way to turn a person away from evil and toward a higher mode of existence is through love, Shaw recommends force as the most effective way of dealing with the bad. Although the idea of loving your enemy has been expressed in a variety of ways in many traditions, the following quote from Martin Buber's *Tales of the Hasidim* (1947) expresses the idea quite well. In the brief tale "More Love," some zaddikim (righteous ones) are discussing how to deal with "wicked or hostile persons"; they

> recalled the advice the Baal Shem Tov once gave to the father of a renegade son: that he should love him more. "When you see," they said, "that someone hates you and does you harm, rally your spirit and love him more than before. That is the only way you can make him turn."[8]

Of course it is much easier (and for some, more enjoyable) to pummel enemies into submission, much as Siegfried, in Shaw's words, "throttles Mimmy until he is speechless" (229). And it is not only easier to use force when you are stronger or have a larger stockpile of munitions but also easy to rationalize your moral superiority, whether or not you really are morally superior to your enemy (and if you are beating him "speechless" you probably are not). Mimmy is a wicked and greedy person, although Siegfried only intuits this at this point. But it should be remembered that Siegfried's grandfather, Wotan, stole the gold that Mimmy covets from Mimmy's brother Alberic, who himself acquired it unjustly when he extracted it from the Rhine at the cost of love. Had Wotan returned the gold to the Rhine instead of handing it over to the giants, the Volsungs would have the moral high ground; but as it is, Wotan is just as guilty as Alberic.

As a moral allegory *The Ring* is not as black and white as it might at first seem. Shaw realizes this, and regards Wotan as corrupted by his dealings with the giants and with Alberic in his lust for the gold. But regarding Siegfried's predilection for violence he has nothing but approval and admiration. My own reaction as an audience member when I saw the *Ring* performed was to sympathize with Mimmy; although he was weak and morally inferior he had spent many years raising the boy, and Siegfried appeared nothing more than an ungrateful bully, instinctively violent and totally lacking in intelligence, moral depth, and sympathetic imagination. Wagner can perhaps be excused for his depiction of the hero as a brutal thug since it is central to his philosophy that aggressive masculine energy needs to be tempered by uniting with the maternal and self-sacrificing energy of the feminine. Siegfried does not become complete until he unites with Brunnhilde; in that last act of the third play when he sees the sleeping Brunnhilde he learns what fear is for the first time, and becomes a new, whole person. Nonetheless, ultimately I have to agree with Gutman, who says that "for all its sublimity, there is in the *Ring* a brutality making it perhaps the ultimate artistic expression of the times."[9] Gutman has in mind the racial theories of Gobineau and the rapidly advancing theory of social Darwinism, with its ethos of the stronger races, such as the Volsungs in the *Ring*, thriving and ultimately replacing the inferior and weaker races, such as the *Ring* represents in the giants and dwarves.

While Shaw is correct in much of his analysis of the *Ring*—for instance Alberic does represent the type of greedy industrialist and Wotan does represent the compromises that our religious and political institutions have been drawn into—Wagner's allegory exists on multiple levels. Key for Wagner was just this aspect of love that Shaw denounces almost pathologically through the extent of his long career. In *The Perfect Wagnerite* Shaw expresses exasperation at what he perceives as Wagner's adulation "of Love as the remedy for all evils and the solvent of all social difficulties" (246). Shaw denounces the last act of *Siegfried* and the final play of the cycle which follows it for two reasons that were essential to Wagner's larger vision. Firstly, Siegfried is not complete by himself but must unite with Brunnhilde, thus fusing the masculine with the feminine principle, or in Jungian terms the animus with the anima. This was central to Wagner's philosophy and, as Rather remarks, is the same principle that compelled him as an artist to unite word and music, to create a "new tonal-verbal language, representing a new level of 'understanding-feeling,' of 'myth-history,' and the attainment of a perfected 'male-female' human being."[10] In other words, the theme of love for Wagner—especially as represented in the final act of *Siegfried*— is more than just a capitulation to the convention of the love duet, or, as Shaw puts it, a simple-minded expression of love as a "panacea" for all of society's ills (245). And secondly, the entire work ends in a consummation by fire with Brunnhilde and Siegfried united in death as she immolates herself in the flames that are engulfing not only her lover but Valhalla as well. Wagner embraced Schopenhauer's philosophy of annihilation of the will, and the final conflagration is a symbol of that act of annihilation. For Shaw's purely political allegorical reading, the cycle should have ended after Wotan's spear of power is broken by Siegfried and before the lone hero entangles himself with a woman.

This deeper allegorical meaning was highly offensive to Shaw, and he expends great energy and large reserves of his famous wit attempting to combat it. It is clear that a political allegory ending in fiery conflagration and destruction cannot be reconciled to Shaw's meliorism, and so he converts Wagner's meaning to a facsimile of his own deeply held utopian longings. For those of us living in the post-Nazi era the cycle is indeed uncannily prescient. In fact, although Wagner might plausibly be described as the unofficial artistic representative of the Nazi movement,[11] the *Ring* was banned after 1942 because the ending could so easily be read as an image of impending destruction for the Reich. Shaw is adamant that "the ultimate catastrophe of the Saga cannot by any perversion of ingenuity be adapted to the perfectly clear allegorical design of The Rhine Gold, The Valkyrie, and Siegfried" (239) and devotes an entire chapter attempting to prove that he understands Wagner's intentions better than Wagner.

In 1898 Shaw saw the *Ring* as illustrating the evolutionary advance from a world ruled by idealists (Wotan) to a world ruled by heroes or supermen (Siegfried). This new imminent epoch he calls "The New Protestantism," and it will bear a strong resemblance to anarchism. But this appearance is an illusion; in truth the "apparent growth of anarchy is only the measure of the rate of improvement" as history shows that "all changes from crudity of social organization to complexity, and from mechanical agencies in government to living ones, seem anarchic at first sight" (250). Wagner's cycle, for Shaw, is the "inevitable dramatic conception" (242), the ultimate vision of the future "embodied by him [Wagner] in a masterpiece" (243). Here we see the "perfectly naïve hero upsetting religion, law and order in all directions, and establishing in their place the unfettered action of Humanity doing exactly what it likes, and producing order instead of confusion thereby because it likes to do what is necessary for the good of the race" (242–43). As we saw in our study of *The Quintessence*, Shaw sees progress depending on man, or at least a certain higher class of man, severing all connection to traditional notions of religion and morality.

In his chapter "Siegfried as Protestant" Shaw places the current evolutionary phase within the historical development that was initiated by the Protestant revolution and which quickly led to the age of reason, where "the boldest spirits began to raise the question whether churches and laws and the like were not doing a great deal more harm than good by their action in limiting the freedom of the human will" (241). Shaw believes Wagner's cycle represents the highest artistic representation of the next phase of evolution because it depicts the hero as free of the restrictions of conscience. "The world has always delighted," says Shaw, "in the man who is delivered from conscience" (240). In popular culture the masses flock to see the man without conscience exercise his unrestricted will, but in the end this villain is always punished. Shaw does not say so, but clearly the masses are vicariously enjoying the id unbound while at the same time preserving their sense of themselves as moral beings (their ego) by the satisfaction they feel at justice restored at the end; their superego may also enjoy a vicarious sadistic pleasure at the rigorous punishment meted out to the rogue at the story's end. Shaw believes that though "men felt all the charm of abounding life and abandonment to its impulses, they dared not, in their deep self-mistrust, conceive it otherwise than as a force making for evil—one which must lead to universal ruin unless checked" (240). But, says Shaw, "if progress were a reality, his beneficent impulses must be gaining on his destructive one" (241). Shaw is of course making the same argument here using Wagner that he made earlier using Ibsen, and attempting to appease the doubts of his readers regarding the destructive forces that may be unleashed by severing law and morality and giving the will an open field.[12] It is interesting that Shaw was writing this at the exact time Freud was in the early stages of formulating his theories on the unconscious, and after Wagner had himself stated his cycle's coherence with

Schopenhauer's theory of the will, which Thomas Mann has described as equivalent to Freud's depiction of the id.[13]

Keeping in mind Shaw's optimism and his blind spot regarding the darker forces of the human will, it is easy to see why he suppressed or rationalized the deeper and darker aspects of Wagner's poem. Rather sees the *Ring* as an expression of a death wish inherent in the nature of Western man, a startling depiction of the suicidal course that humankind has embarked on since the beginning of the modern period, precisely the period when man began to cut loose his ties to a larger cosmological order and hubristically view himself as independent and in control of nature. It is the overbalance of masculine aggression—so clearly seen in Siegfried and admired by Shaw—that is leading the way to this doom. But Shaw implicitly trusts the course the modern world is on, and values just those attributes he should have viewed most skeptically; for it is the lust for power and the need to control and exploit nature more even than the love of money that was and remains the greatest danger to humankind (if in fact the two impulses can even be separated). Capitalism and Sovietism were both equally obsessed with increasing production and both were guilty of exploiting labor; both were dependent on gigantic bureaucracies which effectively remove individuals from the consequences of their actions. In fact Andreas Huyssen has referred to vanguard communism as capitalist "modernization's twin brother."[14] These similarities and dangers Shaw rarely, if ever, acknowledged.

In 1913, Shaw added a chapter to the new German edition of *The Perfect Wagnerite* and expressed his disgust with the Siegfrieds of the world (i.e. the inefficient revolutionaries). Shaw writes that the "end cannot come until Siegfried learns Alberic's trade and shoulders Alberic's burden" for "Alberic's work, like Wotan's work and Loki's work, is necessary work, and that therefore Alberic can never be superseded by a warrior, but only by a capable man of business who is prepared to continue his work without a day's intermission" (270). Wotan here is ruler and lawgiver to the credulous masses, Loki is reason and imagination at the service of the will, and Alberic is of course the man of business who has foresworn love—the villain of Wagner's allegory is now found by Shaw to be indispensable! What caused such a change will have to wait until the next chapter, when we look at Shaw's dramatization of this synthesis in *Major Barbara*.

More needs to be said about the aspect of love in Wagner that Shaw found so offensive. We have seen how the last act of *Siegfried* and the final play of the tetralogy upset Shaw's scheme, and throughout the essay he is constantly alerting the reader to where Wagner has gone wrong. Shaw's powerful need for order and efficiency and manly independence is upset by Siegfried's capitulation to love at the end of *Siegfried*. In fact the sexual element seems to disgust and frighten Shaw, and he describes the uniting of Siegfried and Brunnhilde in language that communicates that feeling when he says that "the womanly mixture of rapture and horror with which she abandons herself to the passion which has seized on them both, is an experience which it is much better, like the vast majority of us, never to have passed through" (248). Most of us probably feel otherwise, as such an experience is integral to living a full human life, but such expressions of hostility are frequent throughout Shaw's career and I believe connected to his longing for control, not just over his own body but over other unruly bodies as well.

In a comparison of Wagner with Shelley, Shaw criticizes them both for their overemphasis on love as a "panacea." In fact Shaw expresses some recognition here of the darker nature of Wagner's poem, of the connection between love and the unconscious. He admits that Wagner's depiction of Wotan is an advance on Shelley's depiction of Jupiter in *Prometheus Unbound* (1820), but that

> there is no progress... as regards the panacea, except that in Wagner there is a certain shadow of night and death come on it; nay, even a clear opinion that the supreme good of love is that it so completely satisfies the desire for life that after it the Will to Live ceases to trouble us, and we are at last content to achieve the highest happiness of death. (247)

Shaw says that such nonsense did

> not occupy more than two scenes of the Ring... the love panacea in Night Falls on the Gods and in the last act of Siegfried is a survival of the first crude operatic conception of the story, modified by an anticipation of Wagner's later, though not latest, conception of love as the fulfiller of our Will to Live and consequently our reconciler to night and death. (248–49)

But in truth the

> only faith which any reasonable disciple can gain from The Ring is not in love, but in life itself as a tireless power which is continually

driving onward and upward...growing from within, by its own inexplicable energy, into ever higher and higher forms of organization, the strengths and the needs of which are continually superseding the institutions which were made to fit our former requirements. When your Bakoonins call out for the demolition of all these venerable institutions, there is no need to fly into a panic and lock them up in prison. (249)

For Shaw love is an impediment to this higher organization and its manifestation in social institutions, and it is not always clear what kind of love he is talking about: eros, philos, or agape. Thirty-five years later one of his mouthpieces will respond to a religious man who clearly means agape when he speaks of love, that love is "a terrible tyranny... a devouring thing. Can you imagine heaven with love in it?"[15] With very few exceptions, Shaw kept a wary distance from all manner of love and its expression throughout his life.[16]

We can see, then, that *The Perfect Wagnerite* and *The Quintessence of Ibsenism* are saying more or less the same thing, that despite the differences in the two artists Shaw is able to use them both to express his own vision of evolutionary advance. Shaw sees the world will, operating through its highest creation, the human being, expressing itself in greater organization and efficiency. All political and religious institutions created in the past and no longer effective should be abolished, and the higher man himself needs to free himself from the burden of conscience, which impedes the free expression of his will. Shaw read Schopenhauer for the first time shortly before writing *The Quintessence*, and he believed he saw this universal urge, this will that permeates all of creation, in the Ibsenite hero; but he discarded the pessimism of Schopenhauer and concluded to his own satisfaction that this universal will was a benevolent force that manifests in more complex human social organization; it has no concern with conscience or morality, yet somehow its manifestation in world historical figures will be for the good of all.

Wagner also read Schopenhauer and explained to his friend Roeckel—then languishing in prison for his part in the Dresden uprising—that Schopenhauer's *The World as Will and Representation* (*Die Welt als Wille und Vorstellung*, 1818) was the key to understanding his masterwork, even though he himself conceived and composed the text of the *Ring* before reading Schopenhauer's book. The *Ring* ends in a fiery consummation and can be interpreted in two disparate ways, as either the annihilation of the will in the act of love and self-sacrifice or as the annihilation of the world that will ensue from the will's aggressive drive to dominate. Both readings were anathema to Shaw, and the reason he disregarded the last play.

Shaw was himself concerned almost to obsession with rulers and with ruling; he wrote about it more than any other single topic, whether in plays like *Man of Destiny* (1895), *Caesar and Cleopatra* (1898), *Major Barbara* (1905), *Annajanska, the Bolshevik Empress* (1917), *Heartbreak House* (1919), *Saint Joan* (1924), *The Apple Cart* (1929), *On the Rocks* (1933), *The Millionairess* (1935), *Geneva* (1938), and *In Good King Charles's Golden Days* (1939)—to name just some of the more salient examples— or in the political treatises he wrote such as *The Intelligent Woman's Guide to Socialism and Capitalism* (1927) and *Everybody's Political What's What?* (1944). It was the all-consuming subject for him. But Wagner's message in the *Ring* is that the desire to rule the world is a mania and brings with it unhappiness and destruction. While it may not have been possible to predict how Shaw would respond to a figure like Mussolini or Stalin when they appeared, nonetheless with knowledge of *The Quintessence* and *The Perfect Wagnerite* it should not have been surprising that he defended them and other dictators the way he did, as Beatrice Webb herself remarked in 1927 during the height of Shaw's mania for Mussolini.[17] To forge a new world order for the betterment of all requires cruelty and strength of purpose, Shaw believed, and the burden of a human conscience was only an impediment to such an enterprise. Siegfried, the realist of *The Quintessence* par excellence, was later incarnated in the era of would-be supermen claiming to lead the way to utopia by sheer force of will, and not afraid of exercising violence to bring it to pass.

Life "as a tireless power which is continually driving onward and upward...into ever higher and higher forms of organization" manifests first in the higher individual who can imagine such organization; these energetic visionaries should not be interfered with, should not be checked by lesser humans at variance with the master plan. Such rulers and their officers must be free to direct society, and to direct evolution itself, so that the lower forms are either industriously involved in making the social machine run or are removed from the gene pool. Antiquated moral conscience must not be allowed to interfere with the will just as political pluralism with its inefficiency needs to be stamped out so as not to conflict with the kind of scientific management that only a totalitarian system offers. Quaint moral considerations must be eliminated from rational planning and the "higher" will proceed unchecked. The Mimes of the world must be reformed or else they "must be killed like snakes," as Shaw's spokesperson says in the 1933 story *The Adventures of the Black Girl in Her Search for God*.[18]

Shaw was not a racist like Wagner, but his concern over Hitler's "Judeophobia" was due not to any moral aversion but to his recognition of its interference in carrying out what he believed were Hitler's larger goals, which he approved of. Writing to his German translator Siegfried Trebitsch, himself a Jew who suffered grievously under Hitler, Shaw writes: "Tell Colonel Goering...that I have backed his regime in England to the point of making myself unpopular, and shall continue to do so on all matters in which he and Hitler stand for permanent truths and Realpolitik. But this racial stuff is damned English nonsense."[19] Later he came to believe that Hitler's many "successes" induced in him a megalomania that spoiled his great promise. Nonetheless, as the quoted letter to Beatrice Webb above attests, he defended Hitler's right to make eugenic experiments. But while in 1938 he defended Hitler's right to deal with the "Jewish problem" in any way he saw fit, in 1945 he refused to believe in the Nazi genocide and instead characterized it as a problem of mismanagement and inefficiency:

> These Germans had to live in the camp with their prisoners. It must have been very uncomfortable and dangerous for them. But they had been placed in authority and management, and had to organize the feeding, lodging, and sanitation of more and more thousands of prisoners and refugees thrust upon them by the central government...Only eminent leadership, experience, and organizing talent could deal with such a situation. Well, they simply lacked these qualities...When further overcrowding became physically impossible they could do nothing with their unwalled prisoners but kill them and burn the corpses they could not bury. And even this they could not organize frankly and competently.
>
> (vol. 5, 637–38)

This is from the preface to *Geneva*, written in 1945 after the reality of the atrocities of the Holocaust had been disclosed. Shaw's sole concern is with criticizing the lack of efficiency and organization, and with denying the purpose of the camps, which was to exterminate human beings.

In reality, as Zygmunt Bauman has shown, the Holocaust is a "textbook of scientific management," a "paradigm of modern bureaucratic rationality"[20] and a warning of what can happen when absolute power is backed by a large bureaucracy charged with administering a utopian design of the rulers' making. Shaw wanted to see Hitler and Stalin succeed; both leaders' attempted to produce a utopian society of their own subjectivist creation, and both had the new tools of modernity to execute their wills. Both dictators determined that certain people did not fit into their design, and as logic demanded got rid of them. Shaw hated democracy because it put power into the hands of the philistines who could then thwart the will of would-be utopian visionaries, not realizing that that is precisely democracy's greatest strength. As Bauman remarks, "In the USSR the systematic destruction of the real and putative adversaries of the system took off in earnest only after the residues of social autonomy, and hence of the political pluralism which reflected it, had been extirpated."[21] It was the same in Germany: once democratic institutions were abolished or entirely under the control of the Party, then the elimination of the Jews and other undesirables could proceed step by step until logic—devoid of any moral residue—arrived at the Final Solution.

Shaw always recognized that to live beyond good and evil was for the elite class of spiritual aristocrats and not for the mass of men and women. Siegfried is admired by Shaw because he resembles what he believes is the best side of Wagner's multi-faceted personality, one of the "most pugnacious, aggressive and sanguine of reformers" (280). I think it is fair to interpret the word "sanguine" in its fullest sense as not only cheerful and optimistic, but as bloody as well; for Siegfried is certainly sanguinary as well as sanguine, as we might expect from an aggressive and pugnacious social reformer. If Plato's *Republic* can be read both macrocosmically and microcosmically, so to speak, as both a blueprint for an ideal society and as a metaphor for the perfectly balanced individual, then I think Shaw's dictators and their elite officers represent the controlling apparatus capable of managing the unruly elements, what in the individual are the natural instincts and primitive drives. In other words the "realists" are the controlling apparatus and the "philistines" are the instincts that need to be controlled or rooted out. As Daniel Dervin remarks in his psychological study of Shaw, "The people, like the appetites and instincts, must be governed; the ruler will decide how."[22] Shaw was at heart an anarchist, as all realists as described in *The Quintessence* are, and he chafed at any external control because he felt he could provide that control himself. But the mass of men need to be externally controlled.

For this reason Shaw recognizes that law and morality and religion are tools that the leaders use to control their subjects, but beyond that have no meaning. Shaw can be confusing, for the hero's "upsetting religion, law, and order in all directions, and establishing in their place the unfettered action of Humanity doing exactly what it likes" (242–43) directly contradicts his proclamation regarding the institutions that must govern the philistines, "Wagner's giants, [who] must be governed by laws; and their assent to such government must be secured by deliberately filling them with prejudices and practicing on their imaginations by pageantry and artificial eminences and dignities" (242). In both *The Quintessence of Ibsenism* and *The Perfect Wagnerite* it sometimes seems as though Shaw is predicting a utopian world where everyone will be free and in control of their lives, and while this may be his larger evolutionary vision—or at least it seems to be by the time he writes *Back to Methuselah* in 1920—nonetheless in these early works the era of freedom from law, morality, and religion is for the elite; the mob must still be controlled by them.

The year of *The Perfect Wagnerite*'s composition was a pivotal year in Shaw's life. He was plagued by a series of physical misfortunes and had to get around on crutches for the better part of the year. After experiencing surgery on his toe he later fell down the stairs and broke his arm. And later again, while trying to ride a bicycle with his one good foot, he fell and sprained his ankle. He also married the Irish heiress Charlotte Payne-Townsend, who had been nursing him. And in 1898 he wrote *Caesar and Cleopatra*. It is curious that Shaw chose to write about Siegfried and Caesar at the same time, especially when he himself was so disabled and dependent on Charlotte for so much; both characters show sides of the conquering hero that Shaw admired: they both show Shaw's disgust with the world as it is and his desire to create a new one out of the ashes of the old, with as little trace of the former remaining as possible.

It is easy to read Shaw and believe that he felt a new world was right around the corner, but in his "Notes to Caesar and Cleopatra" he frankly admits that not only has there been no progress over the previous 2000 plus years but that humankind appears to be going in the wrong direction: "it will strike us at once as an unaccountable fact that the world, instead of having been improved in 67 generations out of all recognition, presents, on the whole, a rather less dignified appearance in Ibsen's Enemy of the People than in Plato's Republic" (vol. 3, 472). His choice for comparison is very telling. *An Enemy of the People*, as we have discussed already, shows the modern democratic world being overrun by a mindless and dangerous mob; and Plato's *Republic*—the first carefully crafted literary utopia—presents a totalitarian world where every aspect of society is managed and controlled, and each person assigned his or her precise place within the hierarchy, a society with three orders, very much like Shaw's tripartite world of philistines, idealists, and realists. Shaw was terrified even as he was thrilled by the possibilities of modernity, and longed for strong commanding personalities to order the chaos he felt around him, much as Plato feared and loathed modern democratic Athens and looked to the iron discipline of Sparta for his model of a properly ordered society.

Like Joyce, Shaw experienced history as a nightmare from which he hoped humanity might soon awaken. But it required a Caesar to do the waking. In *Caesar and Cleopatra* the exotic and passionate world of Egypt requires Roman discipline and Caesar's disinterested puritan work ethic and abstemiousness to bring order. When the library of Alexandria goes up in flames and Caesar shows that he is indifferent to the loss, the horrified Theodotus cries in exasperation that it is the memory of mankind that is burning; Caesar glibly remarks, "A shameful memory. Let it burn" and Theodotus *"wildly"* queries, "Will you destroy the past?" to which Caesar replies, "Ay, and build the future with its ruins" (vol. 3, 407). The same desire is expressed repeatedly throughout Shaw's career, including in *The Perfect Wagnerite* where he describes Siegfried as working at the "bellows with the shouting exultation of the anarchist who destroys only to clear the ground for creation" (232). Unfortunately, Shaw failed to realize that in attempting to expunge the sordid history of mankind one runs the risk of expunging the good as well, and that, as Nietzsche says, "He who fights with monsters should look to it that he himself does not become a monster."[23]

Zigmunt Bauman uses a metaphor that Shaw was also fond of using, the metaphor of society as a garden:[24]

> Modernity ... is an age of artificial order and of grand societal designs, the era of planners, visionaries, and—more generally—'gardeners' who treat society as a virgin plot of land to be expertly designed and then cultivated ... There is no limit to ambition and self-confidence. Indeed, through the spectacles of modern power mankind seems so omnipotent and its individual members so 'incomplete,' inept, and submissive, and so much in need of improvement, that treating people as plants to be trimmed (if necessary, uprooted) or cattle to be bred does not look fanciful or morally odious.[25]

Shaw was such a visionary and planner, and he recognized in Wagner a kindred spirit, an artist who had created the quintessential allegory of the future in his dramatic poem the *Ring*, with its image of the superman

Siegfried, devoid of conscience, ready to destroy his enemies without compunction. In the new world order the law would be obsolete, except where it might be imposed on the lower orders as a means of restraining anti-social behavior. Of course while the "trickle-down theory" in economics has been exposed as a fraud, in morals the theory holds true. As Shaw recognizes in *The Perfect Wagnerite*, when the lower orders realize that the elite no longer subscribe to the rules of law and morality, there is a problem. It was a problem he as yet had not given much thought to. First of all, Shaw himself needed to break free from the constraints of law, the burden of believing in a transcendent moral code, a code that so wracked his conscience as a youth and that he now believed was a sham.

Three decades earlier Dostoyevsky, an author Shaw rarely mentions, wrote *Crime and Punishment* (1866) and expertly illustrated the process whereby a man is destroyed when he sets out to be a Napoleon, free of the moral law, who rationalizes to himself that the murder he carries out will be a crime of social utility. Raskolnikov is destroyed,[26] but because he does have a conscience and is open to love he is still able to experience a kind of resurrection in Siberia. Paul Tillich once remarked that

> the written code in its threatening majesty has the power to kill. It kills the joy of fulfilling our being by imposing upon us something we feel as hostile. It kills the freedom of answering creatively what we encounter in things and men by making us look at a table of laws.

Yet for all this, "There is no way out from the written code."[27] In their madness then as now the Siegfrieds of the world believe there is a way out, and they have left the world in flames.

3
From Hell to Heaven: Creative Evolution and the Drive toward the Military-Industrial-Religious Complex: *Man and Superman, John Bull's Other Island, Major Barbara*

The new century brought a breakthrough in dramatic form and philosophical understanding for Shaw. His marriage to the Irish Heiress Charlotte Payne-Townsend in 1898 and his first economically successful play, *The Devil's Disciple* (1897, produced by Richard Mansfield in America), freed Shaw from financial anxiety, and he soon set off on an entirely new course dramaturgically. After *Caesar and Cleopatra* and *The Perfect Wagnerite* he wrote one more play, *Captain Brassbound's Conversion* (1899), before he set to work on a new kind of play that would mark the beginning of his second and most productive phase as a dramatist. *Man and Superman* was not finished until late 1902, and was published in 1903 with a preface, "Epistle Dedicatory," followed by the very lengthy play, a concluding essay – *The Revolutionist's Handbook*, purportedly written by the central character, Jack Tanner – and finally, appended to the *Handbook*, Tanner's "Maxims for Revolutionists." The Penguin edition runs to 264 pages. Certainly nothing quite like this had been seen before, and Shaw was clearly exhilarated by his breakthrough as a dramatist for the entire work is charged by an energetic sense of discovery, a feeling, sometimes a bit overbearing, that he has hit on the secret of the universe.

After ten years of writing plays that were rarely given a proper chance on the boards, Shaw had become used to the idea of being read rather than performed, which was still a novel idea during the late Victorian and Edwardian years. He had published a third volume in 1900 called *Plays for Puritans* (which included *Caesar and Cleopatra, The*

Devil's Disciple, and *Captain Brassbound's Conversion*), and so was quite accustomed to augmenting his plays with additions, such as prefaces and lengthy stage directions, meant for the reading public as opposed to theatergoers; in fact due to its length he never expected *Man and Superman* to be performed at all in its entirety, and he specified that acts one, two, and four might be acted with the third act omitted while this third act, eventually titled *Don Juan in Hell*, might receive its own independent production. This long act, most of which is a dream sequence, represents Shaw's philosophy of the Life Force in the form of a Platonic dialogue; and even at the end of his life Shaw claimed that *Don Juan in Hell* and *Back to Methuselah* (1921) were the clearest expressions of his philosophical and religious views—in the foreword to a new edition in 1911 he wrote that "the third act, however fantastic its legendary framework may appear, is a careful attempt to write a new Book of Genesis for the Bible of the Evolutionists" (vol. 3, 748).[1] Therefore, it is of the greatest importance to our further understanding of the evolution of Shaw's "utopian vision."

Shaw followed *Man and Superman* with *John Bull's Other Island*, which he wrote initially for the Abbey Theatre in Dublin at Yeats' request. The Abbey did not produce it, however, and the play received its premiere at the Court Theatre in London under the auspices of the new managing partnership of John Vedrenne and Harley Granville-Barker; *John Bull* was their third production, the first being Shaw's *Candida* (1895) and the second Gilbert Murray's translation of Euripides' *Hippolytus*. All three plays were produced in 1904, but *John Bull* was their first unqualified success, and Shaw instantly became the most famous dramatist in London (and soon the world), while the Vedrenne-Barker productions at the Court between 1904 and 1907 (most of them Shaw plays that he himself essentially directed) are among the most important in English theatrical history. In May of 1905 *Man and Superman* was produced, the third act being omitted, with Barker modeling his performance of Tanner on Shaw. And in November 1905 Shaw's *Major Barbara* was performed.

These three plays, *Man and Superman*, *John Bull's Other Island*, and *Major Barbara*, form a philosophical trilogy and are extremely important, not only for their masterful dramatic construction, but for what they reveal about Shaw's overall vision of the world. They show him attempting to work out a synthesis of his religion of Creative Evolution with his political socialism.[2] In *Man and Superman* Shaw is clearly elated by his more comprehensive understanding of the Life Force and its operation within humankind, as well as with his newly mastered dialectical form, his advance with the drama of ideas or discussion play that he had hoped to perfect since he first experienced Ibsen's *A Doll's House*; but in *Man and Superman* there is no sense of how these ideas will play out in the development of political institutions. Tanner, who is Shaw's spokesman, is a bit of a buffoon and his alter ego Don Juan Tenorio can only express himself in the amorphous hell of Shaw's (or Tanner's) imagination. The ideas do not live in the concrete world of political fact.

In *John Bull's Other Island* the action takes place very much in the concrete world of socio-economic and political fact, but intellect, material efficiency, and spiritual vision are isolated from one another in three disparate central characters, and so the optimism of *Man and Superman* is superseded by a dark and frustrated pessimism. In the third play, *Major Barbara*, Shaw unites the three necessary faculties by having the three central characters come together in collaboration at Undershaft's munitions factory. This complex of workplace and residence at Perivale St. Andrews is utopia in miniature, a microcosm of what Shaw hopes to see spread across the globe: poverty has been eradicated, crime is presumably negligible or non-existent, cleanliness and order are the norm, and the violence necessary to maintain such an order is, by the end of the play, in the hands of modern-day philosopher kings, such as Plato first described in his own literary utopia, *The Republic*.

At this point it might be useful to consider Shaw from the perspective developed by Roger Griffin in his book *Modernism and Fascism: The Sense of a Beginning under Mussolini and Hitler*. Griffin aims to loosen up the rigid lines dividing cultural modernism from social and political modernism; he sees all totalitarian movements of the twentieth century, whether Italian Fascism, German National Socialism, or Russian Communism, as alternative modernisms, "revitalization movements" responding to the crisis of modernity and seeking to realize a "temporalized utopia."[3] Playwrights, poets, novelists, and modern artists of all sorts are also responding to the anomy and disjointedness, the temporal rupture that is modernity, and seeking to find relief from the stressful "liminoidality" by creatively discovering new individual or cultural *nomos*.

Artists fall into two general types: epiphanic modernists such as James Joyce and Samuel Beckett, and programmatic modernists such as Shaw:

> There is a common matrix behind modernism in the bewildering heterogeneity of concrete manifestations... this matrix is usefully seen as the search for transcendence and regeneration, whether confined to a personal quest for ephemeral moments of enlightenment or

expanded to take the form of a cultural, social, or political movement for the renewal of the nation or the whole of Western civilization.[4]

Programmatic modernists such as Shaw seek to "inaugurate an entirely new era of society within historical time."[5] Certainly Shaw made no secret of his intention to change the world, both with his playwriting and with his more overtly political work. He had nothing but contempt for what Griffin calls epiphanic modernists and even says in the preface to the very play we are about to consider in greater detail, *Man and Superman*, that "'for art's sake' alone I would not face the toil of writing a single sentence" (vol. 3, 514). The solution to the malaise that is the modern world is effective breeding and the subsequent arrival of a new human being destined to save mankind from itself. The purpose of life is evolutionary advance, a progression to higher and more complex forms of biological and institutional organization. This is what the play announces with such fervor, and Shaw seems to believe that once this is understood human beings can begin to order society accordingly, moving away from the degeneration and decadence that had so concerned *fin-de-siècle* intellectuals.

In 1899–1900 there was a crisis within the Fabian Society, a crisis that would result in the resignation of a significant number of members, including future Labour Leader and Prime Minister Ramsay MacDonald, who was a member of the Fabian executive committee at the time, and Emmeline Pankhurst, future leader of the suffragette movement, to name just two of the more notable to leave as a result of the conflict. The reason for the split was the Boer War. Shaw, Sidney Webb, and other members of the executive committee believed that as the most advanced nation in the world Great Britain needed to be an imperial force, and thus they supported Britain's involvement in the South African war.

In early 1900, the Society published its views in a manifesto that was written by Shaw, although he made a heroic effort to include the many critical suggestions and ideas he had collected from about 150 other Fabians. *Fabianism and the Empire* (1900) is therefore the Fabian Society's definitive view on the issue of imperialism and on the role that the British Empire should play in world affairs. It is important to keep this in mind as it forms the immediate background to Shaw's composing of *Man and Superman*, and indeed marks a new phase of international thinking within the Fabian Society that continued as Shaw wrote the other two plays considered in this chapter. Thus understood, Shaw's lampooning of Roebuck Ramsden takes on greater resonance. Tanner is the type of new revolutionary thinker needed to lead England into her new role in international affairs while Ramsden represents the Liberal anti-imperialists and their outmoded ways of thinking, who "with regard to the British Empire," in the words of Sidney Webb, were "mere administrative Nihilists—that is to say... ultra-Gladstonian, old-Liberal to the finger tips... as hopelessly out of the running as the Gladstonian party," and who have no understanding of the need for "the deliberate organization of the empire."[6]

Webb wrote these words in 1901, about a year before he formed a shadow cabinet or "brains' trust," the Coefficients, a group of twelve highly influential experts in various affairs such as the military, the navy, law, finance, foreign affairs, journalism, science, and municipal affairs. Webb himself was the expert on municipal affairs, Bertrand Russell on science, and H.G. Wells on literature. Webb's intention was ultimately to form a new "party of national efficiency," although this never materialized. It is perhaps worth noting that Russell later felt compelled to resign after "listening to a series of fanatical statements about the empire" and feeling, in his own words, that he would "rather wreck the Empire than sacrifice freedom."[7] Shaw was not an original member of the Coefficients, but was asked by Webb to join later.

While Roebuck Ramsden presents no problems and is rather easy to place in the play, Tanner is somewhat problematical. As mentioned earlier, he comes off as a bit of a buffoon, as someone highly developed intellectually but blind to the concrete reality of everyday life. For instance, he is the last to know that Ann has her sights set on marrying him and not the foolish love-sick poet Octavius (or "Tavy") as he so ludicrously believes. Ramsden is lampooned as a Gladstonian Liberal forever stuck in the heady and progressive 1860s, and as the curtain rises we see him in his office surrounded by representations of the leading intellectuals of a now bygone era: we see the busts and portraits of John Bright, Richard Cobden, Herbert Spencer, T.H. Huxley, and George Eliot. He believes he is the most advanced of men, but rejects out of hand the new wave of revolutionary intellectual as represented by Tanner. In the opening minutes of the play he tells Octavius that he has in his hand "a copy of the most infamous, the most scandalous, the most mischievous, the most blackguardly book that ever escaped burning at the hands of the common hangman. I have not read it: I would not soil my mind with such filth; but I have read what the papers say of it" (vol. 3, 521). Of course the book he refers to is Tanner's *The Revolutionist's Handbook and Pocket Companion*. Ramsden is the quintessential Shavian idealist, who is unable to dispense with ideas and institutions after they have outlived their usefulness; and since such men are very active in civil life and tend to control the levers of power, they present a major obstacle to the advancement of society.

Tanner is more complex, and I think can be seen as serving different functions in the play. Most importantly, he is Shaw's mouthpiece. The ideas he presents are Shaw's ideas, but he does not really get a chance to express them with any kind of fullness until the long dream sequence in the third act, and then he has been transformed into Don Juan. His essay, appended to the back of the book and therefore not available to playgoers, *The Revolutionist's Handbook*, also clearly expresses Shaw's revolutionary ideas. We will have more to say shortly about these ideas, as expressed both in the dream and in the *Handbook*. In the third act dream sequence Tanner, now Don Juan, is suave, fully aware, and in complete command of the situation, unlike his counterpart in the rest of the play. Why does Shaw make Tanner such an ineffectual fool in the "outer" play? A couple of possibilities suggest themselves.

One is taken from Max Beerbohm. Speaking of Beerbohm's initial reaction to the characters of *Man and Superman*, which he felt were caricatures, Michael Holroyd says that for Beerbohm "Shaw was one of those for whom the visible world had largely ceased to exist and was being replaced by a world seen through his mind's eye."[8] Tanner, like Shaw according to this interpretation, is constructing a blueprint world in his mind, a Platonic ideal world more real to him than the actual three-dimensional world of everyday life. Such characters are always amusing when seen onstage for the incongruity of their mental world and the world of hard fact that they inevitably bump up against. Only in the dream world of act three does a Platonic idealist like Tanner (as opposed to the other kind first formulated by Shaw in *The Quintessence*) cease to be funny. Then there is the fact that Shaw as GBS—much to the chagrin of many of his friends, such as William Archer—frequently presented himself as a buffoon as well. So Tanner/Don Juan is a fairly apt representation of GBS/Shaw, right down to the running away from a woman in pursuit of marriage with him and his final capitulation.

Shaw subtitled his play "A Comedy and a Philosophy" and felt it was "useless as an acting play...as long as three Meyerbeer operas and no audience that had not already had a Shaw education could stand it."[9] Nonetheless, the play was performed in 1905 twice and again in 1906 and 1907, but always with the third act omitted; it was the most popular play by Shaw at the Court, with 176 performances; in 1907 the dream sequence of act three was finally performed at the Court as *Don Juan in Hell*. It has remained a popular "play" of the Shaw cannon and has been performed many times over the years independent of the outer play. Nonetheless, *Man and Superman* as a whole is a highly unified play and Shaw's intention as an artist is undermined when it is not performed as originally written, the philosophy adding dimensions to the comedy and vice-versa.

In the outer play we see Tanner's philosophy of the Life Force operating, principally through the character of the unscrupulous Ann Whitefield, "*one of the vital geniuses*" (vol. 3, 530). So it is of course ironic that the articulate espouser of the Life Force is blind to its actual machinations as it operates in the world. He wants to remain a bachelor to better fulfill his role as propagandist of the Life Force, but the Life Force has other plans for him—it wants him and Ann to produce a higher and more complex biological offspring, one step closer to the superman. And this brings us to the central theme of the play, especially when taken as a multi-faceted work of literature, much as Blake's *Marriage of Heaven and Hell* (1793). Beatrice Webb hit on this early on when Shaw first read the play to her and a small group of friends before it was published: "He has found his *form*: a play which is not a play; but only a combination of essay, treatise, interlude, lyric—all the different forms illustrating the same central idea."[10] That central idea is that the way out of the current socio-political impasse is eugenics.

This theme is announced in the preface where Shaw says that "we are all now under what Burke called 'the hoofs of the swinish multitude'" (vol. 3, 502), that "our political experiment of democracy, the last refuge of cheap misgovernment, will ruin us if our citizens are ill bred" (vol. 3, 501), and that we "must either breed political capacity or be ruined by Democracy" (vol. 3, 503). "Plutocratic inbreeding has produced a weakness of character that is too timid to face the full stringency of a thoroughly competitive struggle for existence and too lazy and petty to organize the commonwealth co-operatively" (vol. 3, 503–4). The way out of this muddle, Shaw believes, is for a more responsible state to guide the breeding of its citizens; however, "[b]eing cowards, we defeat natural selection under cover of philanthropy: being sluggards, we neglect artificial selection under cover of delicacy and morality" (vol. 3, 504). Of course, in the play the Life Force needs little assistance bringing Ann and Jack together, despite his sedulous efforts to evade her pursuit once he learns of it, just as in *Major Barbara* the Life Force is able to lead Cusins to the Salvation Army where he remains as a volunteer so he can be near Barbara, certainly a most unusual place for an Oxbridge classical scholar to find himself. But as *Man and Superman* and other dramatic and non-dramatic writings of Shaw make clear, in the name of national efficiency eugenic experiments need to be conducted by the state, reproduction being entirely too important to be left to such indiscriminate pairings.

The word "eugenics" was coined in 1883 by Sir Francis Galton, the brilliant English scientist and nephew of Charles Darwin. Galton was a lifelong advocate of eugenics, or selective breeding, and the principal contributor to the section on eugenics in the *Sociological Papers*, published in 1905 by the Sociological Society. Shaw has a short entry in the publication under the chapter heading, "Written Communications." He says that he agrees

> with the paper, and [would] go so far as to say that there is now no reasonable excuse for refusing to face the fact that nothing but a eugenic religion can save our civilization from the fate that has overtaken all previous civilizations. It is worth pointing out that we never hesitate to carry out the negative side of eugenics with considerable zest, both on the scaffold and on the battlefield... but we take no real scientific steps to make sure that the Englishman, when he gets there, will be able to live up to our assumption of his superiority... men and woman are amazingly indiscriminate and promiscuous in their attachments: they select their wives and husbands far less carefully than they select their cashiers and cooks... I am afraid we must make up our minds either to face a considerable shock to vulgar opinion in this matter or to let eugenics alone.[11]

Shaw's approbation of a "eugenic religion" is an echo of Galton's own sentiment, where he says in the *Sociological Papers* that eugenics "must be introduced into the national conscience, like a new religion. It has, indeed, strong claims to become an orthodox religious tenet of the future, for eugenics cooperate with the workings of nature by securing that humanity shall be represented by the fittest races."[12] The increasing hope placed by elites in eugenics as a panacea for society's ills requires some elucidation.

Toward the end of the nineteenth century the increase in urban population and slums alarmed many intellectuals, who under a Darwinian interpretation of social reality had become convinced that decay and degeneration were on track to destroy civilization, and that it was necessary to create an "imperial race."[13] "In Britain," according to historian J.W. Burrow,

> eugenic concern was a matter first of class... the less able, thrifty and responsible seemed to be outbreeding their intellectual and moral

betters; the survival of the fittest, if not treated as an ironic tautology, seemed in danger of becoming a falsehood. London, too, with its swarming yet partly invisible masses of the unhealthy, ill-fed poor, became something of an obsession.[14]

Shaw had been horrified by the dirt, poverty, and drunkenness found in the urban ghetto ever since he first encountered them in the Dublin slums as a boy; his nurse had a weekly rendezvous there and young George was brought along, much to his horror.[15] All his life long Shaw felt that poverty was the greatest crime, and its eradication by scientific means was sure to appeal to him:

> The idea of science as the means to conscious control of mass society by a rational elite, acting to arrest an otherwise irresistible tendency to regression or degeneration, is also the central idea of Eugenics... one decided whom one wanted to breed and to rear offspring and then tried to arrange the environment accordingly. It was akin to what Darwin in *The Origin* had called 'artificial selection.'[16]

Shaw was of course not alone in his championing of eugenics, although even Karl Pearson, one of the authors of the *Sociological Papers*, felt that Shaw "went further than Galton certainly approved."[17] Both Pearson and Galton were worried that Shaw's powerful rhetoric and propensity for shocking the bourgeois would alarm the public, and Pearson asked Shaw to employ the subtle tactic of permeation that he had learned as a Fabian.[18] With this background we are in a good position to look at act three of *Man and Superman*, according to Shaw one of the two most important philosophical statements of his career, along with *Back to Methuselah*.

Man and Superman

It is significant that both of these works, *Don Juan in Hell* and *Back to Methuselah*, are removed from the everyday world as we know it, each being set in a mythical otherworld and perhaps as Plato's ideal forms more real to Shaw than the sordid world of the nineteenth and twentieth centuries. Most of act three takes place in a nebulous region or void—"omnipresent nothingness" is how he refers to it (vol. 3, 600)—that Shaw calls "hell," where romance, pleasure and love are of supreme value and the mental cogitations and designs of the "philosophic man" maligned. These values are championed by the Devil, who is the surrogate of the love-sick romantic brigand Mendoza. Like Tavy, Mendoza lives only in the hopes of blissful union with the woman of his dreams, and spends his time imagining this union and writing love poetry. The Devil, who absorbs into his person not only Tavy and Mendoza but the whole of the nineteenth-century aesthetic movement of "art for art's sake," proves a formidable opponent of Don Juan, and it is not even clear that Juan wins the debate, although clearly Shaw intends him to. For the fact is that whatever else this long act is, it is the supreme achievement of twentieth-century dialectical drama, the prototype of other exemplars of the genre, such as Peter Weiss's *Marat/Sade* (1964) and Tom Stoppard's *Travesties* (1974).

But while Shaw might arguably be considered the inventor of the modern dialectical drama, the genre really has its beginnings in the dialogues of Plato, Shaw's great mentor formalistically and philosophically. Shaw signals as much in the preface when he calls the dream sequence a "Shavio-Socratic dialogue" (vol. 3, 494). There is a fascinating anecdote, which may or may not be true, which asserts that Plato as a young man desired to join the ranks of the great tragic poets, but that after meeting Socrates and listening to the great man philosophize he gave up his ambition and burned his poems. The anecdote has the ring of truth because, in fact, Plato never relinquished his talent and predilection for dramatizing, as is evident to anyone who has read his dialogues. What he did instead, in direct contrast to his master Socrates who never wrote anything, was create a new literary form based on the Socratic Method with the obvious intention of influencing his countrymen.

This anecdote also bears a striking similarity to the evolution of Shaw's career: Shaw wanted to be a great novelist, but then he heard Henry George lecture on economics, and his life was given new meaning, impetus and direction, concrete efforts at socialist reform superseding creative writing for almost ten years. Later on and with the intention of permeating London society with his revolutionary ideas, Shaw (like Plato with his dialogues) began writing plays, which he finally mastered to his own satisfaction in the third act of *Man and Superman*, the first great species of modern dialectical drama. Plato was doing battle with the conventional thinking of democratic Athens, a form of government that he, like Shaw, despised, and his most influential dialogue is *The Republic*, the first great work of utopian literature: "the act of writing philosophy in dialogues therefore constituted a challenge to existing Athenian culture, that what had previously been done on the tragic stage amid great spectacle and verbal pyrotechnics would henceforth be the task of a new kind of writing... by someone who could reason about the issues."[19] Shaw, as contemptuous of what he called Sardoodledom as Plato was of Athenian popular tragedy, nevertheless borrows liberally from the nineteenth-century melodrama and farce of his day to create a new, modern version of Platonic dialectical comic drama.

The key to a successful Platonic dialogue is providing Socrates with a worthy rival, and thereby penetrating deeper into the reality that lies behind conventions. Plato himself calls this "dialectical science"[20] and remarks that "when there is some contradiction always present... then thought begins to be aroused within us, and the soul perplexed and wanting to arrive at a decision asks 'What is absolute unity?'"[21] Eric Bentley has said of Shaw:

> Nowhere... does one have a sense of dialectic as keenly as in a Shavian play... he has a sense of every conceivable point of view... which climbs by parallelisms and antitheses to a climax, and then sinks with the finality of a conqueror to a conclusion which Shaw will not allow you to evade.[22]

Like Plato, Shaw valued unity above all else, and in the preface to *Man and Superman* places Bunyan, Blake, Hogarth, and Turner above Shakespeare and Dickens because the latter are "concerned with the diversities of the world instead of its unities" and "have no constructive ideas: they regard those who have them as dangerous fanatics" (vol. 3, 508). What I want to argue now is that Shaw in act three of *Man and Superman* puts a great deal of himself into both agonists, the Devil and Don Juan, and that while it is clear that we are to side with Juan in his exposition of the religion of the Life Force, we are also compelled to agree with the Devil's exposition of man's destructiveness, perhaps not realizing that the two together synthesize into what for Shaw was of supreme importance: the ethos of creative destruction.

The most important thing we are to learn from this Shavio-Socratic dialogue is that there is a purpose immanent in the world and that all our efforts should be geared to discerning that purpose and consciously aiding its advance—although in reality only those gifted with some attributes of the future race of supermen will be able to grasp that purpose, the philosophical men and women willing to put forth the superhuman effort needed to discern it and who have the courage and tenacity to put it into practice, those willing to steer against the tide rather than drift with the tide (vol. 3, 646). Socrates was a gadfly to Athenian society and paid for this propensity with his life; Shaw was a revolutionary gadfly who partially concealed his intentions by playing the role of the comic buffoon. Shaw believed, and said so at various times throughout his life, that it was necessary to play the clown if you wanted to avoid the fate of Socrates and Jesus.[23] Shaw also believed that by diffusing his ideas into society via humor, they would take root unconsciously amid the laughter and later bear fruit. It was a form of permeation that did not put the prophet at too much risk, and, hopefully, was equally if not more effective. Shaw's motto was Keegan's great line from *John Bull*: "Every jest is an earnest in the womb of time" (vol. 2, 611).[24]

To arrive at social institutions that serve humankind instead of hindering its progress, Shaw believes, it is necessary to hand the reins of power over to those whom he calls the philosophic men, the "masters of reality" (vol. 3, 616), in essence the philosopher kings who were to rule in Plato's ideal city. The "philosophic man: he who seeks in contemplation to discover the inner will of the world, in invention to discover the means of fulfilling that will, and in action to do that will by the so-discovered means" (vol. 3, 628) is one who must embrace creative destruction without squeamishness, clearing away the rubbish that has accumulated over the centuries. This destruction will sometimes involve physical violence and sometimes it will not. Don Juan drives home his argument persistently throughout the act, insisting that life is "evolving today a mind's eye that shall see, not the physical world, but the purpose of Life, and thereby enable the individual to work for that purpose instead of thwarting and baffling it by setting up shortsighted personal aims as at present" (vol. 3, 628). But the Devil is equally persistent, claiming that

> in the arts of life man invents nothing; but in the arts of death he outdoes Nature herself, and produces by chemistry and machinery all the slaughter of plague, pestilence, and famine... This marvelous force of Life of which you boast is a force of Death: Man measures his strength by his destructiveness. What is his religion? An excuse for hating me. What is his law? An excuse for hanging you. What is his morality? Gentility! an excuse for consuming without producing. What is his art? An excuse for gloating over pictures of slaughter. What are his politics? Either the worship of a despot because a despot can kill, or parliamentary cock-fighting.
> (vol. 3, 619–20)

Shaw's voice is unmistakable in both characters. What is needed to rise above such wanton destruction is the breeding of a higher type of human being, for such human beings are too rare at present. This is indeed why Shaw wrote the play, so that we might recognize the "great central purpose of breeding the race: aye, breeding it to heights now deemed superhuman" (vol. 3, 637). Although such men are all too rare at the present time, it is imperative that we listen to and obey the few who do exist. An early Shavian biographer, R.F. Rattray, remarked in 1951 that Shaw had "an itch that other people's affairs should be managed efficiently," and he quotes Frank Harris who said that when Shaw came to visit you expected brilliant conversation but "before you know where you are, he has chosen a school for your son, made your will for you, regulated your diet, and assumed all the privileges of your family solicitor, your housekeeper, your clergyman, your doctor, your dressmaker, your hairdresser, and your estate agent."[25] Later in life Shaw's frustration at not being obeyed despite believing he held the key to a much more organized, efficient, rational, and sane social structure was palpable, and he remarked disgustedly that the "successful man...is one who has people doing what he wants them to do. But they're always doing what I don't want them to."[26] Shaw certainly considered himself such a higher type of human being, although only a foretaste of what the future would later bring. And he frequently equates this higher type of man with God. In a very favorable book on Shaw, Maurice Valency has said that at the end of his life Shaw "was entirely comfortable in his megalomania. In his moments of exaltation he felt not merely that he was godlike, but actually that he was God."[27] Like God, Shaw embraces both creation and destruction as necessary agents of evolution.

When Shaw was fourteen he had a psychological experience that was to have a profound effect on him, a life-changing internal event he was to describe in various places throughout his life.[28] The transformation is described by Tanner toward the end of act one in the first long scene in which he is alone with Ann: "the change that came to me was the birth in me of moral passion; and I declare that according to my experience moral passion is the only real passion" (vol. 3, 549). Ann responds by reminding Jack that there are other passions as well, "very strong ones." The scene warrants looking at more fully:

> Tanner. All the other passions were in me before; but they were idle and aimless—mere childish greediness and cruelties, curiosities and fancies, habits and superstitions, grotesque and ridiculous to the mature intelligence. When they suddenly began to shine like newly

lit flames it was by no light of their own, but by the radiance of the dawning moral passion. That passion dignified them, gave them conscience and meaning, found them a mob of appetites and organized them into an army of purposes and principles. My soul was born of that passion.

Ann. I notice that you got more sense. You were a dreadfully destructive boy before that.

Tanner. Destructive! Stuff! I was only mischievous.

Ann. Oh, Jack you were very destructive. You ruined all the young fir trees by chopping off their leaders with a wooden sword. You broke all the cucumber frames with your catapult. You set fire to the common: the police arrested Tavy for it because he ran away when he couldn't stop you. You—

Tanner. Pooh! Pooh! Pooh! These were battles, bombardments, stratagems to save our scalps from the red Indians. You have no imagination, Ann. I am ten times more destructive now than I was then. The moral passion has taken my destructiveness in hand and directed it to moral ends. I have become a reformer, and like all reformers, an iconoclast. I no longer break cucumber frames and burn gorse bushes: I shatter creeds and demolish idols.

Ann [bored] I am afraid I am too feminine to see any sense in destruction. Destruction can only destroy.

Tanner. Yes. That is why it is so useful. Construction cumbers the ground with institutions made by busybodies. Destruction clears it and gives us breathing space and liberty.

(vol. 3, 550–51)

Here, we see Tanner acknowledging the inherent destructiveness of mankind, or at least the inherent destructiveness within himself, only now the reformer has taken that destructiveness and channeled it to a productive purpose. The dawning moral passion has dignified what were before merely aimless childish cruelties.

Shaw was fourteen when he had this experience, an adolescent with all the powerful new hormonal feelings that cause such a disturbance at that age, and it is not hard to recognize this behind the new moral passion that was born in him at that time. Shaw was always on his guard against the frightening power of Chaos, the "mob of appetites" within, and thus these chaotic energies were processed through a moral filter and used as a weapon against the very source of their being; as Tanner says: "The moral passion has taken my destructiveness in hand

and directed it to moral ends." The instincts—again, the phrase he uses is very telling— "the mob of appetites" had to be "organized...into an army of purposes and principles." I believe this is a key to the enigma that is George Bernard Shaw: both the body politic and the individual body with all their unruly passions must be regimented and kept under control. Once under control they become an "army" doing battle against the forces of chaos: hence Shaw's abstention from alcohol, his vegetarianism (which in 1938 induced pernicious anemia and forced him to undergo liver injections), his antipathy to tobacco, coffee, and tea, his all-wool Jaeger suit, his celibacy (yet with his tendency to "fall in love" and have incorporeal Platonic "love affairs"). Indeed in *The Revolutionists Handbook* Tanner writes that "the survival of the fittest means finally the survival of the self-controlled" (vol. 3, 703). Shaw's affinity to Plato is again apparent as both deride the body and its passions as an impediment to the mind's upward ascent.

As we see implicit in this play—and as we will see explicitly later on in such plays as *Back to Methuselah* and *Farfetched Fables* (1950)—Shaw imagines evolution as working toward the elimination of the body and its instincts altogether. Juan hopes to spend his "eons in contemplation" (vol. 3, 617) and seems to take for granted that his auditors have followed his argument and could only be in agreement:

> Are we agreed that Life is a force which has made innumerable experiments in organizing itself; that the mammoth and the man, the mouse and the megatherium, the flies and the fleas and the Fathers of the Church, are all more or less successful attempts to build up that raw force into higher and higher individuals, the ideal individual being omnipotent, omniscient, infallible, and withal completely, unilludedly self-conscious: in short, a god?
>
> (vol. 3, 626)

It was young George's sense of powerlessness, of helplessness against the forces of chaos and disorder, that caused him to compensate by imagining the human being as potentially all-powerful, a god totally in control; and he wanted a responsible state to exert the same kind of control.

In a good book on Shaw and the Life Force, Warren Sylvester Smith says that the "passion for order is an underlying force in all of Shaw, reflecting his revulsion against the disorder of his own upbringing."[29] Shaw grew up in a loveless home, and his father's life was destroyed by alcoholism and weakness of character. Shaw himself was timid to the point of social paralysis, yet through effort of will was able to overcome this weakness. His myth of man as incipient superman, all-powerful, all-knowing, an infallible god, strikes me as a myth designed to circumvent the fear of chaos and loss of control as it existed potentially in the individual and in society—it is no accident that Shaw describes the multiplicity of appetites that need to be controlled as a "mob," the word he consistently uses to describe the unruly elements in society, the many small units that make up that most chaotic form of government, democracy, or as he frequently calls it, "mobocracy." Griffin says that eugenics is a "form of social modernism in its own right," that

> [e]ugenics thus represents a supreme example of what [philosopher Reinhart] Koselleck calls 'the temporalization of utopia', a fact illustrated by Galton's brief sketch of a society called Laputa which uses social control to promote hard work. The unholy alliance of science with projects to create an ideal society emerges even more clearly from the uncompleted novel *Kantsaywhere* that he started shortly before his death.[30]

Galton's utopian vision as described here bears a powerful resemblance to Shaw's own blueprint utopia, where eugenic experiments and the scientific control of labor are central.

Shaw had come under the influence of Nietzsche by this time, although it is debatable how far that influence extended. The sections "Of Marriage and Children" and "Of Old and Young Women" in Nietzsche's *Thus Spoke Zarathustra* (1885) may have suggested the idea of woman's primary role as being the bearer of the incipient superman. Shaw himself wrote in a letter to his German translator Siegfried Trebitsch just as he was finishing *Man and Superman* that he wanted "the Germans to know me as a philosopher, as an English (or Irish) Nietzsche (only ten times cleverer), and not as a mere carpenter of farces."[31] Shaw believed the higher class of men that were his contemporaries, such as the Fabians, and the supermen and superwomen of the future would order the world socialistically, while Nietzsche despised socialism as a secular remnant of Christianity. Shaw's aristocrat rules on behalf of the social, economic and "spiritual" welfare of the community while Nietzsche's aristocrat is more concerned with the exercise of his own innate power. Shaw would have absorbed his ideal of the superman from Plato's caste of ruling philosophers as well as from Carlyle's conception of the hero before he ever read Nietzsche. But the Nietzsche vogue and the eugenics movement added energy and plausibility to Shaw's desire, which as we have already seen was inherent in his first major critical essay, *The Quintessence of Ibsenism*, with its vision of the singular pioneering realist, beyond good and evil, standing above the crowd, and ready to forge a new world. And Shaw took his title from Nietzsche. But Shaw would certainly have been attracted to Nietzsche's rhetoric of creative destruction, such as we read in *Ecce Homo* where Nietzsche says that "negating *and destroying* are conditions of saying Yes."[32] However there is a long way to go from a literary artist using the metaphor of creative destruction in his work to a dictator using it as a principle of his regeneration movement. Yet there can be no question that Shaw admired Lenin, Mussolini, Hitler, and Stalin precisely for their willingness to destroy in the name of creation, for their willingness and "courage" to stand beyond good and evil and attempt to create a vital new social and political order, a political or civil religion. Speaking of Mussolini and Hitler, Griffin says that because they were

> [f]reed of the moral and institutional constraints of liberalism, democracy, Christianity, and humanism, both dictators attempted to use the unprecedented concentration of state power to enact primordial longings for a rooted, *ordered* world, its horizon once more fixed and framed by myth, its population cleansed of the cultural, social, and human embodiments of chaos, ambivalence, and degeneracy.[33]

Mussolini and Hitler attempted to create a unified social order, and what did not cohere had to be eliminated. This is why Shaw's creative writing, whether plays like *Man and Superman* and *Major Barbara* or essays like *The Perfect Wagnerite*, requires a more critical perusal of his tendency toward programmatic modernism than has hitherto been the norm. Shaw saw his work as a writer and dramatist as an extension of his work as Fabian socialist and propagandist for the Life Force. While Nietzsche would have been horrified by the mass politics and anti-intellectual violence of the Nazis, Shaw saw the new movement as a necessary break from the desiccated socio-economic and political world that he so abhorred.

After the Devil's long speech on how it is the power of death and not life that governs our planet, Juan counters that on the contrary, while man loves to think he is "bold and bad. He is neither one nor the other: he is only a coward" (vol. 3, 621). "Yet all his civilization is founded on his cowardice, on his abject tameness" (vol. 3, 622). Nonetheless, as the proselytizer of the incipient superman Juan predicts a future state governed by the inculcated sense of universal purpose, a new "Catholicism," where the present cowardice of man will be transformed into its opposite by the force of an idea: "you can make any of these cowards brave by putting an idea into his head" (vol. 3, 622). Here again we see that deep longing for Platonic unity that was the motive force in Shaw's thinking and in his art. Juan says that "this idea of a Catholic Church will survive Islam, will survive the Cross... Every idea for which Man will die will be a Catholic idea" (vol. 3, 622–23). The idea, the purpose that unites mankind and is worth dying for, is no longer the old Enlightenment tropes of liberty and equality; Juan's utopian vision is of a state where perfection of the organism is the animating and unifying principle, where "Liberty will not be Catholic enough, men will die for human perfection, to which they will sacrifice all their liberty gladly" (vol. 3, 622–23). This idea of Juan's expressed here is of extreme importance if Shaw is to be understood. In 1912, the Reverend R.F. Horton, a eugenicist, wrote a book called *National Ideals and Race Regeneration*, which Dan Stone in *Breeding Superman* sums up this way: "Horton's argument ties together the long-standing military tradition of sacrificing oneself for the greater good with the eugenicist's argument that the protection of the national 'germ plasm' is of far greater importance than the life of the individual."[34] The individual as such has no value for Shaw, only the social organism as a whole: the evolution of the human race toward a higher individual – that is the purpose of our being, and the reason for his socialism, which besides reordering the wasteful and chaotic world of twentieth-century capitalism would more efficiently aid in that evolution.

And that is also why he could be so flippant regarding the loss of individual life. In *Bernard Shaw: A Chronicle*, R.F. Rattray, one of Shaw's most fervent admirers, mentions a number of such flippant remarks, such as how when he was told that ninety-eight Soviet citizens had recently been shot for petty offences, Shaw shot back, "only ninety-eight? We shall have to shoot more than ninety-eight people a week to make England fit to live in."[35] And how when Shaw came back from the Front during the First World War, where he had seen a young man lying decapitated in the mud, he wrote a cheeky article about a "gentleman who had lost his head."[36] There are too many such incidents to mention, but I mention these two because Rattray represents a species of Shavian who tends to idolatry in his worship of the man (he actually says that "Shaw was a distinguished philosopher, artist, statesman, publicist, humanitarian, critic of music, art, and literature, of the highest integrity and probity, a prophet, a mystic, a saint"[37]) and because Rattray was genuinely puzzled by this contradiction but was honest enough to admit of it: "In spite of all sensitiveness, compassion and kindness, there was a streak of insensitiveness in Shaw. Examples have been given above. I have discussed this streak with several who knew him intimately. They immediately recognized what I indicated, and they too could not understand it."[38]

Shaw's oft expressed indifference to the loss of life very much resembles the indifference evinced in *Major Barbara* by his purposeful superman Undershaft, who can gleefully announce that "the aerial battleship is a tremendous success. At the first trial it has wiped out a fort with three hundred soldiers in it" (vol. 1, 422). It should be noted that when Shaw does express outrage at the wanton destruction of life it is almost always because such acts are wasteful and stupid, and on such occasions he will let loose his unsurpassed powers of derision at the entity that has so stupidly misdirected its power (usually the Brits). But I do believe it is more complex than Shaw's simply putting the race over the individual; after all, you can feel compassion for the individual who gives his life for a greater good while recognizing the necessity just as you can feel compassion for the recalcitrant ne'er-do-well who, according to the stringent order of the new state, must surrender up his life. As mentioned in the Introduction, George Orwell and Arnold Silver perceived what they believed was a streak of sadism in Shaw, Silver writing a book on the topic.

A part of the reason, though, lies in Shaw's unrelenting utopian vision, his belief that ruthless strength and a formidable will are required of those pioneers charged with putting an end to a chaotic sociopolitical structure and bringing forth a new well-ordered society; he seems to feel that compassion is unhealthy, a sign of weakness; that the realist recognizes that suffering and death accompany life and are indeed a prerequisite to evolutionary advance, and so should not be unduly bothered about them. In one of his "Maxims for Revolutionists" Tanner/Shaw avers that "[c]ompassion is the fellow-feeling of the unsound" (vol. 3, 743). This vision and what it entails is intimated in the third act of *Man and Superman*, as it was intimated in *The Perfect Wagnerite* five years earlier, and it stayed with Shaw all his life; he had an apparently unshakable belief that a well-ordered society purged of poverty and crime would ultimately triumph through the efforts of an intellectual elite, and this is especially apparent later on in his ebullient faith in the Soviet Union (most fully expressed in such works from the early 1930s as *The Rationalization of Russia* and *The Simpleton of the Unexpected Isles*). Yet Shaw's faith in a totalitarian world responsibly led by a visionary technocracy comprising five percent of the population was evident well before the First World War, and the parliamentary stalemates that followed exacerbated his patience with the Western Powers and led him to make more alarming pronouncements and write more overtly political plays. But in these years before the rise of any actual totalitarian states no one could have predicted to what depths European nations would descend in the course of their various utopian projects. Shaw remained insensitive to the untimely loss of life even through the Second World War, it would seem as a matter of philosophic principle.

Juan—who as Tanner we should remember is described by Shaw in the stage directions as "possibly a little mad," and as a "megalomaniac who would be lost without a sense of humor" (vol. 3, 523)—gives a hint of what was to come, chillingly ironic with hindsight. He says that a man

> may be abject as a citizen; but he is dangerous as a fanatic. He can only be enslaved whilst he is spiritually weak enough to listen to reason. I tell you, gentlemen, if you can shew a man a piece of what he now calls God's work to do, and what he will later on call by many new names, you can make him entirely reckless of the consequences to him personally.
>
> (vol. 3, 623–34)

This is certainly a prescient pronouncement, and brings to mind the fascist dictum drummed into the youth of Italy: "believe, obey, fight."[39] Indeed Augusto Turati, Mussolini's party secretary, insisted that the people of Italy "had to be ready to die for fascism or, if need be, to kill," and Mussolini himself had said that "the individual exists only insofar as he is subordinated to the interests of the state, and as civilisation becomes more complex, so the liberty of the individual must be increasingly restricted."[40] Such statements could be multiplied indefinitely. How successful Mussolini was at inculcating such mindless devotion I am not sure, although that kind of fanaticism, so reckless of life, certainly found its fulfillment in the devotees of National Socialism, which has recently been powerfully reproduced in Oliver Hirschbiegel's film *Der Untergang* (2004, *Downfall* in English). According to an early biographer of Shaw, one of his "trinity" of urgent changes needed in society was "the formulation and inculcation of a credible religious creed, to give men a common body of spiritual assumptions on which they can act with lively faith."[41] It seems, for Shaw, that a part of the attraction of fascism was its attempt to instill a civil faith strong enough to withstand the promptings of reason.

Although Ann is the vital genius carrying through the most important work of the Life Force, it is Tanner who dominates the play—if, that is, it is performed in its entirety. It is he who is given the rhetorical task of repeatedly proclaiming in various ways that "[t]he overthrow of the aristocrat has created the necessity for the Superman... King Demos must be bred like all other Kings; and with Must there is no arguing" (vol. 3, 728). Upon reading *Man and Superman*, as opposed to simply seeing it performed, that dominance takes on even more force, as the book concludes with his essay *The Revolutionist's Handbook*, from which the quoted words above are taken, with its suggestion for a State Department of Evolution or some such institution for eugenic breeding.[42] Tanner recognizes that such proposals will be repudiated for being "indecent and immoral" but that we will have "nevertheless, a general secret pushing of the human will in the repudiated direction; so that all sorts of institutions and public authorities will under some pretext or other feel their way furtively towards the Superman" (vol. 3, 725). It will be argued by some, of course, that Shaw is not Tanner and that Shaw's fund of irony was always excessive. I would concur, but insist also that Shaw used irony in the same way that Socrates did: as a way of disarming his antagonists and consequently bringing forward ideas that would otherwise never receive a hearing. He admitted as much.

John Bull's Other Island

After the exhilaration of composing so successfully in this new form wore off there must have followed something of a letdown for Shaw; for while Tanner and his ideas dominate *Man and Superman*, he is seen to have no real power in society, is something of a joke, only becoming a force in the amorphous dream world of act three. He is a nonentity in the concrete world of political fact that was so important to his creator. Mere artistic success was never enough for Shaw, and so his next play is rooted in the hard facts of material life; in fact, rooted in the messy divisiveness of Ireland and its relations with England. The play shows Shaw trying to dramatize political realities in a way its predecessor did not, but ending in utter frustration. *John Bull's Other Island* is a pessimistic play, and as the only major play Shaw ever wrote that focuses specifically on Ireland and Irish characters it is very revealing in a way that the previous play is not; *Man and Superman* reveals Shaw as the Platonic idealist, the cerebral socio-political planner, the Coefficient with specific suggestions for ordering society well beyond anything that had any chance of fulfillment in early twentieth-century Britain. While Tanner is a revealing portrait of one side of Shaw, Larry Doyle the Irish expatriate in *John Bull's Other Island* is very revealing for showing another, less public, side of Shaw. Unlike his usual band of comic characters, Shaw has imbued

Doyle with the kind of rich, tormented, divided inner life that he rarely, if ever, created elsewhere. The play again shows Shaw's preoccupation with unity, and how the necessary qualities must either take root in one man who can lead or else come together in a small group of leaders, as we will see in the next play *Major Barbara*; the whole trilogy is a straining toward unity and utopian reality, if such a phrase is not an oxymoron.

But while Doyle betrays parts of Shaw's character that he was never again to reveal on stage, this is clearly not intentional; in fact Shaw has disguised any similarities an audience might discern by making Doyle a Catholic civil engineer instead of a Protestant writer and social reformer like Shaw. Tanner is a projection of Shaw's image of himself as revolutionary while Doyle is intentionally unlike his author despite their both being Irish exiles. Doyle, through his alliance with the Englishman Tom Broadbent, has emancipated himself from the Irish propensity of indulging in dreams and imagination, yet at a cost. Shaw seems to admire Doyle for making something of his life, but in the end condemns him for his ultimate betrayal of Ireland and the better part of himself. This is dramatized by the manifest antipathy Doyle feels for Keegan, the defrocked Irish priest and mystic, in the last scene of the play, an antipathy we feel is self-directed. Shaw seems to be saying that the realist Doyle needs to be complemented by Keegan's mystic vision as well as by Broadbent's indomitable can-do insouciance. These two exceptional Irish characters have much to teach us about Shaw. The third central character, Broadbent, is an English doer who despite being the butt of much of the play's humor is nonetheless a character who Shaw has a great deal of respect for, as can be seen by how in the next play he has metamorphosed into one of Shaw's greatest supermen, Andrew Undershaft. The essential qualities of these three characters—the mystic, the self-creating man of hard unsentimental intellect, and the man of action—must unite before Shaw's longed-for utopia can become a reality. And while that does not happen in this play, it does in the final play of the trilogy, *Major Barbara*.[43]

The Land Purchase Act of 1903 had given small Irish farmers an opportunity to purchase leaseholds and become landlords themselves. Shaw gives a very unflattering view of the new Irish landlords in the play, showing that their greed and desire to imitate their old masters will simply perpetuate the old problem of the exploitation of labor. Furthermore these new landlords lack efficiency and organization and will be unable to develop the land sufficiently to bring Ireland into the twentieth century.

The central premise of the play has Broadbent and Doyle, partners in a London firm of civil engineers, as well as in a Land Development Syndicate, going to rural Ireland to acquire more land. The scheme is all Broadbent's, although by the end of the play Doyle, who owns stock in the venture, has full-heartedly embraced the plan. Doyle is very reluctant to go back to the Ireland he left for good eighteen years ago, but is convinced by Broadbent to make the trip with him. The play is clearly, in part, a satire on English meddling, on English capitalists' predilection for predatory schemes, and shows Broadbent, the Gladstonian Liberal, proponent of Free Trade and Home Rule for Ireland, and who has the best intentions in the world, walking into Ireland and completely taking control of the place through successful electioneering for the Rosscullen seat in Parliament as well as by making loans to the new Irish landlords that they will never be able to repay, thus in the end acquiring their land. Despite being the target of much of the play's satire, Doyle— and Shaw as well, we feel, and we ourselves—have to stand in awe of Broadbent's energy and determination to get what he wants, as well as his good-natured and very likable personality. It is not until the last moments of the play, when through Keegan Shaw begins to expose the dark underside of developmental capitalism, that we get a hint of Broadbent's perhaps more sinister side. But through most of the play, and even ultimately still at the end, we like Broadbent and tend to agree with Doyle that he is a strange admixture of idiot and genius. For it is Broadbent's self-deception, his uncanny ability to remain unconscious of what it is inconvenient for him to know, that in part propels his success. Shaw did not believe that any person did evil or caused harm willfully, and so must have believed that if Broadbent's amazing capacity for transforming material conditions could be welded with a vision of higher reality, with evolutionary purpose as proclaimed in the doctrine of John Tanner, than perhaps this earth (which Keegan believes is really hell) could be transformed into the paradise Shaw always seemed to believe was realizable, if not inevitable.

Broadbent represents the power of big business, which in 1904 still had its nerve center in London. While Shaw mocked England and excoriated capitalism all his life, he was also strangely drawn to their unparalleled power. He saw the industrial machinery of modernity as an opportunity to build a world where disease and poverty were no longer so ubiquitous. Rather than rejecting worldly power as being antithetical to a life of the spirit, Shaw at this time in his career had come to see the necessity of marrying the two; this culminates in his next play, *Major Barbara*, where he attempts to unite them, but in *John Bull* we only see their inability to come together and the depressing consequences of such estrangement. In a sense this had always been Fabian policy, which believed it could infiltrate the halls of power, the world of government at least, if not business, and convince the leaders of all parties of the necessity of transitioning to a socialistic governmental framework. But now Shaw seems to accept the necessity of a partnership with the captains of industry as well as with the leaders in politics. Broadbent is the philistine utterly contented with the way things are while his opposite, Keegan, is utterly discontented with reality as it is. After meeting a dying Hindu, Keegan had come to believe that life on earth is actually hell, where we do penance for the sins of our previous lives. Thus Shaw has taken the hell of *Man and Superman*—a nebulous place (really a state of mind) where one lives for pleasure only and without any sense of purpose—and moved it into the concrete world of twentieth-century Ireland, and indeed the entire globe.

A universal sense of purpose, an understanding of the reality of Creative Evolution, would presumably be all that is needed to begin to transform this world of hell into its opposite heaven. Keegan represents the side of Shaw that despairs the most of utopia's realization on earth, yet also has the deepest longing for it; and ironically it is this holy Irishman Keegan, who believes Ireland is holy ground, who feels most estranged from a sense of divine unity. This world is hell, and heaven is out of reach. When we meet Keegan at the top of act two one of the first things we hear him say, to a grasshopper no less, is: "If you could jump as far as a kangaroo you couldnt jump away from your own heart an its punishment. You can only look at Heaven from here: you cant reach it" (vol. 2, 528). Keegan is one of Shaw's greatest creations, and one feels that to some extent Shaw turned away from him and his uncompromising rejection of the corrupt world as he tried to find a way into what Doyle calls "the big Powers" (vol. 2, 520). We never see another character like Keegan in the Shavian canon, with the possible exception of Shotover in *Heartbreak House* (1919), another of Shaw's more pessimistic plays, written as the First World War raged outside. Keegan will make no compromise with worldly power, as he is too wise to believe there could ever be a sanctified collaboration between the powers of the world and the powers of the spirit. Yet he longs for a unified heavenly reality on earth, and gives one of Shaw's most famous pleas for a utopian state. After Broadbent describes his dream of heaven as a rather boring and joyless place, Keegan describes his dream of heaven as a

> country where the State is the Church and the Church the people: three in one and one in three. It is a commonwealth in which work is play and play is life: three in one and one in three. It is a temple

in which the priest is the worshipper and the worshipper the worshipped: three in one and one in three. It is a godhead in which all life is human and all humanity divine: three in one and one in three. It is, in short, the dream of a madman.

(vol. 2, 611)

With these words he leaves the stage, and after a brief exchange between Broadbent and Doyle, the play ends. Keegan's prophetic message of the ruin that these capitalist exploiters will bring to Ireland rings out powerfully in this final scene, yet nonetheless (or for this reason) Shaw will not abandon his hope of a united military-industrial-religious establishment, and so he turns to its fulfillment in his next play.

Keegan recognizes that the earth is a hallowed and mysterious place for the working out of sins, a preparation for a higher reality, but longs deeply for a catholic sense of unity on earth right now between all creatures. A defrocked Catholic priest, Keegan is unorthodox, and a connection can be made to his dream of catholic unity and Don Juan's vision of catholic unity in *Man and Superman*, although one feels Keegan would not accept it at the price of the human sacrifice, however willingly made, that Tanner predicts. Shaw was a radical "Protestant,"[44] of sorts, who longed deeply for a catholic, "totalitarian"[45] social organism, a unified coherent state where life's evolutionary purpose is universally recognized. Remarkably, Valency believes that beginning with *Man and Superman* Shaw had barely any real interest in politics or socialism, and that this tendency increased right up until the end of his life; he claims that Shaw was wholly absorbed in dramatically demonstrating the reality of the Life Force via the evolutionary appetite of his characters. I am not sure I would go this far, but, supposing it is so, how might that evolutionary appetite be working itself out in this most ostensibly political of Shavian plays? Broadbent promises the kind of industrial paradise that we will see actually come to fruition in the next play in Perivale St. Andrews:

> Broadbent. The syndicate is a perfectly respectable body of responsible men of good position. We'll take Ireland in hand, and by straightforward business habits teach it efficiency and self-help on sound Liberal principles. You agree with me, Mr. Keegan, don't you?
> Keegan. Sir: I may even vote for you.
> Broadbent [*sincerely moved, shaking his hand warmly*] You shall never regret it, Mr. Keegan: I give you my word for that. I shall bring money here: I shall raise wages: I shall found public institutions:

a library, a Polytechnic (undenominational, of course), a gymnasium, a cricket club, perhaps an art school. I shall make a Garden city of Rosscullen.

(vol. 2, 605–6)

In just a minute Keegan will prophesy a different reality, shifting from subtle Socratic irony to straightforward invective, overturning the likelihood of Broadbent's claims and exposing the dark heart of predatory capitalism:

> Keegan [*with polished irony*] I stand rebuked, gentleman. But believe me, I do every justice to the efficiency of you and your syndicate. You are both, I am told, thoroughly efficient civil engineers; and I have no doubt the golf links will be a triumph of your art. Mr. Broadbent will get into parliament most efficiently, which is more than St Patrick could do were he alive now. You may even build the hotel efficiently if you can find enough masons, carpenters, and plumbers, which I rather doubt. [*Dropping his irony, and beginning to fall into the attitude of the priest rebuking sin*] When the hotel becomes insolvent [*Broadbent takes his cigar out of his mouth, a little taken aback*] your English business habits will secure the thorough efficiency of the liquidation. You will reorganize the scheme efficiently; you will liquidate its second bankruptcy efficiently [*Broadbent and Larry look quickly at one another; for this, unless the priest is an old financial hand, must be inspiration*]; you will get rid of its original shareholders efficiently after efficiently ruining them; and you will finally profit very efficiently by getting that hotel for a few shillings in the pound.
>
> (vol. 2, 607–8)

This jeremiad on the perversion of capitalist efficiency warrants a close look, for we know that efficiency was practically a sacred concept for Shaw and for the Fabians. Shaw hated waste of any kind and always lauded the importance of efficiency. Sidney Webb and his colleagues in his brains' trust, including Shaw, were known as the Coefficients, and what both Shaw and Webb hoped for in England was a new party of national efficiency. Before Keegan's diatribe on efficiency Larry had said that what Ireland needs now is not Keegan's sentimentality about Ireland, but Broadbent's "gospel of efficiency" (vol. 2, 607) and Broadbent concurs, saying that "efficiency is the thing...The world belongs to the efficient" (vol. 2, 607). Through the entire play Shaw has us marvel, even while laughing, at Broadbent's energy and efficiency.

This was a quality that he valued as indispensable, but it needed to be divorced from the acquisitive propensity and married instead to a higher vision of evolutionary purpose. The world cannot be transformed without Broadbent's cooperation.

In 1904, it had been twenty-eight years since Shaw left Ireland, and he had never returned. Like Larry, Shaw left Ireland for London and was apparently reluctant about ever going back. Interestingly, after Shaw wrote *John Bull* he began to make frequent trips to Ireland with his Irish wife. Like Shaw, Larry left Ireland because he felt it was a provincial backwater and he wanted to be active in the real world of men and ideas: "I had only two ideas at that time," Larry says, "first, to learn to do something; and then to get out of Ireland and have a chance of doing it" (vol. 2, 524). He tells Nora that if she marries Broadbent she will have "real life and real work and real cares and real joys among real people: solid English life in London, the very centre of the world" (vol. 2, 600). He believes, as Shaw had claimed to believe himself, that the very climate of Ireland induced one to a life of imagination and dreaming, that an "Irishman's imagination never lets him alone, never convinces him, never satisfies him; but it makes him that he cant face reality nor deal with it nor handle it nor conquer it" (vol. 2, 517). Shaw hated nationalism, but as he makes very clear in his preface to the play, "Preface for Politicians," nationalism is a stage that has to be got through and Ireland needed to become an independent nation before it could become a responsible member of the international community.[46] Larry is a civil engineer, a creator of organized material reality, and an internationalist, like Shaw. He tells Broadbent:

> I'm a metallurgical chemist turned civil engineer. Now whatever else metallurgical chemistry may be, it's not national. It's international. And my business and yours as civil engineers is to join countries, not to separate them... I want Ireland to be the brains and imagination of a big Commonwealth, not a Robinson Crusoe island.
>
> (vol. 2, 520–21)

Yet he cannot disguise the contempt he feels for his homeland and its people—actually his contempt only manifests intermittently, his feelings really being ambivalent; yet on the whole it is his contempt for Ireland and his love for England that hold sway.

After Broadbent tells Keegan that it is "our capital, our knowledge, our organization, and may I say our English business habits, [which] can make or lose ten pounds out of land that Haffigan, with all his industry, could not make or lose ten shillings out of. Doran's mill is a superannuated folly: I shall want it for electric lighting," Doyle says, "What is the use of giving land to such men? They are too small, too poor, too ignorant, too simpleminded to hold it against us: you might as well give a dukedom to a crossing sweeper" (vol. 2, 603). However fair or not such a judgment, we feel that it is only by leaving Ireland and coming to London that Doyle has been able to make something of himself; very much like Shaw. In fact we feel Shaw's description of Doyle in the preface applies equally to himself: "Doyle's special contribution was the freedom from illusion, the power of facing facts, the nervous industry, the sharpened wits, the sensitive pride of the imaginative man who has fought his way up through social persecution and poverty" (vol. 2, 445). By "special contribution" Shaw means to the Broadbent and Doyle firm, and he gives Broadbent credit for its success as well: "The virtues of Broadbent are not less real because they are the virtues of the money that coal and iron have produced" (vol. 2, 445).

In the play it is clear that it is not just Broadbent's money but his energy and ability to get things accomplished as well that Shaw admires. He is described as *"a robust, full-blooded, energetic man in the prime of life, sometimes eager and credulous, sometimes shrewd and roguish, sometimes portentously solemn, sometimes jolly and impetuous, always buoyant and irresistible, mostly likable, and enormously absurd in his most earnest moments"* (vol. 2, 504). Later he sweeps Nora *"into the garden as an equinoctial gale might sweep a dry leaf"* (vol. 2, 598). Clearly, Broadbent is a force of nature as well as efficient in his acquisitive projects. Surely such a creature must have been evolved by the Life Force for something more sublime than the mere fattening of his own predacious self. Both Larry and Broadbent have abilities and talents that the Life Force cannot do without, but divested of Keegan's vision and sense of the sacredness of life, such talents will ultimately only lead to waste and ruin.

Shaw was ambivalent in his feelings for both Ireland and England, but there can be no question but that England, and London in particular, was a vital necessity for him. He lived there and in the neighboring Ayot St. Lawrence all his life. London was the center of the world and Shaw needed to be in the center of things. There was something unreal about Ireland for him, as there was about poetry and feelings too (Shaw's distrust of poetry and emotion is yet another affinity he has with Plato); Shaw needed the active, purposeful world of London, the hard work to be found in the practical everyday world of politics as a defense against the overwhelming power of his own imagination and deeply buried feelings. He was more like Larry than he might have cared to admit. Within ten years of arriving in London Shaw had written five novels, started a career in journalism, and become an executive committee member of the newly formed Fabian Society; he had transformed the inveterately timid and shy George Bernard Shaw into the spellbinding orator Bernard Shaw; he had assiduously applied himself to the task of mastering economics; and in promoting socialism he had found a purpose for his life. London was indispensable, and in joining the Fabians he must have felt as Larry did about his partnership with Broadbent: "it is by living with you and working in double harness with you that I have learnt to live in a real world and not in an imaginary one" (vol. 2, 519). But he may have felt at times like a bit of a traitor, such as Larry is implicitly accused of being by Keegan.

The play satirizes fairly equally both Irish provinciality and English blindness, but the 1906 preface is clearly written in defense of the Irish, and is much more critical of the English. In there he says: "I like Englishmen much better than Irishmen (no doubt because they make more of me)... But I never think of an Englishman as my countryman" (vol. 2, 447–48). But a few years earlier, in the letter quoted on page 81, he had told Trebitsch that in Germany he hoped to be known as an English Nietzsche, only putting in "or Irish" parenthetically. Shaw was ashamed of Irish backwardness as he was ashamed of his father. His ambivalence about London manifests throughout his career, frequently in violent ejaculations such as in *Man and Superman* where he says in the "Maxims for Revolutionists" that the "imagination cannot conceive a viler criminal than he who should build another London like the present one, nor a greater benefactor than he who should destroy it" (vol. 3, 742) or even Doyle's response to Broadbent's remark about the "Celtic race": "When people talk about the Celtic race, I feel as if I could burn down London. That sort of rot does more harm than ten Coercion Acts" (vol. 2, 515). Shaw's ambivalence and sense of self-division, his guilt at attaching himself to England, are betrayed in his portrayal of Larry Doyle, while with Keegan he has created an Irish prophet to balance the portrait. Nicholas Grene puts it aptly regarding both Doyle and Keegan when he says that in

> Larry Doyle Shaw faced the feelings of provinciality, of divided national identity, of emotional instability which confirmed him an Irish exile. But he also faced the self-destructiveness implicit in that aggressive rejection of Ireland. And to transcend Doyle he created Keegan. As a result there is a pressure of feeling in *John Bull*, both in Doyle and Keegan, that is not to be found elsewhere in Shaw's

work. Keegan's Utopian vision may be less than adequate, but his denunciation of present evils has the fierce ring of conviction.[47]

But Keegan is ineffectual; as yet the world has no use for eccentric Irish prophets. London is the hub of the material world and necessary to the evolutionary advance of the species, and, though it does not know it, desperately needs what Keegan has to offer. In Shaw's next play Broadbent—while not exactly shedding his avaricious appetite—goes to work for the Life Force, Keegan is brought in and given real work to do, and Larry becomes one of Plato's philosopher kings. *Major Barbara* is Shaw's way out of the dead end that *John Bull* had led him to, and his first solid portrait of utopia.

Major Barbara

Major Barbara: A Discussion in Three Acts is one of Shaw's most powerful and most controversial plays. Most of the controversy revolves around the central character Andrew Undershaft, the self-made millionaire and armaments manufacturer. Indeed before the play had even been published or performed Gilbert Murray, upon hearing Shaw read a draft of it, felt uneasy about the character and wrote Shaw a letter to tell him so. Shaw replied: "As to the triumph of Undershaft, that is inevitable because I am in the mind that Undershaft is in the right."[48] We will consider shortly just what Undershaft, according to Shaw, is in the right about and why he is so troubling. While Undershaft's charisma and force of personality dominate the play and the characters in the play, his daughter Barbara and her fiancé Cusins are equally important to Shaw's ultimate scheme. Shaw desperately needed to believe in a world that could be cleansed of chaos and disorder, of poverty and crime, and his inability to resolve the political problems dramatized in *John Bull* led him, in the words of Nicholas Grene, to the "innocent totalitarianism"[49] of *Major Barbara*.

To resolve the problem he transforms the English capitalist Tom Broadbent into the English industrialist Andrew Undershaft, purging Broadbent of his self-deception and replacing it with Undershaft's clear vision. Indeed Undershaft's vision is so clear that it has been convincingly argued that he recognizes the necessity of his own extinction, just as Wotan does in Wagner's drama.[50] Likewise Larry Doyle has been molded into the classical scholar and translator Adolphus Cusins who will take over the munitions factory from Undershaft when he retires; thus instead of moving from Ireland to England in order to put his brains to good use, Cusins will move from the classroom to the halls of industrial power as the new chief of Undershaft's munitions factory. And Keegan, with nothing at all worthwhile to do in *John Bull* but fruitlessly censure an impervious capitalist class, is transformed into Barbara Undershaft, a saver of souls at Perivale St. Andrews, where the workers in Undershaft's factory live and work. Together these three will work together inculcating religious truth, destroying enemies, and molding the world into a clean, orderly and efficient image of Undershaft's factory town.

According to Shaw the greatest evil is poverty, and this is what he wrote the play to proclaim and to demonstrate. His mouthpiece here is Undershaft, whose philosophy—referred to in the preface as the "The Gospel of St Andrew Undershaft"— is that every human being's first obligation is to escape poverty. Undershaft is an egoist who is also strangely in the service of a higher will, a self-made millionaire[51] whose position as the nation's leading arms dealer has brought him to the height of power, as he informs his naïve son Stephen:

> *I* am the government of your country: I, and Lazarus. Do you suppose that you and half a dozen amateurs like you, sitting in a row in that foolish gabble shop, can govern Undershaft and Lazarus? No, my friend: you will do what pays us. You will make war when it suits us, and keep peace when it doesnt. You will find out that trade requires certain measures when we have decided on those measures. When I want anything to keep my dividends up, you will discover that my want is a national need. When other people want something to keep my dividends down, you will call out the police and military. And in return you shall have the support and applause of my newspapers, and the delight of imagining that you are a great statesman.
>
> (vol. 1, 416)

It must be perplexing for those who think of Shaw as the peaceful Fabian socialist to contemplate such an unlikely Shavian hero and mouthpiece, yet this pugnacious millionaire arms dealer is one of Shaw's great supermen, facsimile of the pioneering realist first documented in *The Quintessence of Ibsenism*: clear-sighted, bold, ruthless, beyond good and evil, organized and efficient. He is also morally repugnant. While he is meant to be taken as a servant of the Life Force, the philosophy he espouses throughout the play is social Darwinism. He sees existence as the naked struggle of one man against another, with the difference being that once a person has some success in life he or she might then be of some use to society. When Barbara expresses some misgiving about leaving the poor of the east end of London to starve, he says:

> *I* was an east ender. I moralized and starved until one day I swore that I would be a full-fed free man at all costs—that nothing should stop me except a bullet, neither reason nor morals nor the lives of other men. I said "Thou shalt starve ere I starve"; and with that word I became free and great. I was a dangerous man until I had my will: now I am a useful, beneficent, kindly person. That is the history of most self-made millionaires, I fancy. When it is the history of every Englishman we shall have an England worth living in.
> (vol. 1, 435)

In the preface Shaw says that Undershaft's conduct passes the Kantian test while the honest, industrious yet poor Peter Shirley's does not; that if everyone believed and acted as Undershaft rather than as Shirley the "immediate result would be a revolution of incalculable beneficence" (vol.1, 309). This is certainly a specious bit of logic—if we are meant to take it seriously, and I think we are—for Undershaft is a competitive capitalist seeking maximum profits. Regarding this "naked capitalist ethic of self-help," Nicolas Grene asks, "Does Shaw really believe or want us to believe that a Utopian England is to be achieved by a whole nation of would-be millionaires ready to cut one another's throats?" Grene thinks it unlikely, yet admits that "within the debating structure which the play sets up, Undershaft and Undershaftian principles carry the day."[52]

Of course the successful millionaire Undershaft has ordered the complex of Perivale St. Andrews so that it is a comfort to his workers, who are well paid, fully insured and will receive a pension upon retirement; he has created a Garden City much like the one Broadbent claimed he would bring to Rosscullen in *John Bull*, with libraries, schools, and a nursing home. Everything is clean and orderly and its inspectors in the third act are enthralled, Cusins calling it "perfect! wonderful! real! It only needs a cathedral to be a heavenly city instead of a hellish one" (vol. 1, 421–22). As in the previous two plays Shaw brings in the hell metaphor, but in this play it is only the addition of the former evangelist Barbara Undershaft that is needed to convert the Garden City into a "heavenly city."

It must be admitted though that Undershaft's magnanimity grows out of a need for order and cleanliness rather than out of a desire to improve the lives of his workers for their own sake. It has nothing to do with compassion or with pity, which on principle he rejects, calling it the "scavenger of misery" (vol. 1, 438). It is not the suffering of the poor that bothers him, but the affront to his own sensibility that the sight of poverty produces. Like Shaw he is repelled by disorder and dirt and feels threatened by their existence:

> there are millions of poor people, abject people, dirty people, ill fed, ill clothed people. They poison *us* morally and physically: they kill the happiness of society: they force *us* to do away with *our own* liberties and to organize unnatural cruelties for fear they should rise against *us* and drag *us* down into their abyss.
>
> (vol. 1, 434; the italics are mine)

Undershaft's solution to the problem of poverty and slavery is to "Kill them" (vol. 1, 436), and when Barbara asks if violence is his solution for everything he replies: "It is the final test of conviction, the only lever strong enough to overturn a social system, the only way of saying Must" (vol. 1, 436). *Major Barbara* is thus a revolutionary play, perhaps the most revolutionary play that Shaw ever wrote.

Through superhuman self-control and an indomitable will, and unencumbered by any tablet of laws, Undershaft has become a force in society and is one of the most salient examples in Shaw's dramatic cannon of a Nietzschean superman. He also represents more fully the process of sublimated passion intimated in *Man and Superman*. Tanner tells Ann that he has disciplined his "mob of appetites" to make war on disorder and chaos, that those appetites are now an "army of purposes and principles" fired by moral passion rather than physical appetite. In Shaw's language, he has an evolutionary appetite and not a merely sensuous one. Undershaft is creative destruction incarnate, although it might be argued just how creative his destructive propensities really are. He believes in violence as the great governing principle, the ultimate decider, the test of courage and conviction, and the most effective agent of change: "Your pious mob fills up ballot papers and imagines it is governing its masters; but the ballot paper that really governs is the paper that has a bullet wrapped up in it" (vol. 1, 436). He has given his life to providing the means to those with the will to exercise violence.

Undershaft advises Cusins to have the courage of his convictions, daring him to "make war on war" (vol. 1, 440), yet at the same time exhorting him that if he is to come to work for him he must live by the armorer's faith and sell arms to anyone who offers a fair price for them, "without respect of persons or principles: to aristocrat and republican, to

Nihilist and Tsar, to Capitalist and Socialist, to Protestant and Catholic, to burglar and policeman, to black man, white man and yellow man, to all sorts and conditions, all nationalities, all faiths, all follies, all causes and all crimes" (vol. 1, 430). Shaw wrote *Major Barbara* at a time when the age of industrial warfare was reaching its peak, just getting ready to unleash its first cataclysmic explosion in 1914, yet Undershaft's hunger for higher profits and the love he feels for his product would have the whole world armed to the full.

Although it might seem that if Cusins makes war on war he would soon be out of business and in violation of the armorer's faith, it is presumably Undershaft's Wotan-like desire for extinction that is behind what seems to be contradictory advice, with Cusins the Siegfried who will bring in the new utopian world. When Cusins reminds Barbara that the munitions factory is ultimately in the power of the forces of capitalism, and that Undershaft is really their slave, Undershaft reminds Cusins that the armorer's faith requires that he sell weapons to the good as well as to the bad, and that "If you good people prefer preaching and shirking to buying my weapons and fighting the rascals, dont blame me. I make cannons: I cannot make courage and conviction. Bah! you tire me, Euripides, with your morality mongering" (vol. 1, 432). So it is not really war that Undershaft advises Cusins to make war on; rather he advises Cusins to make war on his enemies, which presumably once vanquished would leave the way clear for the Millennium, and war would be no more. In other words, Cusins is to initiate the "war to end all wars," as was said of the First World War. In Shaw's scheme Undershaft's efficiency and organization has created an ideal industrial infrastructure and the Life Force has led him to the republican Cusins, a brainy poet and translator of Euripides, who is to be, Shaw implies, the philosopher king that Plato had prescribed to rule in his utopian city state.

But Cusins seems an unlikely successor to Undershaft—this Siegfried would never be able to break Wotan's spear. In the same letter to Gilbert Murray quoted earlier Shaw said he wanted Cusins to lack "physical robustness or brute determination." The character was modeled on Murray, and Shaw made him of frail constitution, even somewhat sickly; he is totally overshadowed in the play by the robust and brutally determined Undershaft. Shaw did not want Cusins to be a theatrical strong man, he said, although that is precisely what he has made Undershaft. Shaw told Murray that he thought Undershaft was in the right and Barbara and Cusins "very young, very romantic, very academic, very ignorant of the world."[53] Undershaft is clearly to train them in leadership and courage and augment their natural talents and idealism with his own philosophy, with the desired result being the future philosopher kings of Plato's *Republic*. Undershaft tells Cusins: "Plato says, my friend, that society cannot be saved until either the Professors of Greek take to making gunpowder, or else the makers of gunpowder become Professors of Greek" (vol. 1, 439). Initially revolted by Undershaft, Cusins agrees to align himself with the industrialist for reasons very similar to Doyle's aligning himself with Broadbent. Shaw wrote to Murray that the

> fascination that draws him [Cusins] is the fascination of reality, or rather—for it is hardly a fascination—the impossibility of refusing to put his hand to Undershaft's plough, which is at all events doing something, when the alternative is to hold aloof in a superior attitude and beat the air with words.[54]

In Shaw's revision of the gospel, Jesus would succumb to the devil's bribe in the desert, supposedly to the good of humanity.

While selling his soul does not trouble him, for life is nothing so much as a perpetual selling of the soul for one thing or another, Cusins tells Barbara: "What I am now selling it for is neither money nor position nor comfort, but for reality and for power" (vol. 1, 442). Doyle found Ireland unreal: it was peripheral, ineffectual, of no account, a place where imagination and dreams predominate and reality is lacking; he needs the bustling materiality of world-leading London and finds a place that will put his talents to work in the firm of Tom Broadbent, a pragmatic, efficient, and indomitable Englishman. In the same way, by aligning himself with Undershaft, Cusins now feels useful, engaged in the real, material world. But rather than simply making money, like Doyle, he is going to take the massive industrial machinery of death that he is inheriting and make war on all he finds unjust. He believes that "all power is spiritual" and wants now to "give the common man weapons against the intellectual man" (vol. 1, 442). In this last scene with Barbara it seems he has already absorbed Undershaft's catechism on violence, for he now says that this

> power which only tears men's bodies to pieces has never been so horribly abused as the intellectual power, the imaginative power, the poetic, religious power that can enslave men's souls... I love the common people. I want to arm them against the lawyers, the

doctors, the priests, the literary men, the professors, the artists, and the politicians, who, once in authority, are more disastrous and tyrannical than all the fools, rascals, and imposters.

(vol. 1, 442)

He has a grievance it seems against the whole of the intellectual and professional classes, and is prepared to make war on them, with "the people" behind him. Interestingly, Cusins is described in the stage directions as having "*an appalling temper...capable possibly of murder, but not of cruelty or coarseness*" (vol. 1, 352). Cusins has a cause, and now a formidable arsenal that he will not be afraid to use; he will henceforth be a dangerous man, a revolutionary.

The final piece in the puzzle for Shaw was Keegan: how to get this prophet and religious genius into this new class of elite rulers. Barbara has her mother's gift of ordering people about, but with the difference that she is committed to a higher calling; she defies the tradition of upper-class feminine frivolity and instead goes to work for the Salvation Army, becoming a major and feeding the souls of the poor. It is only her father's demonstration that convinces her that it is solely by bribing the indigent with bread that she is able to get them to accept her sermons, and that anyway the Salvation Army and indeed all religious institutions are implicated in the crimes of their benefactors, the whiskey distillers and the arms merchants. The unorthodox Keegan is defrocked for his eccentricities while Barbara voluntarily withdraws herself from what she now sees as a hypocritical institution. Shaw has Barbara, and indeed everyone else in the play, fall in love with the orderliness and cleanliness of Perivale St. Andrews. It is here, among the well fed and the well scrubbed whom she will not have to bribe, that she will supposedly be able to inculcate the higher truths of reality.

Undershaft has discerned in Barbara a rare gift, and is determined to lure her away from the Salvation Army. He tells her to scrap her old religion and find a new one that works; he wants a triumvirate that will use the power he has amassed to carry forward the work of the Life Force, "the will of which [he is] a part" (vol. 1, 431). Yet although Barbara and Cusins have an apparent love for the common people, such love fills Undershaft with contempt: "I am a millionaire; you are a poet; Barbara is a savior of souls. What have we three to do with the common mob of slaves and idolators?" (vol. 1, 388–89). Shaw detested the masses— Irving Howe once said that "Shaw was the petty bourgeois, resentful of his rulers but hating the 'Yahoos' "[55]—and he was fearful of their rapidly growing numbers; he was appalled by their ignorance and frivolity, their dirty surroundings and propensity for drunkenness and bad living, yet ultimately he envisaged a democracy of aristocrats and hoped that a gifted technocratic yet visionary ruling class might be able to lift them out of the squalor and uselessness of their lives. His was definitely a top-down approach. In *Major Barbara* he has brought the visionary poet and intellectual, the mystic saver of souls, and the efficient industrialist together to work in combination to make that democratic aristocracy a reality, with indifferent success—for despite the power of the ideas in this play to hold the stage, Shaw's utopian dream is not credible, and what it really signals is his need to believe in almost any unorthodox regime with a programmatic vision to deracinate the corrupt and purposeless society that alarmed him so profoundly.

In *Man and Superman*, Juan says, "It is not death that matters, but the fear of death. It is not killing and dying that degrades us, but base living, and accepting the wages and profits of degradation. Better ten dead men than one live slave or his master" (vol. 3, 623).[56] In *Major Barbara*, Cusins asks: "Then the way of life lies through the factory of death?" (vol. 1, 445). The answer he receives from his new partner at the munitions factory, the former Major Barbara, is: "Yes, through the raising of hell to heaven and of man to God, through an unveiling of an eternal light in the Valley of The Shadow" (vol. 1, 445). Undershaft, Cusins and Barbara will raise the hell of the previous two plays to a new heaven; the manifest efficiency and order of Perivale St. Andrews will be augmented with the eternal truth that Barbara intuits and, with the aid of violence, spread throughout the world. Shaw was evidently in earnest about seeing such a utopian world brought to fruition, and believed (or desperately needed to believe) that this was the direction in which Creative Evolution was tending. He believed that fierce leadership and iron will were needed to aid the Life Force. In *Man and Superman* Shaw chose to explore the theme of breeding a higher race of human beings capable of circumventing the many problems modernity had brought to bear, that is, positive eugenics; the theme of *Major Barbra* is negative eugenics, that is, not how to selectively breed a higher type of human being but rather how to eliminate the bad through violence. Undershaft states categorically that violence is a legitimate and necessary means of solving problems. On the wall of the office of the munitions factory we learn that each of the Undershafts has placed a motto:

The first Undershaft wrote...IF GOD GAVE THE HAND, LET NOT MAN WITHHOLD THE SWORD. The second wrote up ALL HAVE

THE RIGHT TO FIGHT: NONE HAVE THE RIGHT TO JUDGE. The third wrote up TO MAN THE WEAPON: TO HEAVEN THE VICTORY. The fourth had no literary turn; so he did not write up anything; but he sold cannons to Napoleon under the nose of George the Third. The fifth wrote up PEACE SHALL NOT PREVAIL SAVE WITH A SWORD IN HER HAND. The sixth, my master, was the best of all. He wrote up NOTHING IS EVER DONE IN THIS WORLD UNTIL MEN ARE PREPARED TO KILL ONE ANOTHER IF IT IS NOT DONE. After that, there was nothing left for the seventh to say. So he wrote up, simply, UNASHAMED.

(vol. 1, 430–31)

Initially Cusins is in rebellion against Undershaft's philosophy, but reluctantly concurs that he is right, that violence has been the great agent of change throughout history, that, in Undershaft's words, "When you shoot, you pull down governments, inaugurate new epochs." But he adds that it "ought not to be true" (vol. 1, 436). Undershaft expostulates: "Ought! ought! ought! ought! ought! Are you going to spend your life saying ought, like the rest of our moralists? Turn your oughts into shalls, man. Come and make explosives with me" (vol. 1, 436).

In *The Revolutionist's Handbook* Tanner had made the exact same point, that every movement of reform in history has been produced and maintained by violence, from the disestablishment of the Irish Church to the first reform bill of 1832; even

> if the nation adopted the Fabian policy, it would be carried out by brute force exactly as our present property system is. It would become the law; and those who resisted it would be fined, sold up, knocked on the head by policemen, thrown into prison, and in the last resort "executed" just as they are when they break the present law.
>
> (vol. 3, 710)

Of course Tanner is arguing for the necessity of breeding out of man's nature his violent tendencies, and there is no question but that in *Major Barbara* Shaw is shocking his audience into recognition of the reality of violence in our everyday world, and emphasizing the unpleasant truth of its necessity as we advance further. But in *Major Barbara* the theme of the virtue of creative destruction, of political violence wielded by the Righteous, is so emphatic that it overshadows the virtues of cleanliness and order, the eradication of poverty, the ostensible theme of the play.

It is hard to imagine what Barbara's religion will be now that she has left the Salvation Army (although the play would seem to suggest it will be Dionysian, or vitalist, however, that plays out)[57] but the play is very clear in its rejection of Christianity. As we know from his two major essays of the 1890s, the Christian virtues of love, charity, and forgiveness have had their day and must be discarded. While in *Major Barbara* Cusins takes the role of Siegfried, who will usher in a new era free of religion and law, it is Undershaft who displays all the attributes of that amoral hero, and he preaches a defiantly anti-Christian message. Compassion feeds on misery, we learn, forgiveness is the refuge of beggars, we are told, and as for love, Undershaft contemptuously tells Cusins that he does not want it: "By what right do you take the liberty of offering it to me? I will have your due heed and respect, or I will kill you. But your love! Damn your impertinence!" (vol. 1, 439). Shaw's religion of Creative Evolution is not about love, charity, or forgiveness—that is, the essence of all the world's major religions—but is rather about the advancement of higher intelligence and its supersession of the lower forms of life. As he puts it in the section titled, "NOT LOVE, BUT LIFE" in *The Perfect Wagnerite*, his religion is about life "as a tireless power which is continually driving onward and upward... into ever higher and higher forms of organization."[58] In a sense his religion is that of Nietzsche's; it is a will to power.

But while negative eugenics only gets implicit endorsement in the play itself, Shaw is explicit in the preface. He concludes his essay by saying that "there are two things that must be set right, or we shall perish" (vol. 1, 337). The first is that every human being shall earn through his or her own exertions the equivalent of what they consume as well as enough of a surplus to maintain them in their old age. Secondly, the inhumane practice of judicial punishment must be eliminated from our so-called justice system. Incarceration is inhumane and it strengthens criminal propensities; and the maintenance of criminals is a waste of resources. Therefore, incorrigible law breakers should be painlessly put to death: "We shall never have real moral responsibility until everyone knows that his deeds are irrevocable, and that his life depends on his usefulness" (vol. 1, 338). Oddly, despite the fact that Shaw proposed exactly this over and over again for most of his adult life, many critics still maintain that he was just joking—even when there is obviously no attempt at humor, such as the last pages and indeed most of the preface to *Major Barbara*.

In fact, critics do not even attempt to argue that he is joking and present their case; they just assume it is self-evident. In one of the better essays on *Major Barbara*, "Giving the Devil More than His Due," Nicholas Grene rightly acknowledges the Swiftian tone of Shaw's suggestion earlier in the preface that in our efforts to abolish poverty it might be worth considering that "every adult with less than, say, £365 a year, shall be painlessly but inexorably killed, and every hungry half naked child forcibly fattened and clothed" (vol. 1, 308). Grene agrees with Eric Bentley that Shaw liked playing the devil's advocate, but that by using the word "painlessly"

> Shaw shrinks from using the fierce tactics of Swift; he pulls his punch in proposing mass executions by adding qualifying phrases about humane killing. The result is at once to lessen the outrageous impact of the proposal and to give it a partial plausibility. What starts as a shock-tactic, a deliberate horrific suggestion to awaken people's conscience, is palliated to the point where it begins to sound as if it were in earnest.[59]

I too have trouble believing Shaw would condone the deliberate murdering of the poor no matter how grievously their sight pained him, and recognize the Shavian propensity for exaggeration here, but I also know that Shaw's jokes should never be merely dismissed, and that "painless liquidation" was a theme of his that extended over many years.

At least Grene takes Shaw seriously and questions his motive; yet like Barbara Bellow Watson in her essay "Sainthood for Millionaires,"[60] Grene only comments on this bit of Swiftian wit and ignores the more straightforward recommendations for the painless killing of undesirables found throughout the essay. In 1947, at the age of ninety and with only three more years to live, Shaw wrote again that criminals incapable of reform, as well as "our asylums idiots," and even "shirkers" and "tramps" charged with being "vermin in the Commonwealth," should be "killed without malice"; in sum, all those who are unable "to prove their social solvency" should be "painlessly liquidated."[61] Despite the fact that Shaw had been saying exactly this for well over forty years, critics like Bernard Crick think we should consider such statements as "Shavian dramatic hyperbole" or "clownish melodramatic exaggeration."[62] Crick goes on to say that Shaw unfortunately did not realize on time that the totalitarian dictators were not joking about the elimination of the unfit and unsocial.[63] But Shaw definitely knew of Stalin's efforts to "weed the garden," as he liked to put it, and defended his right to do so; he also had an excessive admiration for revolutionary terrorist Felix Dzerzhinsky, as we saw earlier, and kept a picture of him above his desk in his office.[64] In the 1930s, he repeatedly and with great approbation told the story of Dzerzhinsky's murdering of two employees who did not obey his orders.[65] Dzerzhinsky is nothing if not a Soviet version of Undershaft.[66]

In 1910, the *Daily Express* reported that Shaw had given a lecture at the Eugenics Education Society where he stated that if eugenics were implemented as state policy,

> [w]e should find ourselves committed to killing a great many people whom we now leave living, and to leave living a great many people whom we at present kill...A part of eugenic politics would finally land us in an extensive use of the lethal chamber. A great many people would have to be put out of existence simply because it wastes other people's time to look after them.[67]

These were the kinds of public statements that worried Pearson and Galton, who advocated selective breeding and never endorsed "the lethal chamber." But Shaw, whatever his intentions and whatever the dose of levity, frequently brought up the idea of liquidating recalcitrant citizens in a lethal chamber. In the preface to *Major Barbara* he says of criminals that it

> would be far more sensible to put up with their vices, as we put up with their illnesses, until they give more trouble than they are worth, at which point we should, with many apologies and expressions of sympathy, and some generosity in complying with their last wishes, place them in the lethal chamber and get rid of them.
>
> (vol. 1, 337)

And in 1922 in his preface to the Webbs' *English Local Government*, he remarked that the

> moment we face it frankly we are driven to the conclusion that the community has a right to put a price on the right to live in it...If people are fit to live, let them live under decent human conditions. If they are not fit to live, kill them in a decent, human way. Is it any wonder that some of us are driven to prescribe the lethal chamber as the solution for the hard cases which are at present made the excuse for dragging all the other cases down to their level, and the only possible solution that will create a sense of full social responsibility in modern populations?[68]

Shaw's tone lacks all jocularity here, and considering that it was prefaced to an entirely serious and rather dry book on English local government by those most serious utilitarian colleagues of his in the Fabian Society, Sidney and Beatrice Webb, it would be foolish to argue here that Shaw is joking. Clearly Shaw was serious about the quick and efficient scientific elimination of those unwilling or unable to raise themselves to utopia's level. Regarding the idea of a lethal chamber for ending the lives of those not conforming to a certain standard of social behavior, Dan Stone asks a rather haunting question:

> Here I want only to ask, since the field of eugenics was established in Britain, and was eagerly taken on board by German scientists, might it not also be the case that the notion of the 'lethal chamber', which had existed in British literature on eugenics since the turn of the century, also fed into the fantasies which eventually led to the gas chambers?[69]

This is a compelling question, whatever the answer might be. And *Major Barbara* becomes even more fascinating in the light of such a question, for the munitions factory at Perivale St. Andrews was modeled on Krupps, the German armaments company that later provided weapons to the Nazis.[70]

Shaw wrote plays for the same reason that he gave speeches, wrote essays and pamphlets, and served on the executive committee of the Fabian Society: he wanted to be a useful member of a class of men and women who were actively bringing forth a new society, totally unlike any that had ever existed before. In other words, he was a revolutionary. He was also an impatient man who had excessive reserves of patience, if I may avail myself of a Shavian-style paradox. Of all of Shaw's supermen and superwomen, from Undershaft to Joan, the greatest of all was perhaps Shaw himself. He worked tirelessly as a playwright, pamphleteer, journalist, orator, and Fabian agitator, and even for awhile served as a vestryman for the St. Pancras City Council, meeting regularly to discuss the most mundane matters. He would speak anywhere he was asked, and like Socrates would not accept a fee, just a third-class train ticket there and back. He was obsessed with changing the world, and realized it would not happen overnight; yet for all that he violently desired its immediate eradication, and as a creative artist he was able to give expression to these sorts of fantasies. Although he worked with his Fabian colleagues for decades, and quietly accepted the Fabian policy of gradual change over cataclysmic transformation, he was in his impatience predisposed towards just such a cataclysm.[71] As early as 1889, in the first edition of *Fabian Essays*, he concluded "The Transition to Social Democracy," one of his two contributions to the book, with this paragraph, which warrants including in full:

> Let me, in conclusion, disavow all admiration for this inevitable, but sordid, slow, reluctant, cowardly path to justice. I venture to claim your respect for those enthusiasts who still refuse to believe that millions of their fellow creatures must be left to sweat and suffer in hopeless toil and degradation, while parliaments and vestries grudgingly muddle and grope toward paltry installments of betterment. The right is so clear, the wrong so intolerable, the gospel so convincing, that it seems to them that it *must* be possible to enlist the whole body of workers—soldiers, policemen, and all—under the banner of brotherhood and equality; and at one great stroke to set Justice on her rightful throne. Unfortunately, such an army of light is no more to be gathered from the human product of nineteenth century civilization than grapes are to be gathered from thistles. But if we feel glad of that impossibility; if we feel relieved that the change is to be slow enough to avert personal risk to ourselves; if we feel anything less than acute disappointment and bitter humiliation at the discovery that there is yet between us and the promised land a wilderness in which many must perish miserably of want and despair: then I submit to you that our institutions have corrupted us to the most dastardly degree of selfishness. The Socialists need not be ashamed of beginning as they did by proposing militant organization of the working classes and general insurrection. The proposal proved impracticable; and it has now been abandoned—not without some outspoken regrets—by English Socialists. But it still remains as the only finally possible alternative to the Social Democratic program which I have sketched to-day.[72]

Shaw's desire for putting "Justice" on her throne with "one great stroke," and acceding to the longed for "promised land" without delay, is manifest here in his powerful rhetoric; and the seeds of his eugenic utopianism are implicit in his frustrated desire to mold the "human product" into an "army of light," although he recognizes that it would be tantamount to gathering grapes from thistles.

The years between this writing and the writing of his great trilogy had only increased his impatience. At the time of their composition England's supremacy as "workshop of the world" was under threat by

Germany and the US, especially the former. An unprecedented arms race had begun between Germany and England, and war seemed a definite possibility in the near future. Despite the economic threat from Germany and elsewhere and calls for tariff reform to protect England's economic standing, the economy had fully recovered from the Great Depression of 1873–95, and capitalism, on shaky ground in 1889 and the early 1890s, seemed by the early twentieth century securely without rival. Perhaps it is for this reason that in 1905 Shaw seems oddly reconciled to capitalism, and to believe or hope that the necessary transition to socialism will come from the capitalists themselves.

Major Barbara evinces Shaw as radical Libertarian Anarchist with a powerful desire for cataclysmic change, rather than the interminable crawl of Fabian gradualism. He would like to see his utopian designs put into immediate effect, but such is not possible; so he writes a play like *Major Barbara* and creates a character like Undershaft, the kind of individual he feels England and the world desperately need, but which is really a fantasy, a fantasy that will shortly become a reality. Undershaft, Shaw tells us in the preface,

> is not the dupe of that public sentiment against killing which is propagated and endowed by people who would otherwise be killed themselves... [and] if we were all as resolute and clearsighted as Undershaft, an attempt to live by means of what is called "an independent income" would be the shortest way to the lethal chamber.
> (vol. 1, 309)

Writing *Man and Superman* and *Major Barbara* was Shaw's way of participating in that will that would finally mold chaos into a race of gods, burn away the rubbish, and transform the environment into a heaven-on-earth, as he once wrote to Henry James:

> What is the use of writing plays?—what is the use of anything?—if there is not a Will that finally moulds chaos itself into a race of gods with heaven for an environment, and if that Will is not incarnated in man, and if the hero... does not by the strength of his portion in that Will exorcise ghosts, sweep fathers into the chimney corner, and burn all the rubbish within his reach with his torch before he hands it on to the next hero?[73]

Writing the two plays was Shaw's way of permeating the social and political milieu with the idea—or meme—of scientifically molding a new environment, and ultimately a new species; and in *Major Barbara*, at least, he was also able to express his own aggressive frustration with utopia's delay. Shaw, Webb, and the Fabians had hoped that England would lead the way in instituting the necessary reforms, and when it did not Shaw at least was very excited when Russia, Italy, and later Germany, seemed, through men of will, to be pushing in the right direction.

As a revolutionary Shaw was not taken seriously in his lifetime, and that habit has continued among Shavian critics. Perhaps when we accept the absolutely radical nature of the program for social change that Shaw advocated, and how it coalesced with so much of what was actually happening in the 1930s and 1940s—although utopia had turned to dystopia—we can begin to reevaluate his powerful plays, and these three would be a good place to start. Despite his propensity for clowning, Shaw desperately wanted to be taken seriously. He says in the preface to *Major Barbara*,

> Here am I, for instance, by class a respectable man, by common sense a hater of waste and disorder, by intellectual constitution legally minded to the verge of pedantry, and by temperament apprehensive and economically disposed to the limit of old-maidishness; yet I am, and have always been, and shall now always be, a revolutionary writer.
> (vol. 1, 336)

Is it not time we began to take him at his word?

4
Shaw's Modern Utopia: *Back to Methuselah*

> Our leaders have not loved men: they have loved ideas, and have been willing to sacrifice passionate men on the altars of the blood-drinking, ever-ash-thirsty ideal. Has President Wilson, or Karl Marx or Bernard Shaw ever felt one hot blood-pulse for the working man, the half-conscious, deluded working man? Never. Each of these leaders has wanted to abstract him away from his own blood and being, into some foul Methuselah or abstraction of a man.
>
> D.H. Lawrence[1]

After the success he had with his great philosophical trilogy, Shaw continued to explore and expand the possibilities of the discussion drama, most especially in *Getting Married* (1908), which has hardly any pretension toward plot at all, consisting merely of various personages engaged in a serious disquisition on the institution of marriage. Between *Major Barbara* in 1905 and the advent of the First World War in 1914, Shaw wrote a number of other important plays as well, including *The Doctor's Dilemma* (1906), *The Shewing-up of Blanco Posnet* (1909), *Misalliance* (1910), *Fanny's First Play* (1911), *Androcles and the Lion* (1912), and *Pygmalion* (1913); but while *Blanco Posnet* and *Androcles* deal with the manifestation of the Life Force, they, like the others, eschew the momentous political and philosophical questions that preoccupy Shaw in the plays of his trilogy. During the war Shaw wrote what some believe to be his greatest play, *Heartbreak House* (1919), a tragicomic look at the ruling class that led England into a disastrous war, but it was not until after the war in his massive five-play cycle *Back to Methuselah* that Shaw returned to the serious philosophical play. Written during the years 1918–20, *Back to Methuselah* is Shaw's most ambitious play, what he described in the preface as "a contribution to the modern Bible" (vol. 2, xix), and what he himself considered his most important work.

Before proceeding to our analysis of this key play in the Shavian canon, it is necessary to address the impact of the war, and determine what, if any, changes it may have wrought in Shaw's utopian thinking. In an important essay from 1971, "Shaw and Revolution: The Politics of the Plays," Shaw scholar Martin Meisel claims that while Shaw may have been initially somewhat apocalyptic or catastrophic in his thinking, in joining the Fabians he came to accept gradualism over catastrophism, or sudden violent revolution. The strategy of the early plays works to leave a "residual impression" by which the audience will be moved to contribute to such gradual change. Consequently Meisel is "not content to take what seem to be important elements of catastrophism and impossibilism in the plays as the 'real' Shaw, or even as the suppressed Shaw breaking out in the irresponsible dreamwork of art as personal expression."[2] Beginning with *Heartbreak House*, though, Shaw's frustration with gradualism and parliamentary procedure is apparent and he gives way to a new strategy in his plays, a strategy that stayed with him to the end of his career; in other words, an anti-Fabian message is delivered to his audience regarding the futility of parliamentary procedure. Shaw did not want revolution by violence, Meisel claims, but as his pessimism increased after the war—and as he reflected on the revolutions in France and Russia—he became convinced of the inevitability of violence in bringing forth the desired social transformation. Nonetheless gradualism to some degree was still necessary, as evidenced by Lenin's switch from instant collectivism to the New Economic Policy.

This is an important essay and close to my own contention, but with one crucial difference. In my view, and as we have seen in previous chapters, the "catastrophism and apocalyptic violence" are continuous, deeply embedded in Shaw's psyche and frequently apparent in pre-First World War writings—as Meisel himself admits—even as his political persona and conscious political activity faithfully adapted to Fabian policy. In other words, I do not believe the war provoked a radical disjuncture in Shaw's thinking, or even greatly altered his strategy as a political playwright, although it clearly did influence his patience. In fact Meisel's essay, despite his thesis, seems to bear out my own contention; for even Shaw's first play, Meisel says, "aims to prepare and capture the will, not the reason; and...the will is conceived as revolutionary and catastrophic in its changes, concerned with ends rather than means, and with justice rather than prudence."[3] And a little later

Meisel says that the "prospect of revolutionary violence as an answer to inclusive institutionalized disorder becomes explicit for the first time in *Major Barbara*," and that there are intimations as well in *Androcles* and *Misalliance*.[4] Meisel does not seem to find a radical disjuncture in Shaw either, although he does descry a more conscious commitment to catastrophism after the war.

In any case, the war surely left its mark, and it is a fascinating fact that one of Shaw's most pessimistic plays, *Heartbreak House*, is followed by one of his most utopian, *Back to Methuselah*. Shaw's most notorious publication during the war was not a play at all, but a long essay called "Common Sense about the War" which was issued as a companion to the *New Statesman* in November 1914. By the end of the year 75,000 copies of the pamphlet had been bought and Shaw, whose fame and popularity had only grown since *Pygmalion*, was reviled throughout England for assigning equal blame to England and to Germany for the start of the war. He followed this with another long essay titled, "More Common Sense about the War," which was written in 1915 but not published. Shaw wrote other essays and short articles as well, and a number of short plays published in 1919 in a volume titled *Heartbreak House, Great Catherine and Playlets of the War* (*Great Catherine* was written in 1913, before the advent of the war). Reading through Shaw's war writings now one is left with the impression, first of all, that his allusions in the titles to his common sense is entirely apposite. Shaw did indeed resist the war fever and jingoism that gripped England and provides a sensible analysis of the conflict. He assigns the blame for the war to the "Junkerism" and militarism of both Germany and England; and he accurately predicted that outrageously burdensome war reparations exacted on Germany would lead to another world war.

What is also apparent in these writings is Shaw's simultaneous hatred of and fascination with war. As has been remarked by J.L. Wisenthal and Daniel O'Leary in their edition of *What Shaw Really Wrote About the War* and Stanley Weintraub in his book *Journey to Heartbreak*, Shaw's ending of *Heartbreak House*, where Ellie and Hesione long for the return of the bombers, is taken directly from Shaw's own experience.[5] And in his account of visiting the front line in "Joy Riding at the Front" (1917) Shaw states:

> I spent a week in the survey of all this ruin, with the booming and whizzing of its unresting progress continually in my ears. And I am bound to state plainly, as a simple fact to be exploited by devils or angels, according to its true nature, that I enjoyed myself enormously

and continuously, in spite of exposures and temperatures that finally gave me my first taste of frostbite.[6]

Shaw is characteristically provocative as he exclaims throughout this essay what a great time he had amid the terror and destruction, how he enjoyed his "week at the front much more than I enjoyed my last week at the seaside,"[7] but what he makes clear throughout, and especially as he concludes the essay, is the great respect he has for the military efficiency of England in comparison with the bombastic foolishness of the civil authorities in the government and in the press, and he longs to see the ethos of service that mostly characterizes life at the front supersede the ethos of predation and individual grasping that characterizes the commercial world away from the frontline.

Back to Methuselah was begun during the last year of the war and Shaw was still revising it in the first months of 1921. It consists of a five-play cycle, a 30,000-word preface, a "Postscript after Twenty-Five Years," and a one-act fragment called "A glimpse of the Domesticity of Franklyn Barnabas" that was excluded from the play proper when it was published in 1921 but eventually published in *Short Stories, Scraps, and Shavings* in 1932 and finally performed in New York in 1960. *Back to Methuselah* is the definitive product of Shaw's enduring utopian imagination, and a work of utopian literature in the strictest sense of the genre, with perhaps one qualification. Classical utopian works such as More's *Utopia* (1516), Campanella's *City of the Sun* (1602) and Bacon's *New Atlantis* (1624), to name just three of the best known, had depicted static societies, "perfect and static States, a balance of happiness won forever against the forces of unrest and disorder that inhere in things."[8] But the modern utopia, befitting a post-Darwinian age, as H.G. Wells continues, "must not be static but kinetic, must shape not as a permanent state but as a hopeful stage, leading to a long ascent of stages."[9] Shaw's magnum opus is intended in all seriousness as a work of religious literature for a new age, a mythical master narrative of Creative Evolution, which is the "genuinely scientific religion for which all wise men are now anxiously looking" (vol. 2, xix). It is astonishing to me that all the surveys of utopian literature that I perused failed to include *Back to Methuselah*, with the exception of Frederic Jameson's *Archaeologies of the Future: The Desire Called Utopia and Other Science Fictions*.[10] Shaw's utopia spans untold thousands of years, beginning with, appropriately enough, "In the Beginning," with Adam, Eve, and the Serpent in the Garden and concluding with "As Far as Thought Can Reach," which depicts a summer afternoon in the year 31,920. Like all utopias it satirizes the present state of things (the second play, "The Gospel of the Brothers Barnabas," is contemporary with Shaw's writing) and imagines an alternative more or less perfect state of things. The final three plays, "The Thing Happens," "Tragedy of an Elderly Gentleman," and "As Far as Thought Can Reach," present Creative Evolution leading humankind to a state of omniscience and omnipotence, just as Shaw predicted it would in *Man and Superman* twenty years earlier.

Utopias were resurgent in the latter part of the nineteenth century, and Shaw was very much influenced by a number of them, as has already been remarked. It is my belief that Plato's *Republic* may have had a greater influence on Shaw's inveterate utopian thinking than any other book he ever read. Although he does not mention it nearly as often as he mentions *Pilgrim's Progress* (1678), it seems to have impressed his mind indelibly. So did More's *Utopia* and Swift's *Gulliver's Travels* (1726). But of contemporary works, Bulwer-Lytton's *The Coming Race* (1871) and Edward Bellamy's *Looking Backward* (1888) made a profound impression, as did Samuel Butler's *Erewhon* (1872). Why were utopian works so prevalent at the end of the nineteenth century, and why was Shaw so inclined to be influenced by them and to produce them himself? According to Northrop Frye:

> the typical utopia contains, if only by implication, a satire on the *anarchy* inherent in the writer's own society, and the utopia form flourishes best when anarchy seems most a social threat. Since More utopias have appeared regularly but sporadically in literature, with a great increase around the close of the nineteenth century. This later vogue clearly had much to do with the distrust and dismay aroused by extreme laissez-faire versions of capitalism, which were thought of as manifestations of anarchy.[11]

As this study should have made amply clear by now, it is the threat of chaos, both from within and from without, that accounts for many of Shaw's idiosyncrasies and stimulated much of his literary and political activity throughout his life.

Because *Back to Methuselah* is a utopian work of dramatic fiction, it contains a picture of the world as Shaw wished to see it and evidently believed the Life Force was leading it. It is meant to stimulate the imagination, fire the will, and become reality. As the Serpent says at the start of the play: "You imagine what you desire; you will what you imagine; and at last you create what you will" (vol. 2, 10). This is no idle wishful thinking for Shaw, but sound Lamarckian evolutionary theory, as he avers in the preface, with its "fundamental proposition that living organisms changed because they wanted to" (vol. 2, xxii). Shaw had no quarrel with Darwin, whom he says admitted that Natural Selection—"Circumstantial Selection," in Shaw's lexicon—was only part of the story; it was only the neo-Darwinians who made it the whole story, abrogating will and purpose from the story of evolution. Shaw states that "Creative Evolution is already a religion, and is indeed now unmistakably the religion of the twentieth century, newly arisen from the ashes of pseudo-Christianity, of mere skepticism, and of the soulless affirmations and blind negations of the Mechanists and Neo-Darwinians" (vol. 2, lxxx). In order to advance this new twentieth-century religion, Shaw wrote *Back to Methuselah*, to be a part of the new Bible, as he says in the preface; for Creative Evolution "cannot become a popular religion until it has its legends, its parables, its miracles" (vol. 2, lxxx). Therefore, we should expect to find in Shaw's play everything he wished to see in the body politic as well as in the bodily organism of the future. Shaw subtitled his play *A Metabiological Pentateuch*, and the extreme importance he placed on bodily control is as evident in this play as it is anywhere else in the Shaw cannon.

Shaw was apparently greatly impressed by the superhuman race depicted in Bulwer-Lytton's utopian novel *The Coming Race*. He mentions the novel in a lecture on fiction that he gave in 1887, and we know from this lecture that Shaw was already thinking about what evolutionarily advanced men and women of the future would be like: serene, wise, passionless, self-controlled – in fact they are nearly omnipotent in their relative power over the material world.[12] The novel depicts an engineer who encounters an advanced race living in the bowels of the earth. Much of the force of the novel is in the contrast between the ordinary man and the race of supermen and superwomen he encounters. Like the ancients in the final play of Shaw's cycle, the Vril-ya, as they are called, can paralyze with a stare, move matter with their power of volition, and indeed have practically absolute control of their will and their environment. All creatures judged hostile to life are destroyed, but to destroy anything—even an insect—that is not deemed hostile is a grave wrong. When the Tur, their leader, decides to kill the engineer who has stumbled on their subterranean society, he says, "[B]e his end painless and prompt."[13] This sounds like an echo of Shaw's frequent call for the quick and painless liquidation of recalcitrant citizens, but of course it is not an echo because it preceded Shaw's first recorded utterances to that effect by almost thirty years.

Back to Methuselah dramatizes the ideas presented by Don Juan in the third act of *Man and Superman*, the central idea being that the Life Force is evolving to a state of omniscience and omnipotence. Shaw says that as a young playwright back in 1901 he was forced to dress his philosophy up with a great deal of comedy to please the tastes of the time, and so no one noticed "the new religion in the centre of the intellectual whirlpool" (vol. 2, lxxxix). There is no missing it this time, for while there is debate in the dialectical manner, the chief difference between *Man and Superman* and *Back to Methuselah* is that in the later play the ideas are given concrete dramatic expression rather than simply debated about—and over five fairly short plays rather than one long act. And in *Back to Methuselah* it is also urgently declared—in both the play and the preface—that it is necessary to extend the life span of human beings, and not just by a few years or decades, but from three score and ten to three hundred years or more.

According to Shaw, our life spans are too short for us to take life seriously. Much of Shaw's preface was taken from a 1906 Fabian lecture on Darwin; in the years since that lecture Shaw had become increasingly convinced that "the human animal, as he exists at present, is incapable of solving the social problems raised by his own aggregation, or, as he calls it, his civilization" (vol. 2, xii). Shaw claims that although the appalling destruction of the war confirmed this ever growing conviction, the seeds of his doubt on the matter actually extend back forty years to the start of his public work as a socialist (vol. 2, xi–xii). In the previous chapter, I remarked that in *Man and Superman* Shaw put a great deal of himself into both the Devil, who expounded on man's inventive powers of destruction, and Don Juan, who espoused the reality of the Life Force and its ineluctable march to greater powers of organization. Although the Devil's arguments were quite persuasive, it was clear that for Shaw nothing could stop this marvelous power, which would even appropriate the powers of destruction to its own purposes. That is clearly still Shaw's opinion, but the youthful insouciance of the earlier play is gone. Social Darwinism and society's lack of any serious religion has nearly wrecked civilization, and the time has come to muster the will to lift us out of this morass. Consequently there is a greater tension between hope and despair in *Back to Methuselah* than in his earlier plays; it is as if the less Shaw had reason to believe in utopia, the more extreme and doubtful were his projections of it, and the more wildly he pinned his hopes on dubious supermen like Hitler and Mussolini, as would soon become apparent.

Back to Methuselah posits a world where the human race is split into two factions: the "grown up children" who for their own good and the good of the race should probably be exterminated (the biologically inferior, called the short-livers) and the responsible citizens, who through an unconscious manifestation of will have begun to live to a very great age (the biologically superior, called the long-livers). In other words, in *Back to Methuselah* the race of supermen Shaw always longed for has become a reality; the philistines and idealists that had always frightened him begin to decrease in numbers until finally the race of supermen (guardians, they are also called, as in Plato's *Republic*) consider wiping them out for good and for all. In the last play the triumph is complete; there are only supermen, and if there is an atavistic throwback he or she is usually descried early and destroyed.

Shaw presents a totalitarian world in which all that is messy disappears: recalcitrant egoistic citizens, the family, sexual difference, human touching, sleep, dancing, and metaphor; and even art and sensual pleasures are relegated to a primeval stage of development for a couple of years between the ages of birth and four years old—in fact, after the age of four social intercourse itself is more or less eliminated. The human body is becoming ethereal, and it is intimated or at least hoped that we will soon be leaving the body behind as we become vortices of pure Thought. Gestation no longer occurs within the body of the female, for we have somehow become oviparous. (We have become, essentially, a new species.) The world Shaw presents, ostensibly a utopia, has unintentionally become a dystopia: the ancients are isolated, cold, revile nature, and terminate the lives of any newborns who they feel are in any way inadequate. In the 1887 lecture on fiction mentioned above, Shaw tries to allay his audience's doubts about the evolved human beings of the future by telling them that he has "no doubt that if the tigers and monkeys were to express their opinion of mankind they would vote us cold, passionless, calculating, and mysteriously dreadful."[14] For all Shaw's justified concerns about the political incompetence of our leaders and the destructive propensities of the human race, it is not hard to see why the human race might choose the hot blood-pulse and half-conscious delusions that epitomize us as we are now, to paraphrase the epigraph from Lawrence at the head of this chapter, rather than the cold isolation of his ancients, despite their miraculous ability to grow new limbs at will.

"In the Beginning"

The first play in Shaw's cycle takes us back to the beginning of human history, and introduces us to a central problem: the problem of immortality. According to Lamarckian evolutionary theory, nothing is simply "natural." Everything we do habitually—breathing, circulating blood, dying—was "willed" by our ancestors in the remote past via functional adaptation, which is another way of saying Creative Evolution. We *wanted* to come out of the water, so we exchanged our gills for lungs and began to breathe the air and roam the earth. Or it might be said that as the water receded it became necessary to develop lungs if we *wanted* to live in this new environment. The play opens with Adam confusedly contemplating a fawn that has tripped and broken its neck. What if this happens to him or Eve? For although they cannot die naturally, they may die accidentally—in fact such an occurrence is inevitable given the sempiternity of their existence. Then the one would be alone without the other. But Adam had been brooding about the hell of sempiternity anyway. Who wants to live forever in the Garden clearing briars and thistles? (In fact, it is just because Adam expects to live so long that he tends the Garden so meticulously; a key point for Shaw.)

The problem is solved by the Serpent, the first pioneering realist, in the Shavian sense. The Serpent sees things as they are, but also as they might be instead; she experiences dissatisfaction with the status quo and imagines a better reality. She says to Eve: "You see things; and you say 'Why?' But I dream things that never were; and I say 'Why not?'" (vol. 2, 7). The Serpent, who has learned to renew herself by shedding her skin, has also learned to multiply herself. She did these things because she wanted to. They are miracles, and she teaches Eve of miracles: that which is not possible yet is suddenly possible anyway. The problem that Adam and Eve are grappling with can be solved, the Serpent teaches Eve, by giving life to another Adam and another Eve to take their place; then they may die and take their rest. Eve says, "I will give life myself. I will tear another Adam from my body if I tear my body to pieces in the act." The Serpent tells her: "Do. Dare it. Everything is possible" (vol. 2, 9). Adam and Eve fix their lives at one thousand years, but the introduction of their child Cain in the second act alters this by his invention of murder, war, and conquest. Thus the problem of immortality is solved, but a whole host of new problems are set in motion by this functional adaptation.

Shaw's antipathy to sex is apparent in the way he closes the act, and indeed it is apparent throughout the cycle, especially in the later utopian plays when his relatively ideal social and biological structures come into view. The act closes with a stage direction describing a tableau. The Serpent is whispering in Eve's ear the "secret" of sex and regeneration: "*Eve's face lights up with intense interest, which increases until an expression of overwhelming repugnance takes its place. She buries her face in her hands*" (vol. 2, 19). St. John Ervine objected to Eve's squeamishness when he read the play and expressed his opinion to Shaw, who told him that "what made the God of the Eden legend incredible was His deliberate combination of the reproductive with the execratory organs and consequently of love with shame."[15] And when Cecil Chesterton asked Shaw if he was a "puritan in practice," Shaw told him that "the sexual act was to him monstrous and indecent and that he could not understand how any self-respecting man and woman could face each other in the daylight after spending the night together."[16] And from the same source it is reported that "Shaw doubted whether children should know who were their parents or the parents be able to identify one another. The most satisfactory method, thought Shaw, would be for a crowd of healthy men and women to meet in the dark, and then to separate without having seen one another's faces."[17] The last idea sounds as though it were absorbed from Shaw's reading of Plato's *Republic*. While one might be inclined to regard some of these quotes with skepticism, it should be borne in mind that they all come from Hesketh Pearson's authorized biography of Shaw, which came out with Shaw's approval (and assistance) while he was alive. In any case, they are certainly characteristic of Shaw and evidence of similar repugnance to sex and intimacy can be found from other sources as well, not least in his plays, essays, and stories, including the one we are now considering, as we will see shortly.

Act two introduces Cain, and some of the best dialectic debating of the cycle occurs between Cain and his mother Eve.[18] Cain is an innovator, and like his facsimile in the fourth part of the cycle, Cain Adamson Charles Napoleon, he would have claim to being a Shavian superman, except in this utopian play Shaw is able to illustrate for his audience what the genuine superman of the future will be like. Consequently Shaw is able to present the admirable qualities of Cain and Napoleon while at the same time satirizing the bellicosity of the great warrior personality. In the future there will be no more warriors, and thus the Cains and Napoleons of the world look foolish in comparison. But it is Cain who moves the human race to another level, despite all the new problems he introduces at the same time. Adam and Eve are stagnant, and it is Cain, like the Serpent a pioneer, who strives for something more, however ineffable that something is as yet: "I do not know what I want, except that I want to be something higher and nobler than this stupid old digger" (vol. 2, 30). He contemptuously scolds his father for his philistine complacency: "Still digging? Always dig, dig, dig. Sticking in the old furrow. No progress! no advanced ideas! no adventures!" (vol. 2, 20). Like Undershaft, he feels no shame for the blood on his hands: "I am the first murderer: you are only the first man. Anybody could be the first man: it is as easy as to be the first cabbage. To be the first murderer one must be a man of spirit" (vol. 2, 20–21). Cain is a destroyer; he destroys lives but he also destroys settled ways of being; he invents hunting, fighting, and war, he exults in his courage, and he looks to something higher: "There is something higher than man. There is hero and superman" (vol. 2, 24). He also invents conquest and slavery, and therefore introduces feudalism into society. He is a Nietzschean superman, a creator of new values. He has no fear of God, saying:

> I am not a child to be afraid of a Voice... The Voice does not speak to me as it does to you. I am a man: you are only a grown-up child... And a man does not listen and tremble in silence. He replies: he makes the Voice respect him: in the end he dictates what the Voice shall say.
>
> (vol. 2, 26, 27–28)

Cain reminds one of Siegfried in *The Perfect Wagnerite*.

It is significant that Cain calls his father a grown-up child, for in the later plays that is exactly what the long-livers call the short-livers. Cain also invents (or discovers) the devil, and is therefore like Nietzsche's Zoroaster the pioneer who introduces dualism into the world: "There must be two Voices: one that gulls and despises you, and another that trusts and respects me. I call yours the Devil. Mine I call the Voice of God" (vol. 2, 28). Cain is in revolt against the present order of things and is what Robert Brustein would call an existential rebel,[19] in defiance against the very order of existence:

> I revolt against the clay. I revolt against the food. You say it gives us strength: does it not also turn into filth and smite us with diseases? I revolt against these births that you and mother are so proud of. They drag us down to the level of the beasts.
>
> (vol. 2, 29)

Cain, for Shaw, is thus an essential figure in the destiny of the human race, at least in so far as he is presented in this myth within the Bible of Creative Evolution. His intense desire to transcend the need for food, to escape the body of clay, and to get past propagation by sexual contact are all realized or in hope of being realized many millennia later in Shaw's utopia.

Cain is a representative of what I called in the last chapter creative destruction. For Shaw, externally inflicted death (liquidation) is sometimes necessary. He frequently remarked that it is occasionally necessary to kill a man as it is always necessary to kill a snake or a tiger. Cain is clearly someone who enjoys battle, who enjoys risking his life and killing his antagonists. This is not the type of killing that Shaw normally approves, although he has a great deal of respect for the great warrior (Caesar, Cromwell, and Napoleon being three of his most esteemed), and his introduction of murder and war into the world has wrought all kinds of problems. Yet he has "an instinct which tells [him] that death plays its part in life" (vol. 2, 32–33) and scores a victory when he turns his parents' accusations of him against them: "Tell me this: who invented death?" (vol. 2, 33). They are dumbfounded by this question, and at first have no retort. Eve eventually replies that he invented murder, which is different. When Adam admits that it was they who invented death, Cain responds, "You did well: I, too, do not want to live for ever. But if you invented death, why do you blame me, who am a minister of death?" Adam replies: "I do not blame you. Go in peace. Leave me to my digging, and your mother to her spinning" (vol. 2, 33). Shaw would not blame Cain either, who is only exercising his extraordinary energy and has no predominating acquisitive instinct. But his innovations have caused new problems that will eventually have to be solved when man's invention leads society into the age of industrial warfare. Cain leaves and Adam and Eve are alone; we learn that, figuratively speaking, Thanatos, child of Cain, is gaining on Eros, that through Cain "and his like, death is gaining on life" (vol. 2, 33). This first play in the cycle closes with Eve's remark that man does not live by bread alone and that someday we will learn what that other sustenance is, a time when there will be no more digging, spinning, fighting and killing—in other words, utopia.

"The Gospel of the Brothers Barnabas"

The next play moves into the present, taking place a few years after the war in the comfortable middle-class London study of Franklyn Barnabas, an independent religious thinker who, along with his brother Conrad, a biologist, has written *The Gospel of the Brothers Barnabas*, from which the play takes its title. Franklyn and Conrad are Creative Evolutionists and thus serve as Shaw's spokesmen. Much of their dialogue can be found in so many words in Shaw's preface: "It is now absolutely certain that the political and social problems raised by our civilization cannot be solved by mere human mushrooms who decay and die when they are just beginning to have a glimmer of the wisdom and knowledge needed for their own government" (vol. 2, 69). These words are uttered by Conrad to Burge and Lubin, two politicians who represent opposing sides of the Liberal party, and whose only response to the ideas of the brothers is to contrive how they can spin it to win votes. Thus the play is a satire on the idiocy of politicians whose only concern seems to be electioneering, although they are hardly to be faulted for not taking the idea of the brothers seriously. At first they assume the brothers have an elixir or potion or something, and are credulous enough, but when they learn that the solution to the problems of contemporary society is the willing of longevity they are obviously not so credulous. The two characters are modeled on H.H. Asquith and Lloyd George, and a good deal of discussion about the handling of the war occurs; the two figures are the butts of much invective, but ultimately they are exonerated since their "task was beyond human capacity" (vol. 2, 69).

This second play is one part satire on the incompetence of politicians trying to deal with immense problems considerably beyond their small capacity, and another part propaganda for Creative Evolution. The brothers explain that the "most scientific document we possess at present is... the story of the Garden of Eden" (vol. 2, 74). They summarize the most important points from the previous play, starting with the problem of immortality in the Garden—the frightful thought of living forever and the equally dismaying thought of extinction, which was the catalyst for the solution—followed by the Fall: death by murder, war and general recklessness, which followed the solution to the initial problem. When Lubin expresses skepticism regarding the scientific importance of the document, Franklyn explains:

> The Book of Genesis is a part of nature like any other part of nature. The fact that the tale of the Garden of Eden has survived and held the imagination of men spellbound for centuries, whilst hundreds of much more plausible and amusing stories have gone out of fashion and perished like last year's popular song, is a scientific fact; and Science is bound to explain it.
>
> (vol. 2, 78)

And one advantage that the Garden story has over most other attempts to explain life's origin is that it accounts for vitality: God breathed in through the nostrils and animated the first creatures. This is important because, as Shaw remarks in the preface, a dead body and a live one have the same chemical components, and no one has ever been able to explain what it is that makes for the difference. This leads to a discussion of Creative Evolution, the "pursuit of omnipotence and omniscience.

Greater power and greater knowledge...Evolution is that pursuit and nothing else. It is the path to Godhead. A man differs from a microbe only in being further on the path" (vol. 2, 76).[20] Shaw's thesis here is exactly the same as in *Man and Superman*, and some of his language echoes the earlier play; when Conrad says that the "power my brother calls God proceeds by the method of Trial and Error; and if we turn out to be one of the errors, we shall go the way of the mastodon and the megatherium and all the other scrapped experiments" (vol. 2, 82), we are immediately reminded of a very similar passage that mentions the megatherium in that earlier gospel of Creative Evolution.[21]

"The Gospel of the Brothers Barnabas" demonstrates the power of Shaw's method of instruction or propaganda. For the great joke of the play is also a perfect illustration of Shaw's method as a revolutionary playwright. Haslam is a young rector with absolutely no sense of religious vocation, and indeed only seems to be serious about one thing: his amorous relationship with Franklyn's daughter Savvy. He gives very little thought to the ideas discussed in his presence; or at least he does not take them seriously. Yet it is he and the parlor maid (who has glanced through the brothers' book) who have assimilated the ideas of the Gospel, which have gone to work in the depths of their unconscious. This is the central reason why nothing that Shaw says, and especially the things he says over and over again and which may seem outrageous or simply a joke, is to be disregarded. The play ends with Franklyn asserting that they had better hold their tongues, since everyone seems to be laughing at them. Conrad replies, "I daresay. But Creative Evolution doesnt stop while people are laughing. Laughing may even lubricate its job." When Savvy asks what he means by that, Conrad answers, "It means that the first man to live three hundred years maynt have the slightest notion that he is going to do it, and may be the loudest laugher of the lot" (vol. 2, 88). As the 275-year-old Archbishop Haslam says in the next play, regarding his unusual situation: "Like all revolutionary truths, it began as a joke" (vol. 2, 109). Shaw disseminated the ideas he wanted instituted via jokes and seemingly outrageous comments, hoping these ideas would take root in some of his audience and eventually become a reality in the world.

"The Thing Happens"

The third play in the cycle takes place 250 years later in the year 2170 in the office of the President of the British Islands, Burge-Lubin, who, as his name implies, is a conflation of the two incompetent politicians from the previous play. But he is merely a figurehead, for the country is now run—in an ironic reversal of British Imperialism—by exported foreigners from China and Africa. The socialism that Shaw worked so hard to institute has become a fact of life, as has the leap in biological evolution predicted by the sagely brothers in the previous play. For of course it is a leap we have been talking about, and Shaw addresses any doubts on that issue in the last play when Lubin expresses his understanding that evolution works by infinitesimally slow and imperceptible gradual change. In answering him, Shaw gets in a dig at both politicians and Fabian orthodoxy by having Conrad reply that it is "only the politicians who improve the world so gradually that nobody can see the improvement...Nature always proceeds by jumps" (vol. 2, 80–81). In "The Thing Happens" Shaw lets us know that socialism is not enough, that the destiny of life on earth requires a leap toward the superman. Nietzsche had said that man was a bridge to the superman, and Shaw clearly agrees. In this play many of the reforms Shaw propagandized for throughout his life have occurred, such as the 1969 Act for the Redistribution of Income; the institution of a lethal chamber to liquidate the lives of those decreed by the state to be idle, feeble or insane; the teaching of the value of work (beginning at age three) and the organization of labor by the state (everyone becomes self-supporting or nearly so by age thirteen, retiring at forty-three to a state pension).

But as a close reading of many of Shaw's previous plays makes clear, socialism is meant to serve Creative Evolution and not Creative Evolution to serve socialism. *Man and Superman* is about the importance of breeding the superman; *John Bull's Other Island* shows the inadequacy of even the best men, one having energy but no brains and another brains but no spiritual depth, and so on; and while *Major Barbara* is about an elite group organizing the machinery of the state to serve the interests of the entire community, it also affirms the importance of Cusins and Barbara as biological progenitors, as Cusins makes clear to Undershaft when he tells him that he *must* marry Barbara,[22] and as the movie of *Major Barbara* (1941) makes even more clear by the new opening scene that Shaw wrote specifically for the film. This tendency is especially pronounced in "The Thing Happens," where it is intimated that the long-livers, small in number and isolated from one another, will now come together and begin to reproduce. Feeling themselves prodigious anomalies, each one believing that he or she is the only one, they have kept their secret to themselves; but as the Archbishop (formerly Haslam) and Mrs. Lutestring (formerly the parlor maid) are adventitiously thrown together, Confucius realizes that the Archbishop will now "advertize in terms which only the longlived people will understand. He will bring them together and organize them. They will hasten from all parts of the earth. They will become a great Power" (vol. 2, 133). And as Confucius, who also more or less runs the government, realizes, despite how alarming this turn in events might be, "We cannot in our souls really want to stop it: the vital force that has produced this change would paralyse our opposition to it, if we were mad enough to oppose. But we will not oppose. You and I may be of the elect, too" (vol. 2, 133). Shaw's Calvinistic terminology is important. For despite the relative wisdom of Confucius, if he is not one of the "elect" he is by definition one of the reprobate and destined for destruction, as the next two plays in the cycle make clear. For even here there is a suggestion that these two factions are at war, and Barnabas, who is nothing like his illustrious forebears, has a powerful instinct to destroy the long-livers, telling Burge-Lubin that they should: "Kill them...Lock them up. Sterilize them somehow, anyhow." When asked why, he responds: "What reason can you give for killing a snake? Nature tells you to do it" (vol. 2, 128). His instinct for self-preservation is not unwarranted, for earlier Mrs. Lutestring, foreshadowing the position of the Colonizing Party of long-livers in the next play, tells Burge-Lubin that she does not regard him as a completed soul, and that he has good reason to be afraid of her, for there "are moments when your levity, your ingratitude, your shallow jollity, make my gorge rise so against you that if I could not remind myself that you are a child I should be tempted to doubt your right to live at all" (vol. 2, 122). The right of the short-livers to live becomes a contentious political issue in the next play.

"Tragedy of an Elderly Gentleman"

In the penultimate play of the cycle, "Tragedy of an Elderly Gentleman," Shaw introduces an important theme of the *Methuselah* cycle: the despair, or "discouragement" as he calls it, that the short-livers feel in the presence of the long-livers. It is now the year 3000 and the two factions are geographically separated from one another. In *The Quintessence of Ibsenism* Shaw delineated humankind as 0.1 percent realist (the supermen), 29.9 percent idealist (the intellectual and professional classes that Cusins wants to see wiped out in *Major Barbara*), and 70 percent Philistine (the complacent and self-satisfied). Now, a thousand years in the future, the realists or long-livers have become a power just as Confucius predicted they would. They occupy Ireland as

(As we will see in the final play of the cycle, language is disappearing entirely among the ancients as they revert to the prelapsarian stage of Adam and Eve before the Serpent taught them language.)

The Elderly Gentleman is met only with confusion when he says that blood is thicker than water or that the remedy is in your own hands because the long-liver can only understand these words literally. The words that we learn have gone out of circulation indicate the radical change in the nature of the social structure, as well as the beings within it: trespass, decent, sneer, moral sense, liberty, married, private property, questionable taste, and embarrass have no meaning here; and Shaw has a joke with the word landlord. When asked by the Elderly Gentleman if she is a landlord the secondary replies, "There is a tradition in this part of the country of an animal with a name like that. It used to be hunted and shot in the barbarous ages. It is quite extinct now" (vol. 2, 144). It is interesting that, while the violent part of the long-livers' nature is supposed to be almost extinguished, Shaw gives a hint here of a violent past, and intimates the violent extirpation of the landowning class that at the time of his writing was actually taking place in the Soviet Union.

When finally the Elderly Gentleman erupts in frustration, "Pray, is there no one in these islands who understands plain English?" Zoo—a youngster of fifty assigned to watch him—replies, "Well, nobody except the oracles. They have to make a special historical study of what we call the dead thought" (vol. 2, 149). The oracles in this play would seem to be filling the role of the clergy in the medieval period, the commissars in Soviet Russia, and those in the upper echelons of the Nazi Party in Germany. As in all totalitarian systems there seems to be a "priestly" caste that has a monopoly on the wider reaches of mental life, and it is difficult to escape the impression that Shaw's long-livers, at least in this fourth play, have circumscribed intellects. Later the Elderly Gentleman confesses to Zoo that one of his two goals is to see the ruins of London. But it turns out that Zoo has never heard of London, and anyway "ruins" are not tolerated. It is becoming clear why a short-liver in this environment would get "discouraged," which in this play means more than simple discouragement and is an actual malady which results in a losing of the will to live. In fact, we learn that occasionally a short-lived child is born to the long-livers, and although their policy is to "weed them out" (vol. 2, 172) in actuality this involves no interference: "If one of us has no self-control, or is too weak to bear the strain of our truthful life without wincing, or is tormented by depraved appetites and superstitions, or is unable to keep free from pain and depression, he naturally their base and are occasionally visited by short-livers who want either to consult the oracle or to try to acquire the mental flexibility that the climate induces. As it happens, those consulting the oracle do not really want to gather the fruits of oracular wisdom, but rather want to exploit the prestige of the oracle for political gain back home.

The play offers an interesting perspective as we see both groups together in about equal number, unlike in the previous play where long-livers are a minority and the final play where the short-livers are extinct. Thus we see the two sides of Shaw, the totalitarian and the anarchist, which has caused such confusion for many. The long-livers have no law, no judiciary, no police; they are totally free to do as they like because they are biologically advanced and have no need of authority; they are self-governing. The short-livers have very strict rules and must be accompanied at all times by "a nurse," one of the guardians or long-livers. When the Elderly Gentleman wanders off without his nurse he is scolded for breaking the rules, which he assumes are only for the lower classes: "There are only two human classes here: the shortlived and the normal," he is told. "The rules apply to the shortlived and are for their own protection" (vol. 2, 143). Thus we see Shaw's belief that the "elect" require no restraint whereas he takes a paternalistic position toward the less elevated.

But interestingly, there is a kind of class system or at least hierarchy within the long-livers and it intimates a sort of totalitarian world even within the anarchic freedom of these elect beings. We learn that the long-livers are divided among three types and each type is indicated by a hat with the number one, two, or three on it. At the start of the play the Elderly Gentleman has wandered away from his nurse and is accosted by a woman with a number two on her cap. Although her "*age cannot be guessed: her face is firm and chiseled like a young face; but her expression is unyouthful in its severity and determination*" (vol. 2, 139). In fact, she is somewhere between the ages of 100 and 200, and designated as a "secondary," the "2" on her cap signaling this rank. Those in the first centenary are called primaries and those in their third tertiaries.

I call this budding utopia "totalitarian" because mental outlook has narrowed as language potential has atrophied, while at the same time knowledge of history is only available to a hieratic class. At the very start of the play the Elderly Gentleman is having trouble communicating because his interlocutor is unable to comprehend metaphor and metonymy and because her vocabulary has been significantly reduced.

becomes discouraged, and refuses to live" (vol. 2, 172). If it turns out that one of these atavistic offspring is "thoroughly degenerate" (vol. 2, 169) and does not die from discouragement, then he or she emigrates to the short-lived territory, which Zoo admits is for them a convenient dumping ground.

Despite what Zoo says about the weeding-out process involving no killing, she had already told him that they do in fact kill children who are deemed "evil." When the Elderly Gentleman insults Zoo she has an impulse to kill him, which she has never experienced before. The impulse is of the "kill or be killed" variety, and she explains to him that while the impulse to strike at him is new, there is no moral reason to restrain her from killing him. When he says to her that doubtless his old age emboldens her to threaten him, she retorts: "[*fiercely*] Old! You are a child: an evil child. We kill evil children here. We do it even against our own wills by instinct. Take care" (vol. 2, 168). This impulse to kill has induced her to reconsider her political position as a conservative. As it happens, the Elderly Gentleman has arrived at a time when there is a debate going on between the two parties of long-livers, the Colonization party and the Conservative party, regarding the option of committing genocide against the short-livers, and Zoo, having changed positions, confesses to him that "our true destiny is not to advise and govern you, but to supplant and supersede you. In that faith I now declare myself a Colonizer and an Exterminator" (vol. 2, 171).

For all Shaw's criticism of social Darwinism, what he is dramatizing in the *Methuselah* cycle is the slow attrition of the "weaker" members of the human race, until finally a conscious decision is made by the superior beings to finish off the job with deliberate intention: "What is the use of prolonging the agony? You would perish slowly in our presence, no matter what we did to preserve you" (vol. 2, 172). While Shaw is critical of the neo-Darwinian rationalizations used by proponents of laissez-faire capitalism, he has accepted those same rationalizations for the opposite measure: the use of state intervention to assist the supposed fittest members of the race and ensure the speedy elimination of the less fit. But for Shaw the fittest are not the greedy and cunning capitalists, but those he believes are aligned with the Life Force. Shaw remarks in the preface that if man is not up to the mark then the Life Force will supersede the human race with another creature that can serve its intentions better; alternatively, we (the short-livers), as Zoo remarks, can decimate ourselves and "begin all over again as half-starved ignorant savages, and fight with boomerangs and poisoned arrows until you work up to the poison gasses and high explosives once more, with the same result" (vol. 2, 185). Her better idea is that the superior elements of society (in this play, the long-livers) "have sense enough to make an end of this ridiculous game by destroying you" (vol. 2, 185). Shaw's utopia is thus extremely sinister, especially as it was written at a time when very similar ideas would become pervasive in the totalitarian regimes that were about to unsettle still further Western civilization. And this planned genocide becomes even more sinister when we learn that the Colonizers are in "favor of beginning in a country where the people are of a different color from us; so that we can make short work without any risk of mistakes" (vol. 2, 189). Shaw was not a racist, but all planned utopias begin by deciding who belongs and who does not and making "short work" of the unlucky outcasts.

Before moving on to the final play of Shaw's *Metabiological Pentateuch*, we should perhaps take a quick inventory of what changes have either been instituted by the long-livers or have become manifest biologically. We have already discussed the narrowing of language's possibilities.[23] The long-livers also need little or no sleep, one of the long-livers saying, "I am nearly a secondary. I never sleep" (vol. 2, 148). Beginning in their second century they start to develop incredibly powerful force fields, potentially lethal to short-livers (this is one of Shaw's many borrowings from *The Coming Race*). And at least their oracles (if not the others; it is not clear) lack physical substantiality. When the Elderly Gentleman, speaking figuratively, says that he throws himself on the oracle's indulgence Zoo interrupts him, saying, "Dont throw yourself on anything belonging to her or you will go right through her and break your neck. She isnt solid, like you" (vol. 2, 196). The mature long-liver, like one of Plato's guardians, does not laugh. Responding to the puerility of the Elderly Gentleman, one long-liver "*smiling gravely*" says, "It must be at least a hundred and fifty years since I last laughed. But if you do that any more I shall certainly break out like a primary of sixty" (vol. 2, 141). They wear silk tunics, with numbered caps, and they have abolished the family unit. While we do not learn the specifics of child-rearing, we do learn that at least the more fecund women of the long-livers, such as Zoo, have many children ("After eight or nine children become quite uninteresting") and do not bother about them after the age of ten—Zoo declares she would not know her two eldest if she met them (vol. 2, 152).

While it is not stated directly it is obvious that their fecundity coupled with their longevity would make colonization a necessity, and their claim that the short-livers' "lives are too short to be worth living" would seem to be a rationalization for the contemplated genocide (vol. 2, 179). In fact, the Nazi concept of *Lebensraum* was based on precisely this same rationalization: the Master Race needed more living space, and expansion and colonization—in fact, genocide—were deemed necessary to their "success." The theory followed through to its logical conclusion would eventually have all non-Aryans superseded by this supposed most biologically advanced race.

"Tragedy of an Elderly Gentleman" ends with the Gentleman's euthanasia by the oracle. Confronted with the dilemma of returning to a benighted society to which "nothing is real" or staying among these beings so superior to himself, he begs to be able to stay:

> The Oracle. My friend: if you stay with us you will die of discouragement.
> The Elderly Gentleman. If I go back I shall die of disgust and despair. I take the nobler risk. I beg you, do not cast me out.
> *He catches her robe and holds her*
> The Oracle. Take care. I have been here one hundred and seventy years. Your death does not mean to me what it means to you.
> The Elderly Gentleman. It is the meaning of life, not of death, that makes banishment so terrible to me
> The Oracle. Be it so, then. You may stay.
> *She offers him her hands. He grasps them and raises himself a little by clinging to her. She looks steadily into his face. He stiffens; a little convulsion shakes him; his grasp relaxes; and he falls dead.*
> The Oracle [*looking down at the body*] Poor shortlived thing! What else could I do for you?
>
> (vol. 2, 202)

We can assume that the demise of the Elderly Gentleman will be repeated on a grand scale in the near future. Of course the extermination of the short-lived race will eliminate their usefulness as a dumping ground for the occasional evolutionary throwback, and such occurs to the Elderly Gentleman, who hoping to preserve his kind reminds Zoo of their usefulness: "if you carry out your plan of colonization, and leave no shortlived countries in the world, what will you do with your undesirables?" Zoo replies, forthrightly, "Kill them. Our tertiaries are not at all squeamish about killing" (vol. 2, 173). For Shaw, such ruthlessness was necessary in the provisional supermen of today if the genuine supermen of tomorrow were to become a reality.

"As Far as Thought Can Reach"

Shaw's horror of the body culminates in the final play of the cycle, which takes place in the year 31,920, and where we learn that the human race has apparently become a different species, giving birth oviparously and neither ingesting food nor evacuating waste. The short-livers are gone, and to maintain conflict, so necessary to drama, Shaw makes the youth of the species relive all the traits of the extinct short-livers in their first couple years of life. In this way *Back to Methuselah* remains a satire to the very end.

The play starts impressively with youths dancing gracefully to flute music in what looks like a Greek temple. Shaw's stage directions tell us that none of these dancing youths looks under the age of eighteen, but we will learn shortly that they are all in their first few years of life. Into this impressive ceremony appears one of the ancients, as if in a trance; he is "utterly bald" and except "for his eyelashes he is quite hairless" (vol. 2, 205). Unconscious of his surroundings he walks into one of the dancing couples, thus initiating the dialogue and establishing one of the lines of conflict in the play. Upsetting their dance, he apologizes, saying that he did not realize that "there was a nursery here" (vol. 2, 296). Of course as audience or reader we are bound to feel a slight shock to hear the ancient refer to this august temple as a nursery, for we have been taught to revere those most sapient ancient Greeks and their solemn ceremonies, and these do not appear to be children, but graceful young men and women. We learn that these youths have vowed never to leave behind their dancing, love-making, and art to become one of the dreaded ancients ("cold fish," they are called), thus exhibiting what we would now consider typical adolescent rebellion. But of course their behavior is perfectly normal and they will in due time (between the age of three and four) leave behind these childish antics for a life of solitary contemplation.

The play is a satire and denunciation against the body and all sensuous enjoyments, from the most base to the most sublime. Shaw has never been more Platonic than in this play, denouncing not only singing and dancing, but art itself as a remnant of the immaturity of the human race. But unlike in Plato's ideal city there is no need to ban sensual entertainments because biology has provided an inner censor. And besides, even in *Man and Superman* Juan recognizes the value of art in sensitizing the organism; in that play and in this art is recognized as part of the education of sensibility of those not yet advanced to the higher stages of the contemplative life—in other words, Shaw was very ambivalent about the pleasures of art, as was his master, Plato.

Early in the play we see a heartbroken Strephon pleading with Chloe not to break his heart.[24] He is two years old and fell immediately in love with Chloe when he was born, but she is now approaching her fourth birthday and no longer cares for such childishness. At first "[n]othing existed" for her but what she "tasted and touched and saw"; but now she wants "to get away from our eternal dancing and music, and just sit down by myself and think about numbers." Strephon says he expected as much: "you are getting flat-chested...you are bored with us...you talk to the ancients when you get the chance" (vol. 2, 209). It sounds ridiculous out of context, and no doubt in context as well, as this is a satirical comedy and meant to provoke laughter even as we, hopefully, absorb its lessons.

Much of the play is an extended debate about art with the youths taking disparate positions, but which ends with the ancients—the He-Ancient and the She-Ancient—pronouncing the final word, not only on art but also on the body:

> The She-Ancient. Yes, child: art is the magic mirror you make to reflect your invisible dreams in visible pictures. You use a glass mirror to see your face: you use works of art to see your soul. But we who are older use neither glass mirrors nor works of art. We have a direct sense of life. When you gain that you will put aside your mirrors and statues, your toys and your dolls.
> The He-Ancient. Yet we too have our toys and our dolls. That is the trouble of the ancients.
> Arjillax. What! The ancients have their troubles! It is the first time I ever heard one of them confess it.
> The He-Ancient. Look at us. Look at me. This is my body, my blood, my brain; but it is not me. I am the eternal life, the perpetual resurrection; but [*striking his body*] this structure, this organism, this makeshift, can be made by a boy in a laboratory, and is held back from dissolution only by my use of it. Worse still, it can be broken by a slip of the foot, drowned by a cramp in the stomach, destroyed by a flash from the clouds. Sooner or later, its destruction is certain.
> The She-Ancient. Yes: this body is the last doll to be discarded.
> (vol. 2, 250)

The debate on art leads to Pygmalion, a very talented three-year-old scientist, bringing to life a pair of "dolls," intriguingly named Ozymandias and Cleopatra-Semiramis, and this is what the He-Ancient is alluding to when he mentions a boy in a laboratory. This amounts essentially to a play-within-the-play, Ozymandias and Cleopatra-Semiramis taking the part of a couple of puppets performing. They are automatons, and meant to represent ordinary humanity as it mostly is now, before the evolutionary leap Shaw hopes to see. A debate ensues between Pygmalion and Martellus, with the latter maintaining that the pair are "only automata" and "have no self-control." Pygmalion contends that on the contrary they have consciousness; and that "there really is some evidence that we are descended from creatures quite as limited and absurd as these" (vol. 2, 234). It should be remembered that in *The Revolutionist's Handbook* Shaw has Tanner write that "the survival of the fittest means finally the survival of the self-controlled" (vol. 3, 703). Margery Morgan is surely right in regarding Swift's *Gulliver's Travels* as a primary influence on Shaw's satire, and Shaw's misanthropy and hatred of the body is as palpable and potent in this final play as in Swift's tale. She quotes from a letter that Granville-Barker sent to Shaw regarding this fifth part of the cycle. He asks, "How far can one use pure satire in the theatre? For satire scarifies humanity. The theatre uses it (humanity) as a medium and must therefore be tender to it ... If you degrade the token ... you falsify your case."[25] For Morgan it is the Elderly Gentleman in the previous play that humanizes the cycle and acts as a sort of emotional center of gravity, as she puts it.[26] I do not find that satisfying as an answer to Barker's complaint myself, but we will come back to the problem in greater detail shortly, as well as to some other questions that Morgan rightfully acknowledges as important, when we conclude our discussion.

There is a parallel between the automatons and the younger of the youths. Shaw has written a coup de theatre by staging the birth of one of these prodigious creatures, and it provides for a great deal of comedy as we witness the birth of what looks to be a comely seventeen-year-old women from a giant shell. It gives us the opportunity as well to view one of the ancients in her role as a sort of doctor, but also as one who has the power of determining who lives and who dies in this brave new world. The Newly Born is impetuous, pure appetite and reflex, just like the automatons, and in fact she falls immediately in love with Strephon after she cracks through her shell. As Ozymandias and Cleopatra-Semiramis perform their stage act as a couple of egoistic creatures driven by appetite and impulse, she is a sort of mirror image in the audience, Strephon telling her to "Control your reflexes, child" as she *"kisses him impulsively"* (vol. 2, 234). As might have been predicted one of the puppets, Cleopatra-Semiramis, kills her creator, causing something of a crisis for the youths. Their "performance" concludes, in the fashion of a melodramatic tragedy, with their deaths as they both die of discouragement in the presence of the He- and She-Ancients, who have intervened when they intuited their presence was needed. At first the automatons beg for their lives while the youths clamor for their destruction, but the He-Ancient demands silence, saying that they are merely "Automata: they cannot help shrinking from death at any cost. You see they have no self-control, and are merely shuddering through a series of reflexes" (vol. 2, 242). Somehow, he infuses them with some of his vitality and they then die of discouragement. Here we see both the He- and the She-Ancients acting as authority figures, rather like Prospero on his island—judges who do not need to hand down a verdict but merely guide the event to its proper conclusion.

The She-Ancient makes her first appearance in the play when the Newly Born is ready for birth. She is described as being *"like the He-Ancient equally bald, and equally without sexual charm, but intensely interesting and rather terrifying. Her sex is discoverable only by her voice, as her breasts are manly, and her figure otherwise not very different"* (vol. 2, 214). As the soon to be Newly Born rocks her shell, kicking violently and screaming to be let out, the She-Ancient takes her instruments and rips open the shell. The Newly Born gazes in wonder at the world she has just entered while she is washed and dressed and reprimanded for her bad manners and impulsive behavior. The She-Ancient then inspects her critically, feeling for bumps "like a phrenologist," shaking her limbs, gripping her muscles, examining her teeth, peering into her eyes and finally pronouncing: "She will do. She may live." The Newly Born is *"indignant"* when she realizes that this severe figure has just passed judgment on her life, as well she might be. But in answer to her query she is told that "Children with anything wrong do not live here, my child. Life is not cheap with us. But you would not have felt anything." When she is appalled that the She-Ancient would have murdered her she is told that murder is "one of the funny words the newly born bring with them out of the past" (vol. 2, 217). I quote this section in some detail to illustrate what was something of an obsession with Shaw, and something that would resonate profoundly in the political environment just then taking shape. This authority figure who wields the power of life and death, and who cavalierly pronounces after a brief five-minute inspection that the Newly Born may live, and who may just as easily have pronounced her death, is representative of the leaders whom Shaw would passionately defend even as the consequences of their murderous actions became apparent to those with their eyes open. The painless death of those who do not fit in for whatever reason had been a staple of the program that Shaw had been advocating for two decades at the time of this play's composition, and he seems to think it a token of his humanity that he is conscientious enough to tell the victim, "you would not have felt anything." As if that somehow makes it all right.

The play testifies, among other things, to Shaw's pragmatism. In the first part Adam's fear and uncertainty induce him to invent marriage, with its vow of life-long fealty to another. The Serpent, as spokesperson for the Shavian point of view, reminds Adam that if he binds the future by making a vow he binds his will also, and if he binds his will he strangles creation (vol. 2, 18). That idea is emphasized again in this final part when Chloe tells Strephon that the vow she made is invalid because of changes that have occurred; "it has broken itself" (vol. 2, 213). Chloe, or The Maiden as she is delineated in the text, represents a number of the more puritanical of Shaw's points of view. We have already heard her denouncing dancing and singing and love-making and we were amused by her desire to exchange such childishness for the contemplation of numbers, but she has a long speech that I want to quote at some length because I believe we can hear Shaw plainly enough in her complaint:

> I have hundreds of years to live: perhaps thousands. Do you suppose I can spend centuries dancing; listening to flutes ringing changes on a few tunes and a few notes; raving about the beauty of a few pillars and arches; making jingles with words; lying about with your arms round me, which is really neither comfortable nor convenient... making a business of sitting together at fixed hours to absorb our nourishment; taking little poisons with it to make us delirious enough to imagine we are enjoying ourselves; and then having to pass the nights in shelters lying on cots and losing half our lives in a state of unconsciousness. Sleep is a shameful thing.
>
> (vol. 2, 210)

This, as frankly much else in the cycle, is in contradiction to some of the realities we have learned or will learn of life in this utopia. For instance, although she speaks of eating here, later in his lecture Pygmalion will say that "there are certain traces in our own bodies of arrangements which enabled the earlier forms of mankind to renew their bodies by swallowing flesh and grains and vegetables and all sorts of unnatural and hideous foods, and getting rid of what they could not digest" (vol. 2, 232–33). And later Lilith says that their "breasts are without milk: their bowels are gone" (vol. 2, 261). Clearly Shaw is venting his disgust with eating, and the social convention of eating communally at meal time, and his hatred of alcohol; he is displaying his disgust at having a body at all as well as some of the social conventions that human society has created around certain of those needs.[27]

As the play nears its conclusion the ancients, as we have already seen, express their frustration with their inability to escape their enslavement to the body. Although they have the ability to grow new limbs at will, the He- and She-Ancient are past the stage of being amused by such games and long only to be done with their bodies. Like Adam before he invented death, these ancients are immortal and simply await their demise through some accident. This final play is called "As Far as Thought Can Reach," but this utopia is marred by the inability of thought to get beyond the body. These immortals lament that the body is a slave that has become "master; and we must free ourselves from that tyranny. It is this stuff [*indicating her body*], this flesh and blood and bone and all the rest of it, that is intolerable" (vol. 2, 256).

The play ends with Adam, Eve, Cain, and the Serpent appearing and commenting on the long road traveled by humankind from their day to this. As they retreat Lilith, Shaw's symbol for the Life Force, appears as well and contemplates whether to wipe out humankind and start again or to let them keep going:

> shall I labor again? Shall I bring forth something that will sweep them away and make an end of them as they have swept away the beasts of the garden, and made an end of the crawling things and the flying things and of all them that refuse to live for ever? I had patience with them for many ages: they tried me very sorely. They did terrible things: they embraced death, and said that eternal life was a fable.
>
> (vol. 2, 261)

In the end she decides that they "have redeemed themselves from their vileness, and turned away from their sins. Best of all, they are still not satisfied... after passing a million goals they press on to the goal of redemption from the flesh, to the vortex freed from matter, to the whirlpool in pure intelligence..." (vol. 2, 261). Although she is pleased, the verdict is not final and she may still destroy them: "let them dread, of all things, stagnation; for from the moment I, Lilith, lose hope and faith in them, they are doomed" (vol. 2, 262).

Her speech makes clear that for Shaw the greatest sin is idleness and complacency and the greatest virtue an active desire and concerted effort to change. This is why Cain, in the first play, for all his sins, is for Shaw a great hero, a vitalist and pioneering realist. It also explains why Shaw could not only approve but admire Stalin, Mussolini, and Hitler. These maniacal criminals were vitalist supermen who sought in a radical way to transform the social institutions of their day. Never mind that they were going, from our standpoint and from the standpoint of many of their contemporaries, in a dangerous, criminal, and retrograde direction. They were, for Shaw, as Roger Griffin would say, "programmatic modernists" creating "revitalization movements," regimes "without historical precedent...realizing the temporalized utopia [and] meeting the material and the spiritual needs of the masses"; and most importantly, rearing a "new breed of human beings."[28] For all the confusion caused by Shaw's support of these dictators and their totalitarian regimes, as I think I have made clear, one only has to look carefully and critically at his plays and major critical essays to dispel the confusion.

Conclusion

Before leaving our discussion of the *Methuselah* cycle, it must be asked whether Shaw really believed that the human race could willfully induce an evolutionary leap to longevity and, eventually, immortality. Some critics have asserted that the longevity theme in the cycle is a screen for something else. Frederic Jameson believes the play is really about History, that the play dramatizes the aftermath of the coming revolution. In fact, by a kind of Brechtian *Gestus*, we see and experience the lower-class parlor maid from "The Gospel of the Brother's Barnabas" in a position of power in the next play while the formerly powerful are reduced to a subservient position. In other words, the short-livers represent the subverted ruling class and the title of the third play, "The Thing Happens," really alludes to the revolutionary event and not an evolutionary leap to longevity—the fact that the event was brought about by such unlikely individuals indicating the unpredictability of revolutionary advance. The discouragement theme also, for Jameson, is a cover for the envy felt by the overthrown class for those newly powerful.[29] This is very ingenious, but I certainly do not think Shaw consciously intended it that way; and there is every indication that he had a lot more faith in Creative Evolution than in a successful uprising coming from untrained revolutionists. Shaw had little faith in the organizational ability of the lower classes, and all his life looked to an elite class of efficient experts to tell the less gifted what to do. However, he did have a lot of faith in the power of the Life Force to make use of unlikely candidates, and therefore Jameson's reading is quite sound from that perspective, and certainly interesting and well argued.

Margery Morgan, too, believes that "[o]nce we cease to be deluded by the fable of longevity into seeing the whole cycle as a straggling chronicle-play, this part ["Tragedy of an Elderly Gentleman"] emerges as the centre of gravity which holds the rest in balance."[30] In her essay Morgan has a lot of interesting and useful suggestions to make; however, I have a difficult time accepting her evaluation of the cycle as a "chronicle-play" built around the flawed and ridiculous Elderly Gentleman, despite the few noble traits that Shaw has given him to conceivably elevate the fourth part of his cycle into a "tragedy." Despite his moral superiority to such base and opportunistic short-livers as The Envoy, he is still, according to the logic of the cycle, a dinosaur doomed to destruction while the long-livers represent the ideal future of Shaw's utopia; and there is no reason to doubt Shaw's stated intention of adding his *Metabiological Pentateuch* to the meager store of legends, parables, and miracles of the new religion of Creative Evolution.

In 1947, Oxford University Press approached Shaw regarding their intention of publishing one of his plays in their World's Classics series, asking him to choose which one it should be. He chose *Back to Methuselah* and wrote a postscript for the new edition, essentially elaborating on the points that he had made in the play and preface some twenty-five years earlier. Clearly the play was very important to him, and it was due to the utopian scheme, not the minor tragedy built around the Elderly Gentleman, which occupies just a small part of the entire cycle. The play is obviously open to a number of valid readings, and both Morgan and Jameson have provided interesting and valuable analyses, but I think we also delude ourselves if we overlook the extent of Shaw's desperate need to believe in utopia and engage in utopian fantasy, which obtruded into the world of hard fact when he used his extraordinary powers of wit and invention to envision, promote, or uphold the utopian fantasies that were emerging as political realities in the 1920s, thirties, and forties.

Back to Methuselah straddles a fine line between the most outrageous hope for the potential of humankind to escape the material conditions of reality (Shaw rejected any hope of the transcendent kind) and absolute despair at the reality of the human condition. And I do not think the despair can be attributed to the recent devastating war, for the despair Shaw feels is for mortality itself and the reality of nature and the body (although the war may very well have increased his sense of mortality). Shaw was in his early sixties when he started writing the play, and felt that he was entering the final phase of his life: "My sands are running out," he says in the preface (vol. 2, lxxxix). Consequently it seems that "Death," the "Arch-Inexorable" and "king of terrors" that he scorned as a young man in *The Quintessence of Ibsenism*,[31] was pushing him into the same kinds of illusions he mocked his idealists for in that early work. Like Cain in his defiance of the body, sexual reproduction, and food, Shaw is in revolt against the most basic facts of existence, and one cannot help but wonder if the sadism that Orwell and Silver observed in Shaw was not, as Silver contends, due to his frustrated sexual life, but rather due to the repugnance he felt for nature and for the body itself; his support for the liquidation of recalcitrant citizens a punishment for those unable to subdue life's importunate demands.

In the first chapter I noted a solipsism or subjectivism that was an unintended consequence of the philosophy articulated in *The Quintessence of Ibsenism*. When one believes in nothing but the self, the self's imminent demise is likely to be a cause for despair, even if living brings no apparent joy. In the final play the She-Ancient describes her turning away from everything but the self: "When I discarded my dolls as he [the He-Ancient] discarded his friends and his mountains, *it was to myself I turned as to the final reality*" (vol. 2, 252, my italics). Likewise, nature itself is viewed as mere dead materiality. The He-Ancient remarks: "I saw that the mountains were dead... your landscapes, your mountains, are only the world's cast skins and decaying teeth on which we live like microbes" (vol. 2, 251). Shaw's contemplative ancients—his incarnation of the superhuman—are utterly alone and self-absorbed, without the consolations of art, religion, or "human" contact; they have retreated from society almost entirely—we learn that the other ancients have in their isolation "forgotten how to speak; how to read; even how to think in your fashion. We do not communicate with one another in that way or apprehend the world as you do" (vol. 2, 256). When they exit the stage for the last time the stage directions tell us they leave alone, in opposite directions. *Back to Methuselah* is the fantasy of a man in rebellion against Eros, against life itself, yet afraid of death, of extinction, which as it happens perfectly describes Adam's position at the start of the cycle.

For all her admiration of the play, Morgan does bring up certain problems that need to be addressed, such as the following:

Is the glorification of the mind only a cowardly flight from emotion? Is the elaborate structure less useful as an objective commentary on the external world than as a means of controlling subjective conflicts? Does the Puritanism in Shaw express a false understanding of human nature (including his own nature)? Does this Puritanism involve an essential devaluing of art, destructive to the integrity of any work in which it is found?[32]

The interpretation offered in this chapter has probably adequately answered some of these questions. It seems to me that Shaw's Puritanism does obscure his understanding of human nature and induces in him a profound misanthropy, most evident in this play. Likewise I believe the elaborate structure is contrived to protect Shaw from the threat he feels from his own deeply conflicted subjectivity, his own emotions. Shaw's feelings regarding art are more difficult to gauge because they are so deeply ambivalent. In the preface he praises artists—artist-prophets, he calls them—whom he believes have served the Life Force and intuited or foretold the coming of the superman: Michelangelo, Beethoven, Goethe, Mozart, Wagner, and Nietzsche. And he maintains that all great art is essentially religious: "the revival of religion on a scientific basis does not mean the death of art, but a glorious rebirth of it. Indeed art has never been great when it was not providing an iconography for a live religion" (vol. 2, lxxxi). Shaw's conflicted feelings regarding art and his own role as an artist, his frequently expressed antipathy to art that is not didactic, does not, I believe, detract from his own worth as an artist any more than Plato's ambivalence detracts from his worth as a great artist. But it does perhaps intimate why Shaw is not often counted among the world's greatest artists, despite his immense talent. The greatest art expresses deeply felt emotion, even if, in Wordsworth's famous phrase, such emotion is recollected in tranquility. Shaw was in flight from such feelings, and it has often been noted that while Shaw is a great satirist his art lacks depth of emotion and he is rarely able to sound the deeper human chords either in his characters or in his audience.

In his classic treatise on modern drama, *The Theatre of Revolt*, Robert Brustein presents an analysis of *Back to Methuselah* which is not dissimilar to my own, and states: "Plagued by such contradictions, Shaw is sometimes pressed away from the perceptions of his art to the earnest Utopianism of his evangelical visions, where, seven degrees removed from the real world, insoluble dilemmas can be resolved in wishful fantasies." And he adds that "for all his humanitarianism, he is dedicated not to recovering man's fading humanity, but rather to inventing something altogether new: in the doctrine of Shavianism, man becomes free only by ceasing to be man."[33] Brustein contends, as I do, that Shaw's revolt is against the very conditions of reality itself. But he does not connect Shaw's dramaturgically expressed revolt with his eugenic or his political utopianism, nor make the appalling connection between the long-livers' extermination of the short-livers and the similar exterminations that were taking place or were soon to take place in the Soviet Union and Germany. In *Heartbreak House* Shotover declares to Hector: "There is enmity between our seed and their seed." "We must win powers of life and death over them both"—both being the capitalist Mangan and the selfish and idle aristocrat Randall (vol. 1, 526). Earlier Shaw had expressed just such a fantasy by handing the state's machinery of death over to the utopian Cusins. But the play ends and we never see the result. Shaw has divided the world into the elect and the reprobate, and at present all that impedes the reprobates' extermination is the elects' lack of power. When that power was wielded by such unlikely utopian outsiders as Mussolini, Stalin, and Hitler, Shaw saw his moment and put his hope in them. It is to that phase in Shaw's life that we turn in the next chapter, scrutinizing some of the plays he wrote while the totalitarian dictators were at the height of their power.

5
Shaw's Totalitarian Drama of the Thirties; or, Shaw and the Dictators: *Geneva, The Millionairess, The Simpleton of the Unexpected Isles*

Shaw followed *Back to Methuselah* with one of his greatest plays, *Saint Joan* (1924).[1] For our purposes the play is notable for its depiction of the singular inspired heroic figure infusing religion and politics in an effort to lead the nation toward its glorious promise. Joan is in the thrall of the Life Force, and the salvation of France depends on its military and political leadership placing blind trust in this visionary outsider. Indeed, in Germany Max Reinhardt produced both *Saint Joan* and Shaw's following play, *The Apple Cart* (1929)—another play that pins the fate of the nation on one superior individual—and according to Michael Holroyd both productions "fed the atmosphere that...was lifting the Nazi regime into power."[2] Holroyd goes on to say that Hitler himself declared Shaw's version of Joan superior to Schiller's, as the Reinhardt

> version emphasized the mystical nature of power vested in someone physically so unimpressive yet gifted with the oratorical magic of patriotic 'voices'. It was this version of Shaw's play that prompted William Mackenzie King, Prime Minister of Canada, to express the conviction that spiritually Hitler 'will one day rank with Joan of Arc'.[3]

After *Saint Joan* Shaw did not write another play for five years. Between *Saint Joan* and *The Apple Cart* he spent three difficult years composing the first of his two books on politics and economics, *The Intelligent Woman's Guide to Socialism and Capitalism* (1928).[4] The impetus for the book was Shaw's sister-in-law's inquiry regarding the nature of socialism, hence the title. Shaw began *Back to Methuselah* during the last months of the First World War and it was finished against the backdrop of the Russian Revolution, civil war, and finally the Bolshevik regime's coming to absolute power. Not long after he finished the play Mussolini took power in Italy, establishing the second totalitarian regime on the continent.[5] *Saint Joan* marks the end of what most critics consider to be Shaw's second and most fecund period as a playwright—the period that began at the start of the century with *Man and Superman*—and *The Apple Cart* marks the beginning of his third and final phase as a playwright, and is the first of a series of plays that are usually termed political extravaganzas.[6] Consequently, we are finally in a position to look at a number of Shaw plays that were written in the environment of fascism and Russian Communism, which has indeed informed this entire study, although more implicitly up to now.

The brave new world that Shaw had prophesied and worked so hard for is finally showing signs of coming to life and many of his plays of the period intimate these birth pangs. I want to ground this chapter in three plays that Shaw wrote between 1934 and 1938, *The Simpleton of the Unexpected Isles* (1934), *The Millionairess* (1935), and *Geneva* (1938), although there is no reason why a chapter that focused on *The Apple Cart*, *Too True to Be Good* (1931), and *On the Rocks* (1933) could not also provide a compelling demonstration of Shaw's utopian thinking.

It might be plausibly argued that Shaw's third and final phase as a playwright could be marked as starting not with *The Apple Cart* in 1929 but with *Saint Joan* in 1924, if we look at the play as the Germans did and pay close attention to the preface as well. But then our focus must be twofold. Clearly Joan can be seen as the inspired leader moved by mystic visions and assuring the nation that she alone can save it from the evil that plagues it; but in the preface Shaw also defends her accusers for executing her and argues quite explicitly against the toleration of those who disturb the equilibrium of society: "We must face the fact that society is founded on intolerance... We must persecute, even to the death" (vol. 2, 302, 303). This would seem to contradict the message of the play, and indeed Shaw's philosophy of Creative Evolution which depends on creative individuals like Joan to move society forward. It is for this reason that the play is sometimes considered a tragedy (for those able to ignore or disregard the epilogue). Shaw avers that there is a tension in society between political tolerance and intolerance, and that "there is nothing for us but to make it a point of honour to privilege heresy to the last bearable degree on the simple ground that all evolution in thought and conduct must at first appear as heresy and misconduct" (vol. 2, 300). He also remarks that the "degree of tolerance attainable at any moment depends on the strain under which society is maintaining its cohesion" (vol. 2, 303). These two remarks taken together might help explain why Shaw became so intolerant as the years went forward. The utopian societies struggling to be born were under a great deal of strain, and so, it would seem, to maintain cohesion dissenters and fence-sitters of all kinds had to be "shoved out of the way as Stalin has shoved them"[7]; and Shaw took it on trust (or had a deep need to believe), especially with Stalin, that the dictators were men of genuine ability who were truly seeking to lead their respective societies toward a post-capitalist utopia.[8]

The Shaw/Salvemini debate on Mussolini

Three years after he wrote the preface to *Saint Joan* Shaw became embroiled in a debate with the anti-Fascist socialists Friedrich Adler and Gaetano Salvemini, which played out over the month of October 1927 in the pages of the *Manchester Guardian*. The correspondence was collected in a small volume in 1928, with the principal agonists Shaw and Salvemini. Despite Shaw's well-earned reputation as a skilled and formidable debater, whether in print or on the stump, it can hardly be doubted that Irving Howe spoke correctly when he remarked that Salvemini gave Shaw "the most merciless polemical drubbing of his life."[9] Reading through the correspondence today, one is astounded by Shaw's obdurate insensitivity and unwillingness to be educated by Salvemini or to admit defeat. He brusquely defends Mussolini's seizure of power in Italy, the political murder of the Italian socialist politician Giacomo Matteoti (a fierce critic of the Fascists, Matteoti boldly published a book exposing Fascist crimes and stood up in Parliament to denounce Fascist violence and fraud) and other high-ranking Italian anti-Fascist ministers, the torturing of dissidents with castor oil (which proved fatal for some), the censorship of his own letter in the Italian press, and many other suppressions of liberties usually taken for granted in the democratic West. Shaw admits that such brutalities are regrettable but insists that they are not particular to Mussolini's Fascist regime, and anyway Italy now had someone in power capable of creating order out of chaos. Salvemini shot back with a list of particulars demonstrating that Mussolini was not only *not* bringing order, but was actually making things a whole lot worse; that besides imprisonment without trial, terrorism, torture and murder, the abolition of free speech, a free press, and the right to assembly, the economy was worse with workers being forced to take a cut in wages while being barred from striking; that in fact, despite what Shaw says to the contrary, the "Italian people never had to choose between bread and liberty. The Fascists first deprived them of their liberties and then cut down their ration of bread."[10] The letter from which this quote is drawn, Salvemini's final letter to Shaw, never received a reply.

It must be emphasized again that although Shaw now had real utopian strongmen in power that he could defend and cheer on, he had been extolling just this type of lawless superman from the very beginning of his career. As early as 1883 in his novel *Cashel Byron's Profession* he has the eponymous boxer expatiate at length on what he calls "executive power," which can be summarized as the possession of knowledge and strength with the courage to use them: "you want to know how to hit him, when to hit him, and where to hit him; and then you want the nerve to go in and do it. That's executive power."[11] Mussolini—from a poor working-class family—was, in Shaw's estimation, a "man of the people,"[12] and in the correspondence with Salvemini he seems impressed by what he might have called Mussolini's executive power: the knowledge, strength, and courage that Mussolini apparently displayed as he fought his way to his position as *Il Duce* of the Italian people—and Shaw would have been most thrilled by Mussolini's jettisoning a parliamentary system that he regarded with contempt.

It is significant that it was primarily his fellow socialists that he was debating with; and it is important to keep in mind that it was chiefly the waste and disorder that resulted from capitalism, and not its inherent inequity, that troubled him. Or put another way, Shaw wanted economic equity because only then he believed would there be an end to the disorder and waste that were apparently the inevitable by-products of capitalism. He writes: "Some of the things that Mussolini has done, and some of the things that he is threatening to do go further in the direction of Socialism than the English Labour Party could yet venture if they were in power."[13] Shaw revels in Mussolini's strength, courage and skill, noting that it was he—and not any of the various factions of communists, socialists, and anarchists—who was able to seize power in Italy. Salvemini reminds him that

> Mussolini was assisted in the civil war (1921–22) by the money of the banks, the big industrialists, and landowners. His black shirts were equipped with rifles, bombs, machine-guns, and motor-lorries by the military authorities, and assured of impunity by the police and the magistracy; while their adversaries were disarmed and severely punished if they attempted resistance.[14]

But Shaw will hear none of this; he insists on believing that Mussolini represents the best chance of breaking the power of a corrupt and scandalously wasteful capitalist system and thus ushering in a new utopian era: "Mussolini will never get rid of poverty and unemployment, of which he has first-hand knowledge, unless and until he breaks the control of *laissez-faire* capitalism."[15] Shaw apparently believed that Mussolini had the strength and resolve and perhaps the ability to finally make an end of poverty and unemployment, although we know Mussolini had no intention of breaking the power of the industrialists who financed him.

This idealized picture of Mussolini bears a remarkable resemblance to one of Shaw's supermen from twenty years earlier: Andrew Undershaft, the millionaire munitions manufacturer in *Major Barbara*, who through superhuman self-control and an indomitable will and unencumbered by any tablet of laws has risen from poverty to become a force in society. Undershaft sees existence as the naked struggle of one man against another, yet paradoxically he recognizes a higher will of which he says he is a part. Having disciplined himself and fought his way to the top, he is now a useful member of society, a servant of the Life Force. In Shaw's language he has an evolutionary appetite, and not a merely sensuous one: "I was a dangerous man until I had my will: now I am a useful, beneficent, kindly person" (vol. 1, 435). So while life seems to be imitating art here, in less than ten years Shaw would begin writing *Geneva*, a play that actually features Mussolini, as well as Hitler, Franco, and a Soviet commissar, as characters, although he changes their names to Bombardone, Battler, and Flanco.

Between 1927, when he engaged in his polemic on Mussolini with Adler and Salvemini, and 1938, when *Geneva* was finally published (the first version was completed in April 1936), much had happened in the political realm that might have been expected to check the first unfettered enthusiasm that Shaw expressed toward the Italian dictator, although if Shaw was not horrified by the litany of abuses that Salvemini enumerated in his letters—of which, by the way, he claimed to be fully aware—it is to be doubted that his humanity would suddenly bloom later. In 1935, Mussolini attacked Ethiopia (or Abyssinia, the only part of Africa still uncolonized by the West) in a massive campaign of bombs and poison gas. Charlotte, Shaw's wife—and most of the civilized world—was horrified. Yet Shaw supported the invasion, writing to a friend that his support had nothing to do with his support of Mussolini generally, but for the cause of "civilization" against "savagery."[16] This was also the reason he gave for his support of the Boer War thirty-five years earlier. Let us now consider the play.

Geneva

Geneva is a satire on contemporary political leadership and centers around a number of complaints brought to the International Court against various world leaders and nations. The play sheds a great deal of light on Shaw's attitude both toward the dictators and toward leadership in general. The world leaders do not make their appearance until act four, the final and longest act of the play, when the Court convenes, still unsure whether they will obey the summons (they do, not because they are compelled, but because they cannot resist the spotlight). Bombardone is the first to enter, and is, according to the stage directions, "*dominant, brusque, every inch a man of destiny*" (vol. 5, 716). Upon entering the Court he says, "I am here because it is my will to be here. My will is part of the world's will. A large part, as it happens. The world moves towards internationalism" (vol. 5, 717). Here he echoes Undershaft in *Major Barbara* when he says that what drives him is "[a] will of which [he is] a part" (vol. 1, 431). When Sir Orpheus Midlander, the British Foreign Secretary, evinces surprise at Bombardone's expressed internationalism, saying that it was his understanding that the dictator was an avowed nationalist, Bombardone alludes to the usurpation of Ethiopia:

> I consolidated my country as a nation: a white nation. I then added a black nation to it and made it an empire. When the empires federate, its leaders will govern the world; and these leaders will have a superleader who will be the ablest man in the world: that is my vision.
>
> (vol. 5, 717)

Shaw hoped the strong leaders that emerged after the First World War would lead eventually to a federation of empires, orderly and efficient and without crime or poverty, like Perivale St. Andrews in *Major Barbara* but on a much larger scale.

Shaw believed that the Life Force inhered especially in extraordinary men and women, and that change came from their superhuman efforts. Creative Evolution worked primarily through individuals of prodigious energy and resolve, the traits he so admired in Hitler and Mussolini. Although we now judge them to be fanatical in their will to power (and lest we forget, so did many of their contemporaries), Shaw saw ability and high purpose, executive power which he hoped was in the service of a higher will. Bombardone says, in words that are unmistakably Shavian:

> [I]f you had ever had God's work to do you would know that He never does it Himself. We are here to do it for Him. If we neglect it the world falls into the chaos called Liberty and Democracy, in which nothing is done except talk while the people perish. Well, what you call God's work, His hardest work, His political work, cannot be done by everybody: they have neither the time nor the brains nor the divine call for it. God has sent to certain persons this call. They are not chosen by the people: they must choose themselves: that is part of their inspiration. When they have dared to do this, what happens? Out of the Liberal democratic chaos comes form, purpose, order and rapid execution.
>
> (vol. 5, 738–39)

A provincial shopkeeper named Newcomer (a liberal democrat and mediocrity that Shaw mostly treats with contempt) says in response to Bombardone's last word, "Yes, the executions come along all right. We know what dictators are." Bombardone responds, also throwing in a word to the pious Deaconess:

> Yes: the triflers and twaddlers are swept away. This trifler and twaddler here can see nothing but his own danger, which raises his twaddle to a squeak of mortal terror. He does not matter. His selfchosen ruler takes him by the scruff of the neck and flings him into some island or camp where he and his like can trifle and twaddle without obstructing God's effectives. Then comes this pious lady to bid me turn to God. There is no need: God has turned to me; and to the best of my ability I shall not fail Him, in spite of all the Democratic Liberal gabblers.
>
> (vol. 5, 739)

According to philosopher and avowed Shavian C.E.M. Joad, the term "God" is used by Shaw "only as a concession to popular modes of thought" and "is simply the principle of change and development in the universe."[17] This makes sense, and explains why Shaw can associate Bombardone and Battler with divinity, as they are primarily agents of change (for the better); and also why Shaw can turn a blind eye to their manifest destruction and cruelty, as God (or the principle of change) functions through acts of destruction, which often cause great suffering—what was referred to earlier as creative destruction—as well as through acts of creation. As a "trifler and twaddler" Newcomer is in the way, is an impediment to change, and therefore Shaw has no compunction about his being dispatched to an island or camp, or indeed executed. And as we know from Solzhenitsyn, Margarette Buber-Neumann, and others, life in a Soviet or Nazi forced labor camp was essentially a death sentence anyway. Finally, if we are in any doubt about Shaw associating the dictators with a higher divine purpose, he has both Bombardone and Battler allude to themselves in the words of God in Exodus 3:14, "I am what I am" (vol. 5, 718, 739). As Job came to learn through his own experience, one does not quibble about morality and suffering when dealing with the Deity, whose purpose is beyond the comprehension of mere mortals.

Bombardone claims that he will transform the chaos of liberal democracy into a society governed with purpose and order. Indeed, this is what he is on trial for. The Judge says that he is accused of the "murder and destruction of liberty and democracy in Europe." Bombardone replies that "[o]ne cannot destroy what never existed" (vol. 5, 731). In Shaw's view liberty and democracy are chimeras; they do not exist as the citizens of the West suppose, but the concepts and platitudes associated with them give cover to a thoroughly rotten plutocratic system that is leading the world to chaos, and quite possibly to an end of civilization. As Shaw frequently remarked, "civilization is perishing from Anarchism."[18] In his debate with Adler Shaw wrote that "we, as Socialists, have nothing to do with liberty. Our message, like Mussolini's, is one of discipline, of service." And in a letter to Ramsay McDonald he uses practically the same words, writing that "[a]t bottom the people know that what they need is not more paper liberty and democracy, but more discipline; and Mussolini's grip of this fact is the whole secret of his command."[19]

One of the high purposes of Bombardone and Battler is their resolve to do away with parliamentary democracy. Newcomer's complaint to the Court is that the new Prime Minister of Jacksonland has locked the opposition parties (of which he is a part) out of the House and "organized a body of young men called the Clean Shirts, to help the police" (vol. 5, 658). In other words, he is complaining of a fascist coup very like that which occurred in Germany after Hitler was appointed Chancellor. When Newcomer asks Bombardone why he is locked out, the dictator replies, "Presumably because you want to obstruct its work and discredit its leaders. Half a dozen such obstructionists as you could spin out to two years the work I do in ten minutes. The world can endure you no longer.

Your place is in the dustbin" (vol. 5, 731). Mussolini and Hitler had taken it upon themselves to rid their countries of what Shaw believed was an outdated, ossified, and utterly ineffectual political system, and for this he was duly grateful.

But in addition to this the two fascist dictators have been able to inspire and inculcate a credible faith to replace the loss of Judeo-Christian belief in the West, which they do in part through their amazing histrionic ability. Battler says that for him the

> object of public speaking is to propagate a burning conviction of truth and importance, and thus produce immediate action and enthusiastic faith and obedience. My technique, like that of my forerunner opposite [Bombardone], was invented and perfected with that object. You must admit that it has been wonderfully successful: your parliaments have been swept away by the mere breath of it; and we ourselves exercise a personal authority unattainable by any king, president, or minister. That is simple, natural, reasonable. But what is your technique? What is its object? Apparently its object is to destroy conviction and to paralyze action.
>
> (vol. 5, 725)

Shaw was himself a gifted orator and reformer, and it is likely that for this reason and for others (such as their being self-created men, outsiders who had climbed their way to the top of their profession) he identified with the despots, almost certainly as well envying their ability to make an indelible mark on society while all his own efforts had seemed to be in vain. These were men of action, Shaw believed, as well as speech givers, and they inspired unity as well as purposeful, directed action in their populations. Shaw's motive in his writing and political work, and the explicit theme of such plays as *Man and Superman*, *Pygmalion*, and *Back to Methuselah*, was the creation of a new being. Battler says of his populace that he has "made better men and women of them. I live for nothing else" (vol. 5, 737). But Battler's professed altruism is challenged by The Jew, who has come to the Court to put in a complaint on behalf of his fellow Jews in Germany, to charge Battler of "murder. Of an attempt to exterminate the flower of the human race" (vol. 5, 731). It is to this debate that we must now turn.

Shaw's later plays, such as *Geneva*, have been criticized for the one-sidedness of their intellectual debates, for not giving the opponents of Shaw's own presumed views a fair chance (as he had done with the Devil in *Man and Superman*, for instance), and yet in the debate between Battler and The Jew it might have been deemed excusable to tilt the debate in favor of The Jew; yet Shaw clearly gives the match to Battler, who defends and sometimes seems to deny the persecution of Jews in Germany, or at least his responsibility for it: "I am sorry. I cannot be everywhere; and all my agents are not angels" (vol. 5, 732). This so upset Lawrence Langner—artistic director of the Theatre Guild and Shaw's chief producer in the United States at this time—that he angrily refused to produce *Geneva*, complaining of The Jew that he was "a pitifully inferior mouthpiece to express his case, thus playing into the hands of the breeders of racial hatred by ranging yourself unconsciously on their side."[20] Langner, like so many others, worshipped Shaw and was deeply hurt by the play, writing to Shaw that although he has

> preached tolerance, justice, love of the common man, freedom, economic fairness, elevation of women; and, in England and America, at any rate, your disciples are numbered by the millions. Yet you seem to justify Fascism with its intolerance, racial hatred, economic slavery, degradation of women, fanning of the war spirit, etc., mainly on the ground that its dictators are 'Supermen' and the Supermen 'get things done.'[21]

Shaw revised the character slightly to please Langner, but otherwise defended his portrayal. As remarked before, Shaw was not a racist and he deplored Hitler's racist policies, which he felt hindered the success of his mission. Nonetheless, *Geneva* concludes with a tasteless racist joke that must have deeply offended Langner, and others. At the end of the play when word comes in that the earth is about to jump to its next quantum, The Jew runs out to exploit his advance knowledge of the situation and make a killing on the stock market.

And yet Battler's main line of defense is quite matter-of-factly wrong and indefensible; and exasperatingly, Shaw himself used the same specious logic when defending Hitler's treatment of the Jews in private letters. Battler says that every state has the right to choose its population and advises The Jew to clear out, saying, "what right have you in my country? I exclude you as the British exclude the Chinese in Australia, as the Americans exclude the Japanese in California"[22] (vol. 5, 731). Battler is of course citing other shameful examples to excuse his own shameful policy. What both Battler and Shaw neglect entirely is the obvious fact that German Jews are—or had been until recently—*German citizens*, many of whom had fought valiantly in the First World War and were every bit as patriotic as their Christian neighbors.[23] Shaw writes in a letter to Trebitsch that "the Germans had as much right to exclude non-Germans from governmental posts as the Americans to reserve the presidency for Americans."[24] He seems to entirely forget that the Jews he is referring to are not "non-Germans" but Germans. Shaw believed Hitler was making a grave political mistake with his Jewish policy, but defended his right to do so.

Shaw was in awe of Hitler and repeatedly refers to him as a messiah, pseudo-messiah, or failed messiah, a political genius whose persecution of the Jews he regarded as a disastrous personal idiosyncrasy, a phobia that undermined his otherwise brilliant vision. Shaw also believed that Hitler's autobiography and political manifesto *Mein Kampf* was a masterpiece that deserved a place next to Marx's *Das Kapital* as one of world literature's seminal treasures. As late as October 1942 we find him writing to Nancy Astor praising Hitler and *Mein Kampf*:

> I have been reading Hitler's Mein Kampf really attentively instead of dipping into it. He is the greatest living Tory, and a wonderful preacher of everything that is right and best in Toryism. Your party should capture him and keep him as a teacher and leader whilst checkmating his phobias. On the need for religion, on the sham democracy of votes for everybody, on unemployment and casual labor, he is superb. The book is really one of the world's bibles, like Calvin's Institutes (written when Calvin was 23), Adam Smith's Wealth of Nations, Marx's Capital: it has changed the mind of the reading world...
>
> Where he has failed is in not making the occupied countries the better for his coming, as Julius Caesar managed to do in Spain. To put it another way, he has failed as Messiah. His army service suited him and made him a Terrorist and a tough. His smattering of cheap science (which is not a Tory subject) filled his head with a crude notion of "the survival of the fittest" which would justify the ruling of the U.S.A. by a Congress of grizzly bears. And so he will be a failure. But then most of the Messiahs have been failures, though they had their points all the same.[25]

And a month later Shaw is still in ecstasies over Hitler's political genius as expressed in *Mein Kampf*, still pondering over how his misguided obsessions and phobias are dooming his political success; but despite this Shaw cannot help but admire Hitler for the sublime "courage of his convictions" which have "nerved him to stake a world war on it." This time he is writing to Beatrice Webb:

> I am seriously thinking of writing an open letter to Hitler, and sending it to *The Observer*, which has asked me for an article. This is the result of reading Mein Kampf right through attentively and seriously. It is a curious combination of an extraordinarily penetrating observation and comprehension of the political and psychological situation with epileptic phobias and conviction of the eugenic value of racial inbreeding. The war, in fact, is a war between inbreeding and cross breeding, between mongrels and pedigrees; and Hitler has the courage of his convictions to a sublime height which has nerved him to stake a world war on it. Altogether a very remarkable fellow this Hitler, though a doomed Impossibilist.[26]

The notion of Hitler as a failed messiah, which he alludes to frequently in prefaces and personal letters, even making a pointed comparison between Hitler and Jesus in one of his very last plays, *Farfetched Fables* (1950), is significant, and is foreshadowed in Shaw's longest essay on Jesus and Christianity, the 100-page preface (written in 1915) to the short play *Androcles and the Lion* (1912).

The essay maintains that Jesus was a brilliant economist, biologist, and sociologist (rather like Shaw) and considers what might have been had he been "a modern practical statesman" with "suitable political machinery" (vol. 5, 323, 369). In other words, the essay is really about a political messiah for our troubled times. Shaw's theory—which is elaborated in this essay but also receives mention elsewhere, and is alluded to in his comparison of Hitler and Jesus in the preface to *Geneva*—is that Jesus finally succumbed to the "psychopathic delusion" that he was the Messiah. Shaw believes that Jesus, for all his genius, ultimately "went mad as Swift and Ruskin and Nietzsche went mad" (vol. 5, 410). This is the danger of greatness, and even the best, such as Jesus, are vulnerable to the creeping dangers of megalomania. In the preface to *Geneva*, Shaw recounts Hitler's career and rapid rise as messiah, but believes that Hitler's successes went to his head and destroyed his chance of ultimate success. In the preface to *Androcles*, Shaw maintains that "all prophets are inspired, and all men with a mission, Christs" (vol. 5, 415), which explains his admiration for those mighty men striving to bring their exalted visions of a better world to fruition: Hitler, Mussolini, Lenin, and Stalin. We might put Shaw himself in this category. These are men in the same class as Jesus, whom, although ranking them highly, Shaw "does not place Jesus above Confucius or Plato, not to mention more modern philosophers and moralists" (vol. 5, 352). It is impossible not to think that Shaw has himself in mind in his allusion to "more modern philosophers and moralists."

Gerald Pilecki, who has written the definitive critical study of *Geneva*, believes that Shaw advocated fascism only as a step in the direction of communism and as a decided advance over liberal democracy, which is certainly true, as far as it goes; but he believes much of the enthusiasm and approbation that Shaw expressed for Mussolini and Hitler was for the most part a way of goading the liberal democratic governments, which is a view taken by many other critics as well. I have intentionally quoted mostly from Shaw's private letters, rather than public articles, to demonstrate that there was a lot more to Shaw's approbation than the mere goading of the democratic powers, although that was certainly *one* of the motivations behind *some* of his public pronouncements. Pilecki also believes that Shaw's principal goal throughout the 1930s was to avoid another war, hence his support of Mussolini's invasion of Ethiopia. While not denying Shaw's stated approval of Mussolini's putative aim of civilizing a backward part of the world, he also believes that Shaw was afraid that strict sanctions by the democratic countries (England and France) against Italy risked starting another world war. Despite this, though, Pilecki does admit that what is

> particularly disturbing in Shaw's remarks about both Hitler and Mussolini ... is the complete lack of concern he shows for the human suffering that was endured under these men. The violence employed by Mussolini he shrugs off as insignificant, and the wholesale extermination of thousands of people he dismisses as one of Hitler's blunders ... Indeed, although he wrote whole tracts against the vivisection of animals, he himself advocated the extermination of the undesirable humans.[27]

Geneva is an important play for understanding Shaw's view of the dictators, at least as he wanted to see them, and we will need to consider it further, especially as we have not even looked at Shaw's presentation of the Soviet Commissar, his representative of Soviet Russia, which he idealized even more than he did the fascist states. But before we get to that I want to consider another play that I believe allegorizes the fascist superman—unlikely as it might at first seem—in its female hero, a character inspired by Hitler and Mussolini, and that will therefore shed additional light on Shaw's thinking on these dictators during the middle 1930s.

The Millionairess

Shaw wrote *The Millionairess* over the course of 1934–35, just before *Geneva*. On the surface it is a simple comedy and we might be tempted to agree with Shaw that it "does not pretend to be anything more than a comedy of humorous and curious contemporary characters such as Ben Jonson might write." Yet Shaw goes on to say, in the second clause of this first sentence of the preface, that nonetheless *The Millionairess* "raises a question that has troubled human life and moulded human society since the creation" (vol. 6, 175). The remainder of the preface is spent considering that question and molding force, which is the "mysterious power that separates" the natural ruler from the rest of us (vol. 6, 176). Shaw titled this essay "Preface on Bosses," and it is a fascinating exposition of Shaw's Machiavellian realism; it also provides a glimpse of the awe that was inspired by those gifted with this mysterious power, such as Mussolini and Hitler, and the admiration as well as the anxiety that such power induced: Would they live up to their potential, or would such awesome power unhinge them?

The play itself, which concerns the capricious behavior of a spoiled millionaire and her eventual engagement to a benevolent Egyptian doctor, would seem to have nothing at all to do with politics. Yet when viewed as an allegory its political meaning becomes apparent enough, especially with the aid of the preface. "Preface on Bosses" considers the attributes that make an individual, such as William the Conqueror, "irresistible: the physical strength and ferocity of a king of beasts, the political genius of a king of men, the strategic cunning and tactical gumption of a military genius" (vol. 6, 180). But behind such obvious admiration there is fear—for without a "religious or political creed all autocrats go more or less mad" (vol. 6, 194). It apparently never occurred to Shaw that Hitler and Mussolini, whom the preface is really about, might have been more than just a little mad before they even achieved power.

But while the preface balances slightly more toward the fear that such a powerful person may induce, in the play it is primarily Shaw's admiration that predominates. As he demonstrated as long ago as *Major Barbara*, it is power wedded to the good that will lead us to the Promised Land, and once again we see Shaw standing in awe of such power: the vitality, the ability to get things done, the access to force, the prodigious responsibility such individuals have chosen to take on their shoulders, the power they wield to mold people and institutions, their being a force of nature, a superman; but he fears such power not being in the service of the Life Force. In that sense the theme of *The Millionairess* is exactly the same as that of *Major Barbara*. In the earlier play it was Undershaft's union with Barbara that wedded power to goodness; and in *The Millionairess* it is Epifania Ognisanti di Pererga's uniting with the altruistic servant of Allah that does the same. Thus she represents the power of a Mussolini or a Hitler, a power fascinating and irresistible, yet dangerous and unpredictable if not wedded to a higher disinterested purpose, which is represented by the Egyptian doctor. Shaw recognized great potential in Mussolini and Hitler; they each had prodigious energy, were fearless, and seemed to command the respect and obedience of their citizens—and each removed the paralyzing obstacle of parliamentary gridlock, not to mention troublemakers of all sorts.

Their will was law, and so Shaw hoped that they were united to the Life Force and would usher in a new post-capitalist era. In *On the Rocks*— a deeply pessimistic play about a Prime Minister's failed attempt to bring socialism to England—Sir Arthur finally concludes that he is not the man to change the political system, and realizes that he "shall hate the man who will carry it through for his cruelty" (vol. 5, 619). If Mussolini and Hitler were aligned with Creative Evolution, they could do wonders despite—or even because of—their cruelty. But if they were not, let the world beware. By uniting the eponymous Epifania with the benevolent servant of Allah, the Egyptian Doctor, Shaw unites fascist energy and vitality with public service and genuine altruism.

Epifania Ognisanti di Pererga is a natural ruler, a master spirit designed to give orders and be obeyed. She is a force of nature, likened throughout the play to a hurricane, a lightning flash, a tornado, an earthquake, and an avalanche (vol. 6, 231, 243, 271), who will do anything to have her will: "I will set fire to the hotel if necessary," is her response to those she wants out of her presence. "Fight him to the last ditch, no matter what it costs," she tells her lawyer regarding her victim's legitimate grievance (vol. 6, 265, 266). She impulsively responds to any real or imagined threat with physical force, and leaves a trail of victims behind her. She is dangerous, but her will is irresistible and her ability to get things done is unmatched.

In Shaw's view of the world there are the masters and the servants, those who command and those who are meant to obey. When a master spirit has a vision he or she wants executed, those lower orders refusing to obey must be compelled; if they cannot be compelled then their useless lives should be terminated without regret or whining. This sounds incredibly harsh, as indeed it is, and Shaw did receive criticism for it (as we saw in his debate with Salvemini), but he believed that it was through such severity that a new world order would come into being. He pictured a tireless and disinterested elite with great brain power and vision, and a managerial class to give orders to a populace that joyfully obeyed; any vision of an egalitarian society of creative and responsible citizens truly was "utopian," and Shaw was as far distant from later utopian visionaries Herbert Marcuse and Wilhelm Reich as it is possible to be. Equality was of incomes only; he was very wary and frankly contemptuous of the masses, and it was a purely top-down social order.

The Life Force attracts the right individuals to each other, as we have seen in *Man and Superman* and *Major Barbara*; and when Epifania sees the Egyptian doctor she has the same response that Cusins has when he first sees Barbara. Prior to that she is willful, but we see no higher purpose to her actions. When the doctor says that it was a stipulation of his mother's that any woman who wished to marry him must pass a test, taking two hundred piastres (about 35 shillings) and earning "her living alone and unaided for six months," Epifania unhesitatingly takes the challenge (vol. 6, 245). From here out she begins to transform the environment, but at a cost.

Epifania's first move is to enter a dreary and impoverished sewing shop run by an unimaginative couple who fear change and innovation. Epifania's imperiousness at first fails to intimidate the couple, but it does not take long for her to cow them into submission. About a minute into the act (act three) the husband responds to her bossiness by saying, "Is that the way to talk to me? You think a lot of yourself, don't you? What do you take me for?" Epifania shoots back, contemptuously, "A worm," to which the husband responds, according to the stage directions, by "*making a violent demonstration*"; but Epifania, undeterred, says simply, "Take care. I can use my fists. I can shoot, if necessary" (vol. 6, 247). After this threat of violence, the couple are mostly entirely subdued.

In the preface to *Geneva*, written after Mussolini and Hitler had proved failures in 1945, Shaw considers whether or not they would have been happier as obscure non-entities, and concludes that the question is irrelevant, since "they were kept too busy to bother themselves about happiness" (vol. 5, 642). And that quality, tireless work in the service of something higher than the self—famously extolled in the preface to *Man and Superman*[28]—a quality Shaw here ascribes to the fascist dictators, he also transfers to his allegorical dictator Epifania. When she says that she wants "to work, to work. I am in a hurry to get to work," and the couple ask what kind of work she can do, she answers, "Brain work... Managing work. Planning work. Driving work" (vol. 6, 251). As she begins to take over the sewing shop she frequently exhorts the couple to "Do as I tell you" (vol. 6, 252) and "[*masterfully*] Sit down. I will deal with Tim" (vol. 6, 254). By the end of this very short act she has taken control of the couple's business, improving its efficiency and slashing away wasteful expenditures. Finally she says, as she gets ready to leave: "There is not enough work here for me: I can do it all in half a day every week." Then this whirlwind departs, leaving the stunned wife only to say: "Do what she tells us, Joe. We're like children" (vol. 6, 255). With those words the act closes.

This was the social dynamic of Shaw's utopia; not the raising up of people to autonomous responsibility (only a few had this capacity, he believed) but rather an elite class of masters acting as the parents to dutiful and obedient children. Earlier we saw how both Battler and Bombardone echo the words attributed to God in Exodus 3:14; those famous words, "I am what I am," are uttered by Bombardone after Newcomer says to him, like a child, "Who are you that I should obey you? What about democracy?" which was itself a response to Bombardone's proclamation that the "place of those who do not understand is in the ranks of silent and blindly obedient labor" (vol. 5, 718). While the rise of mass society has a lot to do with Shaw's point of view, it is hard not to see also Shaw's unstructured, anarchical, and unhappy childhood being a powerful influence on his unrelenting desire for strong commanding leaders and silent obedient subjects, his desire for an ordered and hierarchical political "household."

Epifania next transforms the rundown dilapidated riverfront inn, the Pig & Whistle—the site where she had kicked Blenderbland down the stairs, seriously injuring him—into a flourishing five-star hotel, The Cardinal's Hat. We learn that the provenance of the Pig & Whistle dates back to the time of William the Conqueror, yet it is virtually unchanged through all that time. Shaw seems to borrow from the second part of Goethe's *Faust* (1832) here—a link we will explore shortly—as modernization requires the sacrifice of another old couple. For Epifania to achieve her transformation the old couple who had run the Pig & Whistle for years must be removed, and when Patricia asks the hotel manager if they are "satisfied and happy," the manager—the son of the old couple—responds: "Well, no: the change was too much for them at their age. My father had a stroke and wont last long, I'm afraid. And my mother has gone a bit silly. Still, it was best for them; and they have all the comforts they care for" (vol. 6, 260).

Later when the Egyptian doctor is entertaining doubts about a union with a woman who has so heartlessly uprooted the lives of others, saying that the "hotel looks well in photographs; and the wages you pay would be a fortune to a laborer on the Nile. But what of the old people whose natural home this place had become? the old man with his paralytic stroke? the old woman gone mad? the cast out creatures in the workhouse?" Epifania responds by saying that she "has to take the world as [she] find[s] it" (vol. 6, 273–74). This is Shaw's view, the view of the realist in his 1891 manifesto, *The Quintessence of Ibsenism*. One deals with what is there, and transforming it into something better is inevitably painful for some; there will be sacrifices. Compassion is therefore a hindrance to getting things done. In the previous act when Epifania had offended the husband in the workhouse with her realistic appraisal of the situation, she responded, "You are sensitive about it. I am not" (vol. 6, 253). This is the ruthless nature required for getting a tough job done, and is what Shaw means in *The Perfect Wagnerite* when he describes his hero Siegfried as "conscienceless," living only by the law of his own will.[29]

Siegfried also uses force as his primary means of getting things done, and we see this quality in Shaw's allegorical dictator, the ultra-efficient and productive Epifania. In his excellent book, *All That Is Solid Melts into Air: The Experience of Modernity*, Marshall Berman—who took his title from Marx and Engels' classic utopian work, *The Communist Manifesto* (1848)—discusses modernity as fundamentally a process of rapid change. Starting with Goethe's *Faust*—seen as a proto-modernist work—Berman traverses the nineteenth century and up to the present, examining modernisms, primarily through works of literature and urban development. Faust is seen as a tragic figure of modernism because he embraces change and development—the spirit of modernity—and is aware of the cost, symbolized in the tragic death of the old couple at the end who will not relinquish the property that Faust wants to develop.[30] As mentioned, Shaw appears to be borrowing from Goethe here, one of his favorite authors, although he dispenses with the tragic overtones, which would undermine his essentially comic gifts as well as his fundamentally optimistic spirit. In this sense Shaw is utterly modern, embracing more a political modernism than an aesthetic modernism, the sense outlined by Roger Griffin in his book *Modernism and Fascism*, which we considered in Chapters 3 and 4.

Those perplexed by Shaw's approbation of Hitler might consider Fritz Todt, Hitler's chief engineer and the principal designer of the Autobahn. According to Richard Evans, one of the preeminent authorities on National Socialism, Todt, like "other professionally qualified men in the Party," viewed the Third Reich "as a decisive, energetic, modern movement that would do away with the dithering of the Weimar Republic and impel Germany into a new future based on the centralized application of science and technology to society, culture and the economy in the interests of the German race."[31] Hitler's energetic efforts to transform Germany's economy and infrastructure very much impressed Shaw, and were indeed what he looked for in a leader—likewise Stalin's ruthless efforts to transform and industrialize Soviet Russia. In fact Fritz Thyssen, the German industrialist, predicted, according to Evans again, that the Nazis "would soon start shooting industrialists who did not fulfill the conditions prescribed by the Four Year Plan, just as their equivalents were shot in Soviet Russia."[32] Seen in this light, *The Millionairess* is an allegory of fascist modernism.

Besides her ruthlessness and efficiency, Epifania also inspires blind obedience in the youths who come under her spell (at least the one young man we see). After dispensing with the old proprietors of the inn and utterly refashioning it, Epifania places the old couple's son in a managerial position. We have already seen how he has rationalized the tragic outcome of his parents' forced removal, saying that his father's stroke and his mother's insanity "was best for them." All his allegiance has shifted to Epifania:

> You see, though I could never have made the change myself, I was intelligent enough to see that she was right. I backed her up all through. I have such faith in that woman, sir, that if she told me to burn down the hotel tonight I'd do it without a moment's hesitation.
>
> (vol. 6, 259)

Of course children transferring their love and faith from parents to leader—even to the extent of informing on them—was a phenomenon only too common in all of the totalitarian states.[33] Later when Epifania sees her estranged husband and his girlfriend at the hotel she immediately fires the young manager, who apologizes even though he had no idea who they were: "However, you are always right. Do you wish me to go at once or to carry on until you have replaced me?" (vol. 6, 265). Just as impulsively Epifania changes her mind and keeps him on.

Although we may be able to understand how an impressionable young man might fall under the spell of a fascinating and extremely capable autocrat, we may still wonder how a saintly doctor devoted to a life of service and already "married to science" (vol. 6, 244), as he says, might also fall under that same spell. What ensnares the doctor is the intensity of the Life Force coursing through Epifania's veins, her vitality: "[*Amazed*] Ooooh! I have never felt such a pulse. It is like a slow sledge hammer" (vol. 6, 272). He does not care for women, except as they may need his help as a doctor, but regarding Epifania's superhuman vitality he is moved to exclaim: "But the life! the pulse! is the heartbeat of Allah, save in Whom there is no majesty and no might" (vol. 6, 273). Yet like John Tanner he continues to resist, even responding to her as Tanner frequently does to Ann in *Man and Superman*: "there is no wit and no wisdom like that of a woman ensnaring the mate chosen for her by Allah" (vol. 6, 277). Like Tanner he is able to resist her charm, wit and wisdom for a time, but ultimately he cannot resist her vitality, and as he feels her pulse once more he finally succumbs and the play ends.

The Millionairess is a fascist allegory: the "leader" forcefully invades and "civilizes" the institutions she occupies, causing damage yet improving their condition. Earlier we saw in one of Shaw's letters how he believed that Hitler's mistake was in not improving the conditions of the countries he occupied, as Julius Caesar had done. Epifania clearly improves the institutions that she "occupies," and thus there can be no question that she has Shaw's overwhelming approval. She is unalterably committed and forceful, brooking no opposition and allowing nothing to get in her way—she does not convene a committee, but takes matters entirely into her own hands. She is a realist who refuses to waste energy pitying the necessary casualties of her enterprises. And she inspires confidence in those who recognize her strength and are smart enough to get behind her. She is in fact one of Shaw's greatest "supermen," and like that other earlier great superman Andrew Undershaft she totally dominates the play, leaving the audience spellbound by her vitality and superhuman ability to transform the environment. Moralizing about the destruction which ensues from her actions is like moralizing a hurricane or a tornado for the ruin it leaves in its path; and that is why she is frequently likened, by Shaw's stage directions and by the other characters in the play, to just such a force of nature. In fact, Shaw spoke in exactly this way about the situation in Russia, saying he was astonished by critics who regarded the "monumental triumph of the Bolshevik Revolution" as "a transient riot headed by a couple of rascals...You might as well argue with an earthquake."[34]

It was this unswerving resolve and energetic ability to destroy and rebuild that Shaw admired in the dictators, and the reason he looked to them with such hope. In the "Preface on Bosses" he extols at great length first Mussolini and then Hitler. Of Mussolini he says that with

> inspired precision he denounced Liberty as a putrefying corpse. He declared that what the people needed was not liberty but discipline, the sterner the better. He said he would not tolerate Oppositions: he called for action and silence. The people, instead of being shocked like good Liberals, rose to him. He was able to organize a special constabulary who wore black shirts and applied the necessary coercion.

When these Blackshirts "committed outrages and a couple of murders" the liberal newspapers "shrieked with horror as if nothing else was happening in Italy. Mussolini refused to be turned aside from his work like a parliamentary man to discuss 'incidents,'" and instead threw the liberals who complained into prison. Despite the many complaints about the trampling of the rights of free speech, free press, etc. coming from the foreign press and from a humiliated Parliament, Mussolini "never even looked round: he was busy sweeping up the elected municipalities, and replacing them with efficient commissioners of his own choice, who had to do their job or get out... It was evident that Mussolini was master of Italy as far as such mastership is possible" (vol. 6, 187–88). Shaw goes on in this manner for about two pages, throwing in a few jabs at Salvemini and Company along the way.

Hitler is lauded as well for his strength and use of force, particularly for his handling of the infamous Night of the Long Knives, where

> he was able to kill seventy-seven of his most dangerous opponents at a blow and then justify himself completely before an assembly as representative as the British Parliament, the climax being his appointment as absolute dictator in Germany for life, a stretch of Caesarism no nineteenth century Hohenzollern would have dreamt of demanding.
>
> (vol. 6, 189)

The so-called "Night of the Long Knives" (30 June 1934), when Hitler purged the upper ranks of the SA, also impressed that other Machiavellian, Uncle Joe Stalin,[35] presumably inspiring his own purge of the higher ranks of Soviet commissars a few years later.

But Hitler committed a terrible blunder when he started persecuting the Jews, "which went to the scandalous length of outlawing, plundering, and exiling Albert Einstein, a much greater man than any politician" (vol. 6, 189). Shaw goes on at some length decrying this "appalling breach of cultural faith" (vol. 6, 190), never sparing any of his outrage for the many anonymous human beings who were undergoing this same injustice; and we cannot help but feel that for Shaw Hitler's great sin was not the persecution of an entire people, but the persecution of a single great man. The mass of men and women, for Shaw, were not fully human and thus there was no great sin in their persecution, no matter how unjust, ghastly and barbarous.[36]

In fact in the preface to *Geneva* Shaw even rationalizes the barbarity, providing feeble excuses for the German soldiers in charge of the concentration camps, saying that it "must have been very uncomfortable and dangerous for them... When further overcrowding became physically impossible they could do nothing with their unwalled prisoners but kill them and burn the corpses they could not bury" (vol. 5, 637–38). Expressing pity and concern for those in positions of power, rather than the real victims, is not new with Shaw. We see it elsewhere as well, as in his concern for the "unfortunate Commissars" who are "obliged" to murder "lazy drunkards" to enforce greater efficiency:

> the result was that the unfortunate Commissars who had to make the Russian industries and transport services work, found themselves obliged to carry pistols and execute saboteurs and lazy drunkards with their own hands. Such a Commissar was Djerjinsky, now, like Lenin, entombed in the Red Square. He was not a homicidally disposed person; but when it fell to his lot to make the Russian trains run at all costs, he had to force himself to shoot a station master who found it easier to drop telegrams in the waste paper basket than to attend to them. And it was this gentle Djerjinsky who, unable to endure the duties of an executioner (even had he had time for them), organized the Tcheka.
>
> (vol. 6, 533)

In her classic account *Eichmann in Jerusalem: A Report on the Banality of Evil*, Hannah Arendt describes the process of perverse inversion that we see here in Shaw, the turning of pity from victims to oppressors:

> The trick used by Himmler... consisted in turning these instincts around... So that instead of saying: What horrible things I do to

people!, the murderers would be able to say: What horrible things I had to watch in pursuance of my duties, how heavy the task weighed upon my shoulders![37]

Arendt also remarks that Himmler was very good at conveying a sense of almost divine mission to his staff, suggesting that the grandiosity of their task required them to be "superhuman," or even to be "superhumanly inhuman."[38] Shaw's pressing need to believe in the historic creation of a utopian society had led him into the same delusions.

Shaw speculates that Hitler's "Judeophobia" may derive from Houston Stewart Chamberlain's *Foundations of the Nineteenth Century* (1899, English translation 1911), a book Shaw was very enthusiastic about, writing an "astonishing panegyric"[39] on it in the *Fabian News* when it appeared in Britain in 1911 and, as he says in the preface to *The Millionairess*, recommending it to everyone as a must-read (vol. 6, 191). Chamberlain's biographer Geoffrey G. Field writes that the "extravagance" of Shaw's praise "reveals what we might call 'the other side' of Shaw—his elitist scorn for democracy, the autodidactic quality of his learning, and the deep confusions and contradictions in his ideas—all overlaid by the Shavian love of paradox and assertion."[40] What is especially revealing is that Shaw's enthusiasm for *Foundations*—like his later enthusiasm for *Mein Kampf*—does not seem to be in any way diminished by the extravagant racism of the book. Shaw writes in the *Fabian News* that this "very notable book should be read by all good Fabians" because it is "a masterpiece of really scientific history" that "will show many Fabians what side they are really on, lifting them out of mere newspaper and propaganda categories into their right camp."[41]

But most revealing is Shaw's hearty approval of Chamberlain's outcry "against the lumping together under the general name of 'Humanity' of people who have different souls."[42] While Shaw was not a racist, as Chamberlain and Hitler were, he did differentiate between those of noble soul and those of inferior, those with great souls and those who are not fully human and, in some cases, not worthy of occupying space on earth—as we see so clearly in *Back to Methuselah* in the division between the long-livers and the short-livers. According to Field, Shaw did not believe, as Chamberlain did, that the "battle between Teuton and Chaos still raged," but rather that "Chaos had triumphed," although "the 'short round skull' of a British greengrocer, more than that of the Jew, turns out to be the deadly adversary of G.B.S."[43] While German fascism did not always differentiate wisely between the worthy and the unworthy, it at least exemplified biocratic vision and had the courage to act on its principles, or so Shaw seemed to believe.

As an allegory removed from actual historical circumstances, *The Millionairess*, perhaps even more than *Geneva*, dramatizes Shaw's deepest feelings about Mussolini and Hitler and the hope he placed in them. In Epifania we see the superhuman energy and potential that he saw in the two dictators. Shaw was a keen political observer and was fully aware of the abuses that had outraged more sensitive spectators, but for him the energy, daring, and ruthlessness of Mussolini and Hitler actually made them potentially more effective, despite the dangers inherent in such volatile personalities. Epifania is violent, dangerous, and impossible for mere ordinary mortals to deal with, but she is an irresistible force of nature, and thus, as the play suggests in precise terms, an instrument of God, her vitality the very "heartbeat of Allah, save in Whom there is no majesty and no might" (vol. 6, 273).

Shaw had hoped that Edith Evans would take the challenge of breathing life into his dramatic creation when the play made its premiere. Evans was a brilliant actress, one of the great actresses of the twentieth century, and she had appeared with great success in a number of other Shaw plays, including playing Hesione in the original *Heartbreak House*. But, according to Ronald Bryden, she "smelled a rat"[44] and turned down the role, much to Shaw's astonishment. She felt—again according to Bryden—that Shaw "was asking her to play Hitler and Mussolini, but to make them attractive by her bottomless technique and siren charm."[45] While Shaw was spellbound by the dynamism of Hitler and Mussolini, and hopeful about what they might accomplish, the fact of their being absolute dictators who were ordering their institutions according to their own whims made him nervous. Were they really instruments of Creative Evolution, or might such prodigious power unhinge them? On the last page of "Preface on Bosses" he begins his peroration with a rhetorical pronouncement: "I say cheerfully to the dominators 'By all means dominate: it is up to us to order our institutions that you shall not oppress us, nor bequeath any of your precedence to your commonplace children'" (vol. 6, 202). And this is the difference between the two fascist dictators and that other mighty dominator, Stalin, who, Shaw believed, was operating within an institutional framework and according to a viable creed that could withstand any movement of his toward megalomania. It is to Stalin, then, and to the Soviet Union, that we must now turn.

Shaw, Stalin, and the USSR

In 1933, Shaw wrote in the preface to *Too True to Be Good* that "Stalin and Mussolini are the most responsible statesmen in Europe because they have no hold on their places except their efficiency" (vol. 4, 630). Nonetheless, as far as Mussolini was concerned, Shaw seemed to feel some anxiety, at least by the time he came to write the "Preface on Bosses" three years later. And this is because the fascist states were still groping toward communism, toward "Socialism in One State," whereas the USSR had solidified itself as a communist state with apparent checks and balances for rulers who might spin out of control. A few pages later in that same essay he writes that

> Mr. Stalin is not in the least like an Emperor, nor an Archbishop, nor a Prime Minister, nor a Chancellor; but he would be strikingly like a Pope, claiming for form's sake an apostolic succession from Marx, were it not for his frank method of Trial and Error, his entirely human footing, and his liability to removal at a moment's notice if his eminence should upset his mental balance.
> (vol. 4, 631–32)

Interestingly, "Trial and Error" is the method that Shaw ascribes to God, or the Life Force, and is why he capitalizes the T and the E here. Stalin, even more certainly than Mussolini and Hitler, is a deputy of that creative force that was forging the glorious new future.

In 1931, Shaw made his first and only trip to the Soviet Union, and his observations on Stalin are first-hand, as the Soviet leader granted him and his companions a meeting that lasted several hours. He spent ten days in Russia and believed he was seeing the country as it really was; that there was no attempt on the Soviet side to deceive him in any way, to present a cosmetically modified façade. As he wrote to H.G. Wells, "there was no attempt to humbug me."[46] Shaw knew, of course, as did others, of the labor camps, the liquidations, the intolerance of anything deemed subversive, but he believed that the Soviet Union was ruled by a cabinet of extremely capable men determined to create a socialist utopia and willing to make the sacrifices necessary for that vision to become reality. There is a hint of disapproval toward the rigid epistemology of Soviet Communism at the end of *Geneva* when the Commissar remarks that he is unsure how to respond to the news of the earth's jumping to the next quantum, as the "Marxian dialectic does not include the quantum theory. I must consult Moscow" (vol. 5, 757). And in January 1949 Shaw wrote in the *Labour Monthly* that in Russia "Marx is a Pontif; and all scientists who do not call themselves Materialists must be persecuted."[47] In this article, titled "The Lysenko Muddle," Shaw commends the Russian biologist Trofim Lysenko for being a vitalist, a non-materialist, like Lamarck, Butler, Bergson, and Shaw himself, but because dialectical materialism is the official philosophy of the Soviet Union Lysenko is unfortunately forced "to pretend that he is a Materialist when he is in fact a Vitalist; and thus muddles us ludicrously."[48] But these criticisms were rare and mild, and throughout the thirties and forties Shaw not only had high praise for Russia and its leader Stalin, but considered it (and him) a model for the rest of the civilized world, and was to give dramaturgical expression to this position in some of his plays, especially, as we shall see, *The Simpleton of the Unexpected Isles.*

Shaw thought of Soviet Communism as not only a scientifically advanced political system, but as a new creed, a living faith to replace the ossified Christianity of the West—what he called "Crossianity." This idea is established early on in *Geneva* when an English Bishop and a Soviet Commissar come into conflict. The Bishop is in Geneva to make a formal complaint against the Soviet propaganda that he believes is infiltrating his country, and the Commissar is likewise concerned about British missionaries who have been making mischief in his own country. Although the complaints are identical, the comically Sovio-phobic Bishop is unable to comprehend how Christian missionaries could be perceived as anything other than a force for good and truth. And although he delights in the Russian's company before he realizes who he is, he is horrified, and in fact faints, when he learns that he is a Soviet commissar.

Shaw's view, expressed in this play through the Commissar, is that a true religion has been officially established in Russia while in Britain there is only superstition. We learn from the Commissar, whom we are encouraged to trust, that the missionaries have not been shot without trial, as the Bishop assumes, but after a brief examination have been sent home. During this examination it had been determined that the missionaries had no religion in them, only "tribal superstitions of the most barbarous kind" (vol. 5, 669). The Bishop, already in a shaky state, is horrified even further to hear from the Commissar that "the Komintern is the State Church in Russia exactly as the Church of England is the State Church in Britain" (vol. 5, 670). This is too much and the Bishop faints a second time. When he comes to and mumbles that "Karl Marx—Antichrist—said that the sweet and ennobling consolations of our faith are opium given to the poor" the Commissar contradicts him, saying that in Russia there are no poor. With this he falls dead, although he is presumed at first to have fainted again. When the Commissar learns of his moribund state, he replies, "Was he ever alive?" (vol. 5, 671). The rigid and buffoonish Bishop, representative of a dead institution, is in direct conflict with the energetic, cheerful and kindly Commissar, who represents a living faith.

Many of the letters that Shaw wrote after his 1931 visit to Russia attest to his belief that in the Soviet Union they were creating a new religion, an earthbound heaven or utopia-in-progress where judgment would be transferred from God to an elite bureau of commissars who were leading the way toward this communist utopia. The First Commandment of this new creed might be said to be "Thou shalt work," or, to put it negatively, "Thou shalt not be lazy." Of chief importance is the conditioning of children in the rudiments of the faith as well as the extermination of heretics. Shaw wrote to the Reverend Ensor Walters in 1932 that to "be in a country where the government is fanatically religious and insists on every child being brought up religiously, one of its religious aims being the total abolition of God, is a startling novelty, and one of those things that only a really religious Protestant can understand."[49] That same day he also wrote to his friend, another man of the cloth, William Ralph Inge, Dean of St. Paul's, in similar terms, saying that the

> Russians have "got religion"; and that makes them none the less formidable because one of their 39 articles is that there is no God... They have got hold of the children; and it is very easy to mould human nature if you catch it before it is set. The Russian experiment is enormously interesting and may prove historically momentous.[50]

Shortly after these letters were written, while in South Africa, Shaw would begin writing *The Rationalization of Russia*, although he never finished it. The seventeen-page preface and the unfinished fifty-nine-page first chapter were published in 1964, fourteen years after his death.

Regarding the book, he told his French translator Augustin Hamon that he wanted to

> shew how a revolution made by doctrinaires, who alone have the requisite fanaticism and selflessness, evolves under the pressure of actual experience into a practical government: how points of

doctrine have to be thrown to the winds in all directions and all the revolutionists who will not accept this pressure have to be shot or exiled.[51]

Interestingly, Evans writes that in Nazi Germany words that formally carried a negative connotation, such as "fanaticism," had begun to be used positively. We saw in Chapter 3 that in *Man and Superman* Shaw uses the word "fanaticism" in a positive sense, as he does here.

This brief remark to Hamon also attests to Shaw's political pragmatism. The leaders are "doctrinaires"; they are dogmatic and inflexible about their *ends*, about the necessity of arriving at their blueprint utopia, but entirely flexible regarding their *means*. In another letter to Hamon, Shaw wrote that the "secret to Stalin is that he is entirely opportunist as to *means*."[52] The seeds for this policy of the ends justifying the means can actually be found in Shaw's early work *The Quintessence of Ibsenism*, where the realist is bound by no law or code as he plows toward the creation of a new word order, and in *The Perfect Wagnerite* where the utopian Siegfried is subject to no law but his own will.

Although Shaw never finished or published *The Rationalization of Russia*, he managed to scatter much of its content in the various prefaces that he wrote in the thirties, including the many remarks regarding the extermination of recalcitrant citizens. But the most fascinating dramatic presentation of Shaw's enthusiasm for the Russian experiment—and his desire to see that experiment spread to England and beyond—is found in his 1934 play, *The Simpleton of the Unexpected Isles*. Like his earlier play *Back to Methuselah* and his later play *Farfetched Fables*, *The Simpleton* is a utopian play, set on a remote island that is supposed to have come "up out of the sea" (vol. 6, 562). The island is utopian in that marital and eugenic experiments are carried out freely, its moral code is refreshingly antithetical to that found in England, and in the latter part of the play an exterminating angel descends from the skies to rid the world of its useless parasites and idlers. It is also utopian in that the island is ruled by a small band of exceptional individuals, one of whom is particularly exceptional—in fact a modern day superman (actually, as in *The Millionairess*, a superwoman).

In this play, Shaw's obsession with liquidation gets much more than just a cursory treatment (as it did in *Back to Methuselah*) and is actually the thematic center of the play. Already in this brief description we should be noticing the similarities of this island to the Soviet Union; and in fact the theme of the play is impossible to miss. Yet, for some reason, the few Shaw critics who have written about *The Simpleton* have chosen to exclude from discussion the play's most salient feature. This is especially problematic because the play was written in 1934, when literally millions of peasants were being exterminated in the Soviet Union and in the Ukraine. In 1929, Stalin had dropped the New Economic Policy and implemented a plan of crash industrialization and collectivization, at the same time waging an all-out class war on the so-called "kulaks." In August 1932, he had drafted the infamous "On the Safeguarding of State Property," effectively launching the premeditated famine of 1932–33 that killed millions of peasants. (Most starved to death, but the penalty for keeping back a morsel of food to feed your family was death.) While millions died of starvation, as many as fifteen million were uprooted—two million transferred to industrial projects, labor camps, or simply to the Arctic. On this horrifying plan of mass murder, putatively in the interests of the new state, the Webbs commented: "Strong must have been the faith and resolute the will of the men who, in the interest of what seemed to them the public good, could take so momentous a decision."[53] Besides engaging in this class war, the Soviet elite continued to send to labor camps (and likely death) everyone they considered to be "enemies of the people," such as Mrs Dmitry Krynin, who so earnestly pleaded with Shaw to intervene on her behalf in 1931. This is the socio-political background that informs the play, and its defense is the primary reason for the play's composition.

Although no one with any knowledge of the mass slaughter in Russia and of Shaw's approbation of it would be able to miss the theme of the play, Shaw nonetheless spells it out in his 1935 preface:

> For the Tcheka was simply carrying out the executive work of a constitution which had abolished the lady and gentleman exactly as the Inquisition carried out the executive work of a catholic constitution which had abolished Jupiter and Diana and Venus and Apollo.
>
> Simple enough; and yet so hard to get into our genteel heads that in making a play about it I have had to detach it altogether from the great Russian change, or any of the actual political changes which threaten to raise it in the National-Socialist and Fascist countries, and to go back to the old vision of a day of reckoning by divine justice for all mankind.
>
> (vol. 6, 536)

Note that while the Soviet Union is the primary catalyst for the play, Shaw does include Hitler's and Mussolini's political experiments as being also relevant. The purpose of Shaw's essay is to argue for the necessity of a new inquisition, such as the Cheka then operative in the Soviet Union. This is the raison d'etre for the play's creation, the preface existing to spell it out in plain terms for those who may have missed it in the play. Such an inquisition, Shaw says, is necessary in a world that has lost its fear of hell. Shaw had been hinting at the need for just such an institutional practice for years, and his secretary, Blanche Patch, is wrong to suggest that he might have picked up the idea of "exterminating those who are socially undesirable" from Stalin.[54] Those especially conversant with Shaw's expository prose would find nothing new in reading that "we need a greatly increased intolerance of socially injurious conduct and an uncompromising abandonment of punishment and its cruelties, together with sufficient school inculcation of social responsibility to make every citizen conscious that if his life cost more than it is worth to the community the community may painlessly extinguish it" (vol. 6, 539). Shaw defends the inquisition in Russia and would like to see it emulated in England, and in defense suggests that in some form or another there has always been inquisitorial intolerance, its name simply changing from the opprobrious to the not yet blemished, from the Inquisition, say, to the Star Chamber, or what have you.

Just as he would later justify Hitler's persecution of the Jews by saying that similar persecutions had been committed in America against the Japanese and by the British against the Chinese in Australia, here he legitimizes an egregious attack on human rights—human rights painstakingly won and precariously maintained—because, in effect, "everybody does it." He believes or pretends to believe that after an initial stage of mass killings a Promised Land will be reached in which such killings will no longer be necessary. The Bolsheviks had been killing their enemies, real or imagined, since the revolution began, but over the five years that preceded the writing of the preface those killings had greatly increased; and they would continue for the remainder of Stalin's tenure. In fact, the timing of the play and preface could not be more ominous. While the play was written just after the climax of the peasant extermination, leading Politburo member Sergei Kirov was murdered on 1 December 1934, setting off a wave of killings that was later denominated the "Great Purge." And on 7 April 1935 (the month Shaw wrote the preface) Stalin publicly decreed, to the great outrage of the West, the extension of criminal sentences, including the death penalty, to children as young as twelve. So it is sadly ironic that Shaw could write that the "worst of its work is over: the heretics are either liquidated, converted, or intimidated. But it was indispensable in its prime" (vol. 6, 533). Let us now look at this very unusual play.

The Simpleton of the Unexpected Isles

The Simpleton's structure consists of a prologue of three short scenes followed by two acts, the second being almost twice as long as the first. The curtain opens on two disheveled and unhealthy-looking characters in a cluttered and untidy emigration office in a tropical port of the British Empire. Both characters—a British emigration officer and his clerk—are suicidal, and the scene ends with the officer leaving the office with an upbeat young British woman who would like to emigrate to the islands, after which the clerk, singing "Rule, Britannia!," shoots himself dead. In the next scene, the young officer attempts to kill himself by jumping into the sea, but is encountered at that precise moment by a native priest. The priest says he would never dream of interfering with his suicide, for on this island they "do not encourage them [the island's many suicidal British colonists] to live. The empire is for those who can live in it" (vol. 6, 551). But the priest tells him that this is not the correct place to terminate his life, for this is the haunt of the goddess of the resurrection and the life. He suggests sending for an acolyte who will guide the young man to the "cliff of death, which contains the temple of the goddess's brother, the weeder of the garden" (vol. 6, 550). But instead the priest suddenly kicks him into the sea: it turns out that there are nets below and the priest is merely shocking him into a sense of the value of life. In effect, the emigration officer undergoes a baptism, and when we next see him in the third scene of the prologue he is clean and fresh: a new man.

The island is a utopia, but to experience it as such one must discard the ethos of British life and embrace that of the natives. It was not the emigration officer's fate to die just yet, to be conveyed to the cliff of death, for as it turns out he is one of the elect, one of the "indispensables." Shaw announces his theme in this short prologue, dramatically as we have just seen, but also in plain language; for in scene one the young woman says: "Dispensables and indispensables: there you have the whole world. I wonder am I a dispensable or an indispensable" (vol. 6, 547). It turns out that she is an indispensable, and like the emigration officer will be pushed into the sea at the close of the prologue, in effect also undergoing a baptism. The third and last scene of the prologue takes place on an esplanade before a sacred cave and brings together the remainder of those who will be the ruling class in the play to follow, adding, besides the two Brits and the priest, a priestess and a couple of British tourists who wander into the scene, the woman passing out tracts that say: "Where will you spend eternity?" (vol. 6, 556).

The scene is a sacred festival of sorts, with fruit, bread, and non-alcoholic drinks. Everything is the reverse of British life: here dessert is eaten first, and here the Christian woman is described as a "heathen idolator" (vol. 6, 554). Pra and Prola[55]—the priest and priestess—seem to possess vital powers; their beauty has mesmerized the middle-aged British couple who abrogate their middle-class morality, undergoing a transformation similar to the emigration officer's in the previous scene. But rather than plunging into the water, they are each separately led into the cave—a temple described by the young woman as magical and dangerous (she herself has yet to experience her own baptismal transformation). The trip to the cave is no lascivious excursion, but a spiritual transformation effected through sexual contact in a sacred space. When we see these six characters next in act one, twenty years have passed and in the intervening years they have risen to political eminence on the island. They have also embarked on a familial and eugenic experiment, now being the parents of four gorgeous children, aged seventeen to twenty in act one, and these children are central to the theme of the play.

Thus the prologue sets the scene for the action which follows. The six characters of the previous scene now live together with their children in a stately house on the coast of the island; the emigration officer, *"disciplined, responsible and well groomed"* (vol. 6, 567), is now the political secretary and married to the young woman emigrant: they are now Mr and Mrs Hyering. Sir Charles Farwaters, one half of the pair who stumbled into the festival in the previous scene, is the governor of the island. The three couples, living together polygamously, are engaged in an experiment of plural marriage. Shaw had always advocated experiments in institutional arrangements, and was especially keen on eugenic exploration; he was also frequently antagonistic toward traditional marriage, writing a long preface and play (*Getting Married*) to explore the issue in 1908. The polygamous arrangement is an attempt to merge the flesh and spirit of east and west, and also part of a "plan to open people's minds on the subject of eugenics and the need for mixing not only western and eastern culture but eastern and western blood" (vol. 6, 570).

Unfortunately, the results have not been propitious. The four offspring—a dismally small number after twenty years—are apparently "deficient in conscience." Pra says that he is "convinced that there is something lacking in the constitution of the children. It may be a deficiency of nitrogen. It certainly is a deficiency of something that is essential to a complete social human being" (vol. 6, 570–71). Consequently when the simpleton of the title, Iddy Hamingtap, an Anglican clergyman, wanders into their yard after being released by pirates who had kidnapped him (to provide a respectable front for their marauding), and Pra and Prola learn that he has a morbid excess of conscience, they suggest he couple with their two daughters. Iddy, whose Christian name is actually Phosphor, is himself the son of an English chemist with a powerful propensity for experimentation. His father fed nitrogen to his cows and they produced extremely yellow butter and rich milk, and so Iddy was raised on a diet rich in nitrogen—apparently with the expectation that he might also be the better for it.

The Simpleton is about experimentation. Because of his nitrogen diet, Pra and Prola regard Iddy as possibly a "new sort of man" (vol. 6, 565) and wish to take him into the family as an experiment. He recoils, however, having apparently had quite enough of being the object of other people's experiments. Prola, the real leader of the group, as we shall see, tells Iddy that "All men and women are experiments" (vol. 6, 565). This is the essence of Shavian philosophy, and one of the themes of the play. Shaw believed that there was no omniscient and omnipotent God, but actually a very fallible God working through trial and error toward omniscience and omnipotence. Some of these experiments succeed brilliantly while others, such as cancer and whooping cough, are abysmal failures. Human beings have been created to pursue the experiments that God is unable to perform himself (even though capable of creating them in the first place) and are, taken as a whole, God's greatest achievement so far—although taken individually some are of no worth and dispensable while others are of great value and indispensable. And just as some human beings are dispensable, so are institutions that have become too settled and have outlived their use value. Shaw was himself of course an avid experimenter, whether with diet, clothes, the alphabet, or politics.

Yet this great eugenic experiment has been a failure. The four children are described as having not "a scrap of moral conscience" between them (vol. 6, 571). Lack of conscience here means having a proclivity for sexual unrestraint and mindless vicarious aggression (they never hurt anyone) as well as laziness and superabundant imagination. And so because of his excess of conscience Iddy is enticed to partake in an extension of the eugenic experiment to see if it can be corrected. He had fallen in love with Maya at first sight, but she refuses to have him unless he agrees to marry her sister Vashti as well: for Vashti and Maya regard themselves as one being. Vashti is dark and Maya is fair, just as one brother is young and delicate and the other older and "powerfully framed" (vol. 6, 560). The beauty of the two sisters ultimately overcomes Iddy's repugnance to polygamy and he agrees to enter into marriage with them both. Shaw claims in the preface that these four characters—Maya and Vashti, and their brothers Janga and Kanchin—are merely allegorical, "phantasms who embody all the artistic, romantic, and military ideals of our cultured suburbs" (vol. 6, 541). And we can certainly see from the complementarity that he conceived of them in this allegorical fashion.

These characters have been criticized for being too schematic; yet they are more complex and multi-dimensional than this might imply, and if sensitively directed and well played should be dramatically quite powerful. They are forces of chaos and unrestraint, vital and intensely imaginative. But their vitality and power of imagination is given to play, not to work. When the killing (or, rather, "disappearing") begins in the second act they are the first to go. Indeed, they are the only characters in the play who are disappeared, although there is a section of exposition where we learn of citizens disappearing in England. (Of this we will speak shortly.) Arnold Silver believes that these four characters really represent youth, sexuality, and imagination, and as such are resented by Shaw, who forthwith kills them off.[56] This is a fair reading; they are certainly sensual, erotic, and imaginative. It seems that their sensuality is capable of erasing distinctions and drowning the individual, as the first act closes with Iddy submitting to this "kingdom of love" while Vashti declares that they are now "one life" and the final stage directions tell us that the *"[t]he three embrace with interlaced arms and vanish in black darkness"* (vol. 6, 578). This is hardly an indication that utopia will develop from this union, at least coming from the pen of Bernard Shaw. And the second act confirms our suspicions.

The act opens some years later and we soon learn that the marriage has produced no children, Pra declaring that Iddy is an "impotent simpleton" and his own children "wonderful and beautiful, but sterile" (vol. 6, 581). The act is characterized by an unsteady rhythmic intensification of the forces of disunity and chaos, ending with order being imposed through the extermination of these forces, an order imposed by divine fiat. We learn that the harbor to the island is crowded with bellicose cruisers from other lands, each demanding something irreconcilable with the others. The Church of England demands Iddy's polygamous marriage be dissolved, the Delhi Cultural Minister insists that it shall not be, the Caliph of British Islam says it shall be limited to four wives, and the Irish Free State is adamantly opposed to divorce. In fact, they are unable to agree on anything at all, however inconsequential, and violence is threatened.

The small island household represents a miniature utopia, yet it is a failure in that it is unable to disseminate and expand into the surrounding chaos. Pra says that "we have been unable to advance a step. Our dream of founding a millennial world culture: the dream which...united us all six, has ended in a single little household with four children, wonderful and beautiful, but sterile" (vol. 6, 581). Pra is able to disperse the ships and evade their threatened violence by lying to them, but soon after we learn that another crisis is afoot; and this, rather than calling the children to a sense of responsible action, triggers an extended episode of intense make believe.

This new section of the play starts with a quiet lull. The threatening ships are now gone and the children seem to need a new distraction; they complain how Iddy bores them, and this turns into a new game:

Vashti. The world is tired of Iddy.
Maya. I am tired of Iddy.
Vashti. Iddy is a pestilence.
Maya. Iddy is a bore.
Vashti. Let us throw ourselves into the sea to escape from Iddy.
Maya. Let us throw Iddy into the sea that he may escape from himself.
Vashti. You are wise, Prola. Tell us how to get rid of Iddy. (vol. 6, 583–84)

Iddy strolls lazily into the scene discoursing on what a futile creature he is; but he has been inspired to write two new sermons, one on eternity and the other on love. This shocks his audience, and so we assume that he has not written much since he became involved with the girls—and I believe this inspiration to write is why Iddy appears to be spared from the ensuing purge.

The intensity increases again when we learn from the newspapers that England has withdrawn from the Empire and the island has become an independent republic. The children use this as an excuse to launch into another game; they declare a new kingdom, hailing Prola as absolute ruler. Beneath their play we are to understand that they refuse to embrace the responsibility demanded of a republic's citizens, and instead prefer to put that responsibility on another. They grovel before Prola in obeisance, but fail to obey her command to cease playing and go inside and scrub the floors or "anything that is dirty and grubby and smelly enough to shew that you live in a real world and not in a fool's paradise." Instead they continue pronouncing their pretend expressions of servility: "Obedience is freedom from the intolerable fatigue of thought"; "The voice of authority gives us strength and unity. Command us always thus." Prola retorts that all this is an "excuse for leaving everything to me. Lazy, lazy, lazy! Someday Heaven will get tired of lazy people; and the Pitcairn Islanders will see their Day of Judgment at last" (vol. 6, 593). At this precise moment a trumpet signals that Judgment Day has indeed arrived, and in a minute the Angel descends from the sky into their garden.

As mentioned, although some of the children's dialogue will appear artificial if not handled well, these characters are more than merely emblems of abstract ideas (and if they were not, it would be a serious flaw in the play); they are vivid, engaging, capricious, and lively creatures, and so when they do disappear we should experience their loss as human beings and not as mere symbols. After Judgment Day arrives and Iddy comes on stage to tell the others that Maya has disappeared, a strange scene follows:

Prola. And the others? Quick, Pra: go and find the others
Pra. What others?
Prola. The other three: our children. I forget their names.
Iddy. They said "Our names shall live forever." What were their names?
Hyering. They have gone clean out of my head.
Sir Charles. Most extraordinary. I cant for the life of me remember. How many of them did you say there were, Prola?
Prola. Four. Or was it four hundred?
Iddy. There were four. Their names were Love, Pride, Heroism and Empire. (vol. 6, 604)

Apparently we are supposed to imagine that these four aspects of social existence—love, pride, heroism, and empire—are being eradicated, but it does not really work, and the real experience of the scene is to witness the four children being erased from memory as well as human existence. This is more dystopia than allegory; and indeed from here out the utopia becomes dystopia.

Silver feels that the apocalyptic aspect of the play is a flaw and that Shaw's destructive impulses have intruded abruptly and incongruously, destroying the utopia that he has set up through most of the play.

I strongly disagree: the Judgment Day is the logical outcome to the failed experiments. And in fact it represents the larger experiment that is the real subject of the play. If well-intended experiments, whether by "God" or by human beings, sometimes result in unexpected negative consequences, then what is needed is the honesty and moral courage to undertake a massive clean-up. The exterminating Angel—an imperfect being, admittedly (he has trouble taking off for flight)—announces to the islanders that from now on the "lives which have no use, no meaning, no purpose, will fade out. You will have to justify your existence or perish. Only the elect shall survive" (vol. 6, 598). The four useless children have already disappeared; they are not of the elect, and their memory is fading as well in the minds of the others. Not only must they "disappear," but in this perfect society there can be no memory of their imperfection to spoil the new creation.

It is interesting that Shaw cites love as one of the negative characteristics that must be terminated from the new society. In the preface he uses the term "romance" rather than "love," and so it might be thought that Iddy means romantic love. But Shaw's corpus—the letters as well as the formal literary works—contains many expressions of distrust and antipathy to love in all its forms. His secretary Blanche Patch says that to

> one correspondent after another he would denounce the more emotional interpretations of Christian faith. "God is love" he dismissed as "a lot of charming flapdoodle". Another inquirer is assured that "the sentimental, 'Love one another' and 'Our Father' of Jesus do not fit into a world of thinly veneered unlovable savages. To love them would be unnatural vice".[57]

Iddy says of Prola that she has "never loved anything human: why should you? Nothing human is good enough to be loved" (vol. 6, 586). Pra and Prola in many ways resemble the He- and She-Ancients from *Back to Methuselah*. Even though they seem to inspire love in the Farwaters in the third scene of the prologue, it is not sexual love. They seem to be asexual, the reverse of their children. The sex experience in the cave is a symbol for transformation; they are imbued with some of Pra and Prola's potency. When Iddy first arrives on the island he contrasts the beauty of the four children with Prola's "lovely awfulness" (vo. 6, 563). The two priests are hard and austere, symbols of discipline and power. Prola, the nearest thing to a superman in this play, realizes that she is actually an intermediary working to bring forth the superman of the future. Neither Prola nor Pra has any feelings for their children, whom they regard as failures, dispensable:

> Pra. They grew up to bore me more intensely than I have ever been bored by any other set of human creatures. Come, confess: did they not bore you?
> Prola. Have I denied it? Of course they bored me. They must have bored one another terribly in spite of all their dressing up and pretending that their fairyland was real...
> Pra. The coming race will not be like them. Meanwhile we are face to face with the fact that we two have made a precious mess of our job of producing the coming race by a mixture of east and west. We are failures. We shall disappear. (vol. 6, 609–10)

But Prola does not waste time or energy fretting and has no fear of disappearing. She is an intrepid experimenter, like her predecessor Undershaft in *Major Barbara*. In that play when Barbara is grieving over her lost faith, he brusquely tells her to "[s]crap it," as he scraps his failed experiments in the factories of death (vol. 1, 433). Prola wastes no time grieving for the children she had no love for anyway, nor worrying over whether she is herself a failure.

After the children disappear we learn from a telephone call that disappearances are being reported all over England. In this long section of exposition we learn that the "angels are weeding the garden. The useless people, the mischievous people, the selfish somebodies and the noisy nobodies" are vanishing (vol. 6, 606). Long ago Shaw had Cusins in *Major Barbara* say that he wanted to unleash his newly acquired machinery of death on the professional and intellectual classes and frighten them into using their power for the general good. Now thirty years later in *The Simpleton* it is mostly these same classes that are being expunged in England. This is a highly satirical section of the play, and we learn of the panic gripping London as the exterminating angels hit the stock exchange, the House of Commons, the House of Lords, the Mayfair district, the congregation of Westminster Abbey, a professor of mechanistic biology, almost the entire medical profession, and more than "a million persons... in the act of reading novels" (vol. 6, 605–6). Shaw is no doubt having a good time here, although he risks losing his audience as the dramatic intensity dissipates while reports are read from the papers or repeated from telephone calls. Nonetheless, it is perhaps necessary to the overall moral logic of the play. Only Pra and Prola recognize this as an advance and not a cause for alarm. For them this is about valuation and not punishment (vol. 6, 607).

Of course, this "Newest Dispensation" (vol. 6, 607) is really about awakening the old fear of hell, translating its abode to planet earth, and establishing an environment of coercion and intimidation similar to that of Soviet Russia, where commissars like Felix Dzerzhinsky "carry pistols and execute saboteurs and lazy drunkards" (vol. 6, 533). This police state is a social necessity, Prola believes, and she proclaims that if "the angels fail us we shall set up tribunals of our own from which worthless people will not come out alive" (vol. 6, 606). And indeed the rest of the group is feeling quite anxious after listening to the long list of disappeared, Hyering saying that he has an "uneasy feeling that we'd better get back to our work. I feel pretty sure that we shant disappear as long as we're doing something useful" (vol. 6, 607). Alluding to Voltaire's *Candide* (1759), Shaw has Sir Charles say to his wife that she ought to tend the garden since "gardening is the only unquestionably useful job" (vol. 6, 607). Prola declines Mrs Farwaters' offer to bring her some knitting, saying that she has some thinking to do. This seems a little risky to Mrs Farwaters, who feels far surer about gardening than thinking. But for Shaw, thinking is the highest activity, the cabinet of thinkers occupying the highest rung of the hierarchy in his blueprint utopia—like Plato's philosopher kings, the Fabians themselves, or the Central Committee of the Communist party.

The final lines in the play have Pra and Prola looking to the future. As we have seen, Shaw's conception of utopia is akin to Wells' as outlined in his novel *A Modern Utopia*. Pra and Prola are philosopher kings and committed Creative Evolutionists. In lines that should bring to mind *The Perfect Wagnerite, Man and Superman,* and *Back to Methuselah,* Pra says that he "must continue to strive for more knowledge and more power, though the new knowledge always contradicts the old, and the new power is the destruction of the fools who misuse it." Prola adds that they "shall plan common wealths... We shall make wars because only under the strain of war are we capable of changing the world." And perhaps most significantly, Prola says that she "will abide the uttermost evil and carry through it the seed of the uttermost good" (vol. 6, 610–11). This is truly a chilling line in a play about creating a utopia through the extermination of the "unworthy." And we should not forget that, although Shaw has expressed his political philosophy in a fable about Divine Judgment, his political philosopher par excellence, Prola, is quick to pronounce that if the angels prove slack in their job then they must set up tribunals themselves, "where the worthless people will not come out alive."

In October 1933, Shaw wrote the preface to his most recent play, *On the Rocks*. The preface seemed to have very little, if anything, to do with the play, although it had everything to do with the play he was about to write, *The Simpleton of the Unexpected Islands*; for the subject of the essay is the extermination of recalcitrant citizens, which, as he says in the last sentence of the first paragraph, "must be put on a scientific basis if it is ever to be carried out humanely and apologetically as well as thoroughly" (vol. 5, 479). Extermination is even more the subject of this preface than the one he later wrote for *The Simpleton*, and this was often the case with Shaw, since by the time he came to write his preface he was already preoccupied with the subject of his next play.

Yet the progression from *On the Rocks* to *The Simpleton* is logical and continuous if we consider the socio-political context in which the plays were born, as well as Shaw's psychological disposition. With a worldwide economic depression intimating capitalism's obvious failure, and with the former Fabian and Labour Government leader Ramsay MacDonald as Prime Minister, the time would seem propitious for the implementation of the socialist reforms that Shaw had been advocating for almost fifty years. But MacDonald proved a huge disappointment, and *On the Rocks*, a pessimistic play about a Prime Minister's failed attempt to bring socialism to England, was the direct dramatic result of that disappointment. Shaw had a tendency to follow up pessimistic plays with utopias (for instance, the political stalemate of *John Bull's Other Island* is followed by the hopeful *Major Barbara* while the tragicomic *Heartbreak House* is succeeded by the Bible of Creative Evolution, *Back to Methuselah*), and he looked to the brave political experiments happening outside of Britain to fortify himself against the despair he felt at home; for Shaw's well-known optimism was really an antidote to a most grievous and potentially paralyzing despair. And so he followed his grimmer plays with utopias, and saw political hope where others saw the most blatant tyranny.

The three plays considered in this chapter all deal with Shaw's utopianism as it had evolved in the 1930s under the influence of the totalitarian regimes developing in countries outside Britain. Since Shaw's entire philosophy was based on change and experiment, and all his hopes were grounded in the termination of the status quo in politics and religion, he was inclined to trust these political experiments and ignore their abuses. But at the same time he believed in destruction as inherent in creative progress, and so the destructive propensities of a character like Epifania, while perhaps personally unattractive, are essential for the clearing away of the dilapidated and the inefficient. This principle does not just apply to things and institutions, but to human beings as well. The four "useless" creatures in *The Simpleton* had the highest genetic prospects and received the most enlightened education available, yet they were failures, lazy and irresponsible, fit only for extermination. The quick and bloodless disappearances signifies Shaw's belief that dispensable lives should be terminated "humanely," using the most quick and painless scientifically proved methods available. The four emblematic characters in *The Simpleton*, in my opinion, grew beyond their initial function and came to embody all the forces of chaos that haunted Shaw; and to my mind they are the most fascinating element in the play, giving it an almost demonic or daemonic power that would be easy to lose with weak direction and poor acting. The division of the play into six worthy leaders and four useless philistine/idealists again illustrates Shaw's propensity to view human beings through a binary lens: he fails to see any good on the one side or any evil on the other, and this blind side was his ultimate failing as a man and would-be philosopher if not as a playwright.

Shaw's utopianism cannot be understood if his socialism and Creative Evolution are divorced from each other. It is sometimes maintained that Shaw's Creative Evolution developed out of a frustration with socialism's inability to materialize. Yet as we saw in *Back to Methuselah*, the socialist ordering of society was not enough; human beings must advance biologically beyond their current deplorable condition. Socialism provides a clearing of the ground so that a higher biological species may emerge. In *Bernard Shaw's Marxian Romance*, Paul Hummert correctly asserts that "*The Simpleton* dwells on the painful but necessary process of effecting a society conducive to the working out of Creative Evolution's utopian theories. As in Russia, capitalistic countries must first be purged of the causes of despair before they can prosper."[58]

Shaw was intensely interested in what was happening in the Soviet Union, Italy, and Germany, and his political plays of the thirties were written with them very much in mind. In *Geneva* the Widow tells the Commissar that in Russia she would be shot; the Commissar replies that "a Communist State is only possible for highly civilized people, trained to Communism from their childhood. The people we shoot are gangsters and speculators and exploiters and scoundrels of all sorts who are encouraged in other countries in the name of liberty and democracy" (vol. 5, 695). It is clear from this and much else that Shaw was very much taken in by the propaganda coming out of Russia, but it is also clear that someone as erudite and politically sophisticated as Shaw could not have been so easily taken in if he did not wish to be. Edmund Wilson was also a socialist, but on reading the Kamenev/Zinoviev trial transcripts saw instantly that the whole thing was a fraud.[59] Shaw spent a good part of his life analyzing bluebooks and other political documents; he clearly needed to believe not only in the USSR, but in the other totalitarian countries and dictators as well.

Shaw was continually revising *Geneva* to keep pace with the rapid changes taking place on the world stage, and by the time he wrote the final draft his two fascist dictators had failed politically and were thus condemned. Shaw never condemns Hitler and Mussolini as criminals, but as politicians who failed to live up to their potential. When Battler wants to duel Bombardone for insulting him, the Judge—the most enlightened character in the play—says that their "lives are too valuable to be risked in that way" (vol. 5, 733). This was Shaw's view. For all their mistakes Hitler and Mussolini remained great men. Shaw would never have agreed with the Lutheran pastor Dietrich Bonhoeffer, who was so convinced of the evil that Hitler was bringing on his country that he felt compelled, against his own religious principles and at the risk of his life, to attempt his assassination. In fact, Shaw believed Hitler would soon rank as a "national hero" in Germany (vol. 5, 642), and he argued, before Hitler's suicide, for his honorable treatment after the war. While Shaw did not express any indignation for the many murdered, maimed and plundered at the hands of these dictators, he did express great indignity at Mussolini's execution at the hands of the Partisans. When all is said and done, it must be admitted that Shaw admired power, saw it as existing in a realm beyond good and evil, and hoped it would work for the benefit of all.

6
George Bernard Shaw 1856–1950, Utopian to the End: *Farfetched Fables*

George Bernard Shaw died on 2 November 1950, a little over three months past his ninety-fourth birthday. His wife had died seven years before and his oldest friend and Fabian associate, Sidney Webb, three years earlier. Born in 1856 at the height of the Victorian Age, Shaw lived through the passing of the Victorian and Edwardian years, the two World Wars, the Russian Revolution, the rise of Fascism, Nazism, and Stalinism, and the implementation of the Welfare State in England. Ironically, after the implementation of the Welfare State that he had worked for all his life, Shaw became obsessed with the idea that he was being taxed into penury.[1] Nor was this his only mania. He was also obsessed with what he felt was the prodigious waste of time that accrued from using the twenty-six-letter alphabet, and was assiduous in his campaign to have it replaced by a phonetic alphabet of at least forty letters: "He calculated that, in writing and printing superfluous letters, our 'ancient Phoenician alphabet' cost us the price of a fleet of battleships every year."[2] At his death his Will provided a significant portion of his income to the establishment of a fund to create a new English alphabet along with the translation of a number of literary classics, including two plays of his own, to demonstrate its effectiveness. Additionally, the ideas that had preoccupied him for at least half a century—particularly the theory of Creative Evolution and the movement of the species toward omniscience and omnipotence—remained unaltered by the recent disaster of the war.

The persistence of Shaw's utopian thinking and the fixation of certain ideas that have been explored in this study can be ascertained by a close look at his last completed play, *Farfetched Fables* (1950). This short play, by Shavian standards, is a sort of reworking of *Back to Methuselah*. But instead of a cycle of five plays it consists of six loosely interconnected "fables," which, like the earlier play, extend in time far into the future. Thus this final major play of Shaw's is, like *Back to Methuselah* and *The Simpleton of the Unexpected Isles*, a species of the utopian genre. Most of the themes of *Back to Methuselah* are found in *Farfetched Fables*, except where in the earlier play human beings are evolving toward a bodiless existence, in the latter certain exceptional beings—supermen— have actually attained the coveted incorporeality, subsisting on nothing but air and not visible to the rest of the human race. In the world of corporeal beings an orderly society has finally been established, undesirable citizens are exterminated, and the way is clear for evolution to proceed rapidly and smoothly. Written right after the greatest crime of the century, the Nazi Holocaust, had been exposed and while reports of the other great crime of the century, the Gulag system, were increasingly trickling out of the Soviet Union, Shaw's play, like the earlier one, hovers very near unintentional dystopia, but demonstrates even greater unawareness of very specific moral threats that were imperiling civilization.

The play begins shortly after the end of the Second World War, and starts with a discussion of the realities of atomic and chemical warfare. An avaricious and unscrupulous young chemist realizes during the course of a discussion that the wave of the future is in poison gas, not atomic bombs, which he believes are too destructive to be used again; he therefore rushes off to invent a poison gas that is lighter than air and that will thus kill people but leave the material environment otherwise untouched.

In the second fable we learn that his own government took him for a crackpot and refused to purchase his product, so he sold it instead to the South African government, who then tested it on the Isle of Wight—where the young man had gone to live because he assumed it to be the safest place on the planet. This second fable ends with the gas being dropped on London and killing the two characters of the fable, the Commander-in-Chief and the Foreign Secretary, who had been engaged in a discussion about the gas. Thus, like the second play of the *Methuselah* cycle, "The Gospel of the Brothers Barnabus," these first two short fables center around the recent World War and its aftermath.

Shaw does not give exact dates as he does in *Back to Methuselah*, but the third fable corresponds to the third play of the cycle, "The Thing Happens," in that it is clearly in the future, but near enough in time to still appear recognizable. Like the earlier play, socialism appears to have been established, but in this case no evolutionary change is yet discernable (in "The Thing Happens" a small number of long-livers have begun to appear).

Shaw's intense need for exact measurement and scientific certainty is demonstrated by the implementation of an instrument he had long expressed the need for: an anthropometric device to measure the exact capacities of human beings. This idea is first mentioned by Shaw in the "Maxims for Revolutionists" section of *The Revolutionist's Handbook*, where Shaw (as Tanner) writes that "Government presents only one problem: the discovery of a trustworthy anthropometric method" (vol. 3, 732). The idea appears regularly after that, and is given dramatic presence in this final utopia, where the third fable opens in front of the Anthropometric Laboratory, where three employees are confronted by two characters: a nincompoop who thinks he is a genius and a genius who thinks he is a nincompoop. The location is the Isle of Wight, and we learn that it is "a colony of the Upper Ten" (vol. 6, 499).

Shaw believed that nature produced at any given time a small class, from five to ten percent of the population, capable of directing affairs; thus this colony is for the directors: "Neither Mediocrities nor Anybodies are admitted" (vol. 6, 499). Status is systematically tested at the Anthropometric Laboratory, and there are levels within grades; for instance you can classify as a Mediocrity with honors! (vol. 6, 499). The three characters do "[a]nthropometric work... [c]lassifying men and women according to their abilities" (vol. 6, 500). One of the employees threatens the genius, identified as The Tramp, because he appears in rags and prefers not to work, with arrest, where he will be

> put through the laboratory and classified. That is the law, compulsory for everybody. If you refuse you may be classed as irresponsible. That means that youll be enlisted in the military police or kept under tutelage in a Labor Brigade. Or you may be classed as dangerous and incorrigible, in which case youll be liquidated.
>
> (vol. 6, 501–2)

This corresponds precisely to Shaw's views, which were expressed in some detail in a letter to *The Times* from around the time of the composition of the play: "Had not the ambiguous and confusing terms capital punishment and death penalty better be dropped? The public right and power of civilized States to kill *the unprofitable* or incorrigibly mischievous in self-defense can never be abrogated."[3] He goes on to say that "judicial liquidation" would be the preferable term: "Criminals should be liquidated humanely, not because they are wicked, but because they are mischievous or dangerous."[4] In the printed postcards he had on hand for letters that came to him seeking his views on capital punishment, which he apparently received enough of to warrant printing out a standard reply, he wrote that when we kill a tiger or a cobra it is not to punish it but to prevent its killing us: "Precisely the same necessity arises in the case of incorrigibly dangerous or mischievous human beings, sane or insane, hopeless idiots, or enemy soldiers."[5] He also recommended, like the character from *Farfetched Fables* quoted above, the need to put some people "under tutelage" who are hopeless otherwise but "well behaved and useful" when placed in a position comparable to that of children under a responsible parent.[6]

The fourth fable consists of one character, the Commissioner of Diets, reciting into a dictaphone (which, incidentally, is an example of the efficiency wrought by technology; the time consumed writing things down is obviated by the dictaphone). The chapter of the book he is dictating is called "Living on Air," and is basically a survey of the twentieth century's move away from animal consumption and its substitution first by vegetables, fruit, and grains and then by air and water:

> The British themselves, influenced by a prophet whose name has come down to us in various forms as Shelley, Shakespear, and Shavius, had already, after some centuries of restricted cannibalism in which only fishes, frogs, birds, sheep, cows, pigs, rabbits, and whales were eaten, been gradually persuaded to abstain from these also, and to live on plants and fruits, and even on grass, honey, and nuts: a diet which they called vegetarian. Full stop. New paragraph. Ahem!
> (vol. 6, 504)

The Commissioner goes on to demonstrate that vegetarians were actually more robust and active than meat eaters, contrary to an old superstition that believed the opposite, and were actually "restless, pugnacious, and savagely abusive in their continual controversies with the remaining meat eaters" (vol. 6, 505). But the greatest benefit of the change in diet has been the elimination of the massive waste of labor in breeding animals for human consumption. This would confirm Blanche Patch's statement that Shaw was chiefly a vegetarian because the waste involved in maintaining animals offended his sense of economy.[7]

The Commissioner goes on to announce that the ablest biologists of that benighted age had affirmed that ultimately everything human beings consumed was poisonous, and cites a Russian female pioneer who had contended that one diet had not yet been tried: air and water. Since it has been proved that there is no such thing as nothing, it follows that air is something, and consequently may prove a viable source of sustenance. And indeed the Russian woman attests that she has herself for months lived on only air and water, just as saints and mystics who had undergone prolonged fasts: "This briefly is the history of the epoch-making change in social organization produced by the ending of the food problem which had through all recorded history made men the slaves of nature." Instead the appetite for food and drink has been replaced by "a search for knowledge of nature and power over it, and a desire for truth and righteousness. The supergorilla became the soldier and servant of Creative Evolution. Full stop. Postscript" (vol. 6, 506). The last paragraph tells us that this is a primer on rudimentary biology for infants, now in its tenth edition. The Commissioner orders two hundred million copies.

The setting stays the same throughout the play, with new characters in each scene (in the fourth fable only one) engaged in discussion on a terrace in front of the same façade, yet in each scene the designation of the building changes. In the penultimate fable the sign changes from "Diet Commissioners" to "Genetic Institute." In this scene the history of the human race is also discussed, this time by a group of scholars (or at least inquisitive creatures) who are appalled at the idiocy of their forebears. There are four characters—two men, a woman, and a hermaphrodite—and each wears a uniform which designates their sex. We learn that sexual reproduction as we know it has been eliminated, and now occurs in a laboratory. In the last part of *Back to Methuselah* human beings had evolved into oviparous creatures, and here we find that reproduction is done by scientists using chemical salts and whose job it is to experiment. The characters in this scene are disgusted by the fact that to "initiate births they [their forebears] had to practice personal contacts which I would rather not describe. Strangest of all, they seem to have experienced in such contacts the ecstasies which are normal with us in our pursuit of knowledge and power" (vol. 6, 508–9). We also learn that they share Shaw's antipathy for the non-phonetic alphabet—"[t]hey had not brains enough to make an alphabet capable of spelling their language" (vol. 6, 507)—and that they mistake Hitler for Jesus in their discussion of the death of a prophet who drove the money changers out of the temple and was killed by the authorities. The Hermaphrodite is revolted by the body and says that all their experimentation is worthless if it does not ultimately do away with the body altogether: "I tell you again and again we shall never make decent human beings out of chemical salts. We must get rid of our physical bodies altogether...I dont want to be a body: I want to be a mind and nothing but a mind" (vol. 6, 510). The Hermaphrodite alludes to Shaw (or the ancients from his *Back to Methuselah*) as an example of correct aspiration when he/she adds: "Even in the dark ages of the nineteenth and twentieth centuries there was a man who aspired to be a vortex in thought" (vol. 6, 510). Thus this fourth fable is a discussion held by evolved human beings from the future invested with some of Shaw's ideas and repulsions, and ends with the woman declaring that the "pursuit of knowledge and power will never end" (vol. 6, 511).

The final fable takes place on the terrace in front of a school and involves a Socratic dialogue between five students of different ages (distinguished, as in part four of *Back to Methuselah*, by numbers on caps) although all have passed into the sixth form. These six characters are a throw-back to the types of beings who lived in the twentieth century; they represent no biological advance, and so initially seem to disrupt the theme of evolutionary advance that we have seen from fable to fable. But we learn that there is a theory current in this society that a race of higher beings has evolved— the Disembodies Races or Thought Vortexes—who, it is believed, inspire the embodied creatures by "penetrating our thick skulls in their continual pursuit of knowledge and power, since they need our hands and brains as tools in that pursuit" (vol. 6, 517).

Youth 3, in answer to Youth 1's analogy that they are like black beetles to the supermen, says, "If we were black beetles, the supermen would have tramped on us and killed us, or poisoned us with phosphorus" (vol. 6, 516). But these super beings are not wantonly destructive; they serve Creative Evolution and are destructive only in their pursuit of increased power. Thus, according to this theory, the race of supermen that has evolved is in the precise position of Shaw's theory of God, and his view of creative destruction remains intact, for these super beings inspire to violence as well as to creativity: "for the pursuit of knowledge and power involves the slaughter and destruction of everything that opposes it" (vol. 6, 517). The Teacher elaborates, expounding that even

> the vortexes have to do their work by trial and error. They have to learn by mistakes as well as successes. We have to destroy the locust and the hook worm and the Colorado beetle because, if we did not, they would destroy us. We have to execute criminals who have no conscience and are incorrigible. They are old experiments of the Life Force. They were well intentioned and perhaps necessary

at the time. But they are no longer either useful or necessary, and must now be exterminated. They cannot be exterminated by disembodied thought. The mongoose must be inspired to kill the cobra, the chemist to distill poisons, the physicist to make nuclear bombs, others to be big game hunters, judges, executioners, and killers of all sorts, often the most amiable of mortals outside their specific functions as destroyers of vermin. The ruthless foxhunter loves dogs: the physicists and chemists adore their children and keep animals as pets.

(vol. 6, 517–18)

What is most remarkable about all this is that it was written shortly after the Second World War, and the allusion to amiable chemists creating poison gas by day and going home in the evenings to their loving families is positively chilling. The stunning revelations about Nazi death camps seem to have made no impression on Shaw, nor to have altered his belief in the importance of state liquidation of public enemies in the least. These benevolent killers are inspired by a higher power, the Teacher declares, acting at the behest of the Life Force. She goes on to remind her students of "those children of ours who cannot get beyond the First Form, and grow up to be idiots or savages. We kill them. But we are ourselves a throw-back to the twentieth century, and may be killed as idiots and savages if we meet a later and higher civilization" (vol. 6, 518).

The fable, and the play, ends with the spectacular appearance of one of these Disembodied Thoughts incarnating, whose remarkable entrance is reminiscent of the exterminating Angel in *The Simpleton of the Unexpected Isles*, as he is, like that character, a feathered creature and something of a comedian. He announces himself as an embodied thought, "what you call the word made flesh," and says that they should call him Raphael, as that would be most respectful (vol. 6, 519). Raphael is also reminiscent of the oracle in the fourth part of *Back to Methuselah*, "Tragedy of an Elderly Gentleman" (and also the super beings in Bulwer-Lytton's novel *The Coming Race* that so influenced Shaw) in that he has magnetic power capable of instantly killing these lesser beings. He tells Youth 3, who is saucy with him, that he had better be more respectful for: "I am restraining my magnetic field. If I turned it on it would kill you" (vol. 6. 520). Raphael explains that his intense intellectual curiosity has induced him to incarnate, but, as he says, "I stop short of your eating and drinking and so forth, and of your reproductive methods. They revolt me" (vol. 6, 520). One of the students comments on his apparent lack of passion and Raphael counters, "On the contrary: intellectual passion, mathematical passion, passion for discovery and exploration: the mightiest of all the passions" are his (vol. 6, 520). Thus *Farfetched Fables* demonstrates continual evolutionary advance, and the intensely curious laboratory creations of fable five, who are, like Raphael, revolted by sex and long to be bodiless, have evolved into the supermen of this last fable: bodiless, living on air, lethal, still intensely curious, and capable of intellectual ecstasy.

Before Raphael's appearance one of the students expresses skepticism regarding the possibility of these super creatures, protesting that it is not possible to get rid of the body; but the Teacher corrects him, demonstrating that all through evolution animals have gotten rid of their bodies: their tails, their fur, their teeth: "They acquired thumbs and enlarged their brains. They seem to have done what they liked with their bodies" (vol. 6, 516). Like *Back to Methuselah*, the play asserts and dramatizes a Lamarckian position, where evolutionary change is predicated on a deep desire or need for change: a will to change, or a will to greater power, the body being the ultimate impediment to absolute or near absolute power. In fact the similarities of *Farfetched Fables* to *Back to Methuselah*—similarities in structure, theme, and didactic intent—do not stop at the play, but extend to the preface as well, where Shaw asserts, just as he did in the preface to *Back to Methuselah*, that religions and creeds need fables, legends, and myths as well as logical argument to impress the minds of those more influenced by a good story than by abstract doctrine. We would therefore be justified in supposing that *Farfetched Fables* is meant to be a part of the "Bible of Creative Evolution," just as the earlier play was.

But this brings us to an interesting question. In the preface to *Farfetched Fables* Shaw claims that he, "as a Creative Evolutionist, postulate[s] a creative Life Force or Evolutionary Appetite seeking power over circumstances and mental development by the method of Trial and Error, making mistake after mistake, but still winning its finally irresistible way" (vol. 6, 466). I do not think there can be any question regarding Shaw's sincerity as a Creative Evolutionist, which he first professed almost fifty years earlier in *Man and Superman*, although the theory is inchoate in *The Perfect Wagnerite*.

Yet Shaw spends a good deal of the preface discussing another important element of his doctrine, the Noble Lie, first given expression by Plato in the *Republic*. Shaw had espoused the necessity of deceiving the masses in the interest of order as early as 1898 in *The Perfect Wagnerite*. Shaw's view is that the "masses are governable only by a mixture of cajolery and coercion dressed up in fine phrases, and applied by an energetic minority which knows what it wants and means to have it."[8] This is from an article Shaw wrote in April 1919 for the *Labour Leader* titled "Are We Bolshevists?" and addressed to his fellow socialists in England; it was meant to inspire support for the Bolsheviks in Russia, who were then engaged in a violent struggle for power. In the quote above Shaw is alluding to the Bolshevik elite, especially Lenin, whom he greatly admired and believed used cajolery and coercion in the interests of the people while the capitalist governments used cajolery and coercion in the interests of property. In the preface to *Farfetched Fables* Shaw discusses the need to lie to the masses in the section titled "MENDACITY COMPULSORY IN KINGCRAFT AND PRIESTCRAFT." He quotes Ferdinand LaSalle as saying that "'The lie...is a European power.' He might, however, have added that it is none the worse when it does its necessary job" (vol. 6, 462).

Later in the essay Shaw says that "all the established religions in the world are deeply corrupted by the necessity for adapting their original inspired philosophic creeds to the narrow intelligences of illiterate peasants and of children" (vol. 6, 466–67). I think it is fair to say that Creative Evolution, as expressed in *Back to Methuselah* and *Farfetched Fables*, is not in the category of the necessary lie, but a genuine attempt at the sophisticated dramatization of a doctrine that Shaw *both* genuinely believed in *and* felt was necessary, whether true or not, in a world that had lost its religious foundation. In fact, he says toward the end of the long preface to *Back to Methuselah* that

> civilization needs a religion as a matter of life or death; and as the conception of Creative Evolution developed I saw that we were at last within reach of a faith that complied with the first condition of all the religions that have ever taken hold of humanity: namely, that it must be, first and fundamentally, a science of metabiology.
>
> (vol. 2, lxxxvii–lxxxviii)

Nonetheless, in the "Postscript After Twenty-five Years" he avers that "Creative Evolution, though the best we can devize so far, is basically as hypothetical and provisional as any of the creeds" (vol. 2, cv). It seems that Creative Evolution was, like Stalin and the Soviet Union, an ideal that he desperately needed to believe in to survive, although that would go directly against his theory of the fearless realist who shuns ideals, elaborated in *The Quintessence of Ibsenism*. The masses may need to be fed lies, but it appears that so did Bernard Shaw.

The last section of the preface to *Farfetched Fables* is titled "THE THREATENING FUTURE: HOMILIES NO USE." Here he lambasts the "well-intentioned Utopian amateurs who infest our parliaments and parties" (vol. 6, 489). This is apparently directed at ineffectual Christians and Utilitarians, as he says that they "might as well decree that we shall do unto others as we would have them do to us, or achieve the greatest good for the greatest number, or soothe our souls with exhortations to love one another. Homilies cut no ice in administrative councils" (vol. 6, 489). He goes on, by extrapolation, to disavow not only the play that the essay prefaces, but his entire career as a revolutionary playwright, as he continues, saying that

> the literary talent and pulpit eloquence that has always been calling for a better world has never succeeded, though it has stolen credit for many changes forced on it by circumstances and natural selection. The satirical humor of Aristophanes, the wisecracks of Confucius, the precepts of the Buddha, the parables of Jesus, the theses of Luther, the *jeux d'esprit* of Erasmus and Montaigne, the Utopias of More and Fourier and Wells, the allegories of Voltaire, Rousseau, and Bunyan, the polemics of Leibniz and Spinoza, the poems of Goethe, Shelley, and Byron, the manifesto of Marx and Engels, Mozart's Magic Flute and Beethoven's Ode to Joy, with the music dramas of Wagner, to say nothing of living seers of visions and dreamers of dreams: none of these esthetic feats have made Reformations or Revolutions.
>
> (vol. 6, 489–90)

Although Shaw carries on with his literary work, expressing his vision of evolution and hopes for the future, it seems the nonagenarian had given up any hope of his work making a difference in the world. The one sure course of action "required"—demonstrated by Stalin and his elite cabinet, volubly lauded in the preface—"above all, was boundless daring, cruelty in removing obstacles, and tenacity in seizing power."[9]

Perhaps no author of the twentieth century has caused as much confusion as Bernard Shaw. He has a contingent of followers—academics, playgoers, and general readers—many of whom, it would seem, think he should have been awarded a second Nobel Prize, for peace as well as for literature. Shaw's pronouncements are so various and often contradictory that it can be difficult to sort out just who the real Bernard Shaw was. First of all, it is important to be clear about who Shaw believed himself to be, and what his ultimate intensions were. Shaw saw himself as a modern-day Socrates, shattering mindless conventions and ideals, provoking his contemporaries to actually think about the positions they held; he wanted them to recognize that their positions, ideals, and conventions were most often determined by self-interest, self-importance, and laziness. In this he was remarkably successful and deserves our thanks. Like Socrates he wanted to challenge complacency, especially in religious matters; and he often remarked that it was only through his cleverness—his ability to mask how incredibly revolutionary his suggestions actually were by assuming the role of the fool—that he was saved from the fate of Socrates and other sages and prophets who met a bad end. But Shaw not only modeled himself on Plato's leading character; he also modeled his dramaturgy on the Platonic dialogue, and it might be said that Plato influenced him as much as or more than any other playwright.[10]

Plato's influence was equally powerful in the realm of politics; and the notion of designing an ideal society, a utopia, was central to Shaw's life's work; he really did believe he had devised the blueprint for a more or less perfectly ordered society, and devoted his entire life to its implementation. He remarked in an address aired on the BBC in 1937 that Britain could avoid the war that seemed imminent

> by putting our house in order as Russia had done, without any of the killing and waste and damage that the Russians went through. But we don't seem to want to. I have shown *exactly* how it can be done, and in fact how it must be done, but nobody takes any notice.[11]

Fabian Socialism, in fact, Shaw believed, would be a more accurate description of the system then practiced in the Soviet Union. In his critique of Plato, Karl Popper comes to the conclusion that the philosopher king of his ideal state is actually a surrogate for Plato's own quest for power: "He was reaching for the stars—for god-likeness... [W]e must face the fact that behind the sovereignty of the philosopher king stands the quest for power."[12] Popper goes on to say, in words that I think can be applied to Shaw, that

> Plato, with all his uncompromising canvas-cleaning, was led along a path on which he compromised his integrity with every step he took. He was forced to combat free-thought, and the pursuit of truth. He was led to defend lying, political miracles, tabooistic superstition, the suppression of truth, and ultimately, brutal violence.[13]

Shaw's own quest for power, and his defiance of the Western democratic system and its chaotic economic system, led him along a similar path; although like Plato, despite Popper's brilliant analysis, Shaw still remains a symbol of humanitarianism and integrity.

Shaw often referred to himself as a mystic, and has been so described by others as well, but he really had very little of the mystic's awe of the mysterious. To my mind, Meister Eckhart and the anonymous author of *The Cloud of Unknowing* were mystics, and Shaw has very little in common with them. His energy was directed to greater power and identification with those who had great power and whom he felt used it boldly and wisely. He viewed the human race and the material environment as ultimately knowable and manipulable, and thought that logical analysis and scientific planning could be brought to bear on all aspects of human lives and institutions. This required a small class of directors, a cabinet of thinkers, who were exempt from all laws and regulations: a self-governing elite who were, like Shaw himself, guided by their interest in ordering society for the good of all. This was Shaw's great blind spot; he believed to the end of his life that the Politburo was an altruistic body carefully structured to eliminate members in the rare instances when their actions or intentions deviated from the public good. Human civilization's survival, he believed, depended on the implementation of just such a system in England and elsewhere—a system which had, he maintained, greatly profited from Fabian doctrine. He remarked in one of his last essays that he was happy to have "lived to see the gigantic Russian experiment completely converted to Fabianism by sheer force of experience under Lenin and Stalin."[14]

Basically, there were three key points to his scheme: equal incomes, a new religion to be taught from youth up, and the liquidation of any and all impediments to the advancing evolution of the human race. All of this had been adopted in Russia more or less, with the exception of his equal incomes doctrine, which he later revised in light of Soviet reality. As originally stated, every man, woman, and child was to be guaranteed a basic income by the state, regardless of what he or she did. The problem of how to make people work when they already received an income was solved by the threat of liquidation: all shirkers were to be efficiently, quickly, and painlessly exterminated. As Prola suggests in *The Simpleton of the Unexpected Isles*, tribunals would be set up to determine whether people were pulling their weight or not:

> Theoretically, since there are no indifferent actions, there is for every man a rigid line of conduct from which he cannot swerve one hair's breadth in the minutest detail without injury to the community; and if the community could ascertain that line it would be justified in compelling him to keep to that line, to the entire abolition of his "freedom".[15]

This would solve what Shaw considered the central problem of human civilization: people consuming more than they were producing. As mentioned, Shaw later revised his equal incomes doctrine; when he learned that Soviet elites were earning ten times what their lower-ranking comrades were earning, he calculated that it was alright if the "minority of cultural snobs and genuinely scientific Socialist tacticians" were bringing home eleven times the pay of everyone else.[16] This did not matter, Shaw retorted to his critics, since what mattered was that poverty was eliminated by raising the incomes of everybody else; when that was accomplished it did not matter if a small minority had a bit more cash to spend. He emphasized that he had never been dogmatic about exactly equal incomes. And we can see this in a play like *Major Barbara*, where the elite live in greater style, but the workers at Perivale St. Andrews have had their living standards significantly elevated.

Major Barbara is a good play to examine the other points in Shaw's doctrine as well, even though it was written well before the Russian Revolution. Shaw believed that the Soviet Union had a viable religion, which their children were absorbing from their earliest years, and in *Major Barbara* we see Barbara leaving the Salvation Army to take a position in her father's firm indoctrinating the workers; and in fact her father had already established, even before he had recruited Barbara, a "William Morris Labor Church" (vol. 1, 425). And we have an intimation of the extermination of the parasites holding back the advance of civilization in Cusins' passionate determination to employ the machinery of death now at his disposal to just such a purpose. In fact, many of Shaw's plays will make a lot more sense once the reader or viewer is more familiar with their author's ultimate aim of transforming society, his goal of creating a world already anticipated by Edward Bellamy in his novel *Looking Backward* in 1888 and actually brought to fruition by Lenin and Stalin in Russia during the 1920s and 1930s.

Shaw had logical reasons for all his doctrines. Everything was designed to aid Creative Evolution. Shaw never abandoned his eugenic program, but he realized the best, perhaps the only way to advance the species eugenically was to allow everyone to marry whomever they desired, regardless of class. The Life Force should dictate pairing, not social snobbery or financial need. At present marriage partners are selected by class; no man of the upper classes will marry his char woman regardless of her personal attraction to him, but when incomes are equalized the impediment is removed. Yet Shaw rarely dramatizes in his plays marriages from disparate classes; in *Major Barbara* Cusins and Barbara seem in some regards to be worlds apart, as he is a classical scholar and she is a Christian missionary in the Salvation Army, but they are both well-educated upper-middle-class individuals. While, regarding the working classes, Shaw felt that "*complete State regulation of their lives and thoughts*"[17] was imperative, he must have believed that once poverty was eradicated some members of the lower classes would, as in classical Marxism, find time in their leisure moments to engage in cultural pursuits. Of course the reality is that real life "utopias" never match their blueprint, and in fact rapidly become dystopic nightmares.

Shaw wrote one other play in the 1940s with a political and philosophical theme. *Buoyant Billions* (1948) has a number of features that have by now become familiar to readers of this book, including a character who describes himself as aspiring to "Marx's profession. Lenin's profession. Stalin's profession. Ruskin's profession. Plato's profession. Confucius, Gautama, Jesus, Mahomet, Luther, William Morris. The profession of world betterer" (vol. 1, 754). "World betterer" was the appellation that Shaw ascribed to himself. In *Buoyant Billions* this character intends to rid the world of poverty because living in a world of indigent people is hell to him, and there is no avoiding the wretched many for "[t]he streets are full of them" (vol. 1, 755). As with Undershaft, it is difficult to avoid the impression that it is the offense to his aesthetic sensibility and his general sense of fear rather than actual compassion that motivates him. He is an optimist, like his creator, believing that ultimately atomic power will be used to rid the world of pests—"anopheles mosquito, the tsetse fly, the white ant, and the locust" (vol. 1, 760)—while significantly reducing the labor of humankind; and he complains that he has "no talent for anything but preaching and propaganda. I am a missionary without an endowed established Church" (vol. 1, 760). The play also shows the Life Force bringing together an unlikely pair, engaged to be married at the play's end, and reminiscent of Tanner and Ann Whitefield, Barbara and Cusins, Epifania Ognisanti di Pererga and her Egyptian Doctor.

But perhaps most interesting of all is the mathematician whose greatest passion is for precise measurement, and who in some ways resembles Shaw's creatures from the future as we see them in *Back to Methuselah* and *Farfetched Fables*. Secondborn, as he is called, in the last speech of the play announces that "Mathematic perception is the noblest of all the faculties!" "God is not Love," he expostulates; "Love is not enough: the appetite for more truth, more knowledge, for measurement and precision, is far more universal... Mathematical passion alone has no reaction: our pleasure in it promises a development in which life will be an intellectual ecstasy surpassing the ecstasies of saints" (vol. 1, 803–4). Here we see again the impulse behind Shaw's incessant call for an anthropometric device to accurately measure human beings. This was more than just rhetoric for Shaw, as he tried to establish just such an institutional panel, but when "challenged to produce an anthropometric machine or endocrine or phrenological tests as a means of selection of the right people, he had been forced to admit that no satisfactory ones had been invented."[18] In *Back to Methuselah* his ancients are biologically equipped to accurately measure the capacity and potential of all creatures at birth, and without fuss exterminate those who fail their examination. Shaw's despair at precisely measuring human beings and his thwarted desire for control in governmental selection is felt in both his complaint that such a device had not yet been invented and in his solving of the problem in some of his plays.

Chesterton said in one of his famous debates with Shaw that it "is easy enough to say Property should be distributed, but who is, as it were, the subject of the verb? Who or what is to distribute? Now it is based on the idea that the central power which condescends to distribute will be permanently just, wise, sane," and "[t]hat is what we doubt."[19] Chesterton rightly points out that this central power is likely to become a tyranny. And that is the crux of the problem; Shaw had absolute faith in what he called in *The Quintessence of Ibsenism* the world will, and what he would call later the Life Force. In that same debate with Chesterton he advised his listeners in the audience to take note where otherwise disparate individuals are saying the same thing, because this would then likely indicate that it was the Life Force working through them. The very fact that totalitarian governments sprang up all over Europe at about the same time intimated to Shaw that this was the fruits of Creative Evolution, the Life Force moving the human race forward.

Disorder was pervasive in the twentieth century—especially in the years between the two World Wars—and it took autocrats of strong will to "weed the garden," as Shaw frequently put it. He himself possessed formidable control—had weeded the garden of his own soul, so to speak—and he looked for rulers who would do the same on a larger scale, not knowing to what depths of hell these rulers would lead the world and refusing to believe it when it was later pointed out to him: "The darker the subject, the more light-hearted grew his tone," Michael Holroyd remarked about Shaw's attitude to Hitler and the concentration camps.[20] In *Buoyant Billion* the father tells his world-bettering son: "Power corrupts; it does not ennoble." His son replies that it "does if it is big enough. It is petty power that corrupts petty men. Almighty power will change the world" (vol. 1, 759). It is ultimately a Hegelian position, and can apparently justify anything on the playing field of History as the Will of Spirit working dialectically toward the glorious future.[21]

Very few would deny that Shaw was an indefatigable crusader for a better world. But crusades have rarely inaugurated the Millennium they promised. One of Shaw's "Maxims for Revolutionists" states that "Hell is paved with good intentions, not with bad ones. All men mean well" (vol. 3, 740). This is a Socratic view; it is only ignorance of the good that impedes its flowering. Shaw had good intentions, but was ignorant of the good himself and blind to the destruction of human values all around him: he gave his support to radical evil, and that was his tragedy, as it is ours.

Epilogue

In 1896, the prescient Russian short story writer and playwright Anton Chekhov published a story called, in its English translation, "The House with the Mezzanine." Chekhov took a highly critical attitude toward one of the central characters, and critics in his day were perplexed because this character, Leda, devotes her life to the cause of improving the lives of the poor. How could Chekhov disapprove of such a laudable person? Despite Leda's energetic altruism, the truth is she is cold, severe, controlling, manipulative, intimidating, intransigent, and, worst of all, in her spite destroys her sister's budding love. So in the end all of her fine works are discredited. Her charity does not grow out of compassion for the poor, but out of fanatical zeal to a blueprint utopia. Gary Saul Morson writes that in Chekhov's time the intelligentsia "were expected to adopt one or another grand system of thought that purported to explain all of culture and society and promised an end of all human suffering... the function of the *intelligentsia* was to adopt the right system and make sure that its recommendations were put into practice."[1] Chekhov was highly suspicious of the kind of zealous righteousness that would soon turn soviet Russia into more of a prison than tsarist Russia.

Few writers have Chekov's humane perspicacity, of course, and many besides Shaw fell under the sway of tyrannical regimes and dictators in the years after the First World War—so much so that to make a comparative study would require another book. Yet while my intention throughout has been to keep the focus on Shaw, I think it is necessary before closing to say a few words about some of his contemporaries. Much has been written about the fascist leanings of Wyndham Lewis, T.S. Eliot, W.B. Yeats, Ezra Pound, and others, and the list of Stalinists is even longer. Yet Shaw was unique in that he championed both sides of the ideological divide. Stalin and Hitler and their regimes were much closer than is usually thought, as has already been remarked, and research has shown that Stalin's anti-fascist efforts in the thirties were merely cosmetic, that Stalin admired Hitler and was actively working toward an alliance with him well before the actual Soviet-German Non-aggression Pact of 1939: "The Popular Front proposed an antifascist alliance that Stalin had no intention of joining. He preferred—he had always preferred—an alliance with Hitler."[2] Stalin never dreamed Hitler would be foolish enough to attack Russia, and was initially only worried about the European democracies. The Popular Front was a smokescreen masking Stalin's true intention of inciting war between Germany and the West.[3]

The level of control the Comintern had over Western intellectuals is astounding, and was so pervasive that artists were sometimes married to or sexually involved with Soviet spies. Romain Rolland, for instance, was married to Maria Pavlova Koudachova, "an agent directly under Soviet secret service control," while H.G. Wells was involved with Baroness Moura Budberg, also a Soviet agent; the Soviet spy Ella Winter was married to Lincoln Steffens and when he died in 1936 she married Hollywood screenwriter Donald Ogden Stewart.[4] But despite the expert manipulation and brilliant propaganda, many artists and intellectuals turned against the regime when they learned what was going on there—such as, for instance, Arthur Koestler and John Dos Passos. And Andre Gide, at first an enthusiast, wrote a scathing indictment of the entire Soviet system called *Retour de l'U.R.S.S.* after his 1936 visit to the USSR, while in 1938 Andre Breton wrote a manifesto with Stalin's arch-rival Trotsky that condemned Stalin and the repression in the Soviet Union. Gide and Koestler were two of six contributors to the 1949 book *The God that Failed*, each of whom details their abandonment of Stalin and Russian Communism. Nevertheless, many intellectuals besides Shaw remained steadfast Stalinists.

The atmosphere in France among the intelligentsia after the war was not dissimilar to that in Russia during the time of Chekhov, and the pressure to conform to a Stalinist or pro Soviet position was strong, despite revelations of the gulags. David Rousset was arrested in France by the Nazis in 1942 and sent to Buchenwald. After release he published two books, *The Other Kingdom* in 1946 and a fictional work, *Les Jours de notre mort* (The days of our death), in 1947: "These two works brought into the French language a new adjective, *concentrationnaire*, to describe the camp regime, but they also forged an image of what deportation had been like for political prisoners that remained dominant in France for many years."[5] In 1949, the same year that *The God that Failed* was published, Rousset made an appeal to camp survivors to come forward and participate in an investigation of extant concentration camps, including those in the Soviet Union. Although he won the support of many ex-deportees, "Rousset came under immediate and violent attack."[6] He lost many of his former friends, and in January 1950 Sartre and Merleau-Ponty published *Les Jours de notre vie* (The days of our life) in *Les Temps Modernes*,

> by which they broke off all relations with their comrade. "The truth is that experience, even of something as absolute as the horror of the concentration camps, cannot determine a political position," they wrote, so as to justify their refusal to condemn the Soviet Union—thereby providing us with a striking example of the political irresponsibility that was characteristic of French intellectuals of the period.[7]

But France was not so unique in this regard.

While some might find it odd that Shaw was pro-fascist and pro-Communist (and consider this oddity a reason to believe he was merely jeering the British establishment when he applauded Mussolini and Hitler), I hope this study has made it clear that Shaw had very high hopes for all three regimes—Soviet Communism, Italian Fascism, and German National Socialism—believing them to be, or at least hoping they would be, a positive step on the road to utopia. Stalin's Russia was a near facsimile of the Fabian model state, and the fascist regimes as well, he believed, were a species of political modernism, that is, progressive post-Capitalist states. Shaw was a highly sophisticated political thinker and nothing like Ezra Pound, who believed that there was a Jewish conspiracy of international bankers. The fascist-leaning literary artists in the years between the wars require rigorous analysis and detailed historical contextualization, as I hope I have given Shaw, but some are less ambiguous and more consistent than others in their fascist predilections, such as Pound, who was an enthusiastic supporter of fascism to the end. Wyndham Lewis, on the other hand, recanted from the views expressed in his 1931 book *Hitler* when he got a better idea of what Hitlerism entailed, publishing the pro-Jewish anti-Nazi book *The Hitler Cult* in 1939. But further study is needed; even a seemingly clear-cut case like Knut Hamsun in Norway requires careful scrutiny before judgment is pronounced.

But while many of the fascist-leaning literary artists had a propensity to look longingly back to the pre-industrial past, Shaw never did. He hated the past and would feel no remorse over its complete obliteration. It is true that fascism frequently appealed to "traditional values," but this was mostly for public relations purposes, a way to attract the lower middle classes. Where it was antipathetic to modernity, it was for just those elements that Shaw himself distrusted: liberalism, parliamentary democracy. Fascism was a modernist phenomenon, and Shaw was a cultural and political modernist if not a literary one—although Lawrence Switzky has persuasively argued for loosening up the boundaries of categorization and "recuperating Shaw within the short-lived prewar British avant-garde," which "might help to redefine modernism more expansively."[8] He describes Shaw as a "proto-futurist" who was rejected by the Vorticists, the British avant-garde movement modeled on the futurists in Italy, "despite their similar passions for representing permutations of men and machines to critique and reinvent the world." Switzky sees Shaw as "a figure both inside and outside the teleological narratives of modernism, both a Fabian bureaucrat and a militant counterinsurgent in the avant-garde."[9]

I would agree with Switzky that such a perspective is likely to stimulate new perceptions, especially regarding the connections between politics and aesthetics; Shaw, unlike Pound and Lewis, is normally excluded from considerations of the avant-garde, although he is unambiguously in the political avant-garde, which had a strong aesthetic dimension. As Roger Griffin describes it, fascism "meant breaking out of the ensnarement of words and thoughts into deeds, and using the power of human creativity not to produce art for its own sake, but to create a new culture in a total act of creation, of *poesis*."[10] Shaw was limited, in this sense, to words and thoughts, but of course despised "art for art's sake," and was always about creating a new culture. It is worth remembering that Shaw was an avant-garde artist in the original sense of the term: "Historically," Andreas Huyssen writes,

> the concept of the avantgarde, which until the 1930s was not limited to art but always referred to political radicalism as well, assumed prominence in the decades following the French Revolution. Henri de Saint Simon... ascribed a vanguard position to the artist in the construction of the ideal state and the new golden age of the future, and since then the concept of the avantgarde has remained inextricably bound to the idea of progress in industrial and technological civilization.[11]

Perhaps we should restore that original meaning to the idea of the avantgarde, in which case Shaw would be a central figure.

But fascism also emphasized creating a new human being, or clearing the way for its fulfillment. Modris Eksteins describes Nazism as "futuristic"—"a headlong plunge into the future, toward a 'brave new world.'" "The intention of the movement was to create a new type of human being from whom would spring a new morality, a new social system, and eventually a new international order." "Nazism was a popular variant of many of the impulses of the avant-garde...Above all, it, like the moderns it claimed to despise, tried to marry subjectivism and technicism."[12] In this regard the fascists that Shaw most resembles are F.T. Marinetti and the futurists, as Switzky so compellingly argues in his essay, who were also attracted to those seeming opposites, vitality and the machine, and wanted to see the past expunged from human memory.

Marinetti was of course the epitome of the avant-garde, both political and artistic, and wrote the first great manifesto of the twentieth century. As Martin Puchner has argued, the twentieth-century manifesto has its provenance in the *Communist Manifesto* of Marx and Engels, and is a peculiar fusion of art and politics. Shaw never wrote a manifesto in the manner of Marinetti and so many others, but, as Puchner remarks, he did integrate

> his political pamphlets into his plays. *Man and Superman*, for example, not only revolves around the question of technology, social, and revolutionary modernity but also includes a "Revolutionist's Handbook" as an appendix to the play. And like the Italian futurists working with the manifesto, Shaw was accused of mixing propaganda with art. However, Shaw's dialogues and handbooks, essays and aphorisms never coalesced into the generic form of the manifesto, with all the history and difficulties associated with it.[13]

Shaw was a sort of futurist, of the political avant-garde, and rejected all the blood and soil rhetoric of the fascists. Yet, despite their differences, Shaw would have agreed entirely with the conservative Evelyn Waugh's assessment of Mussolini's invasion of Ethiopia, where he stated that it

> was being attended by the spread of order and decency, education and medicine, in a disgraceful place...It can be compared best in recent history to the great western drive of the American peoples, and the dispossession of the Indian tribes and the establishment in a barren land of new pastures and cities.[14]

Here we see progressivism and conservativism converging, although otherwise the Catholic traditionalist Waugh and the progressive Creative Evolutionist Shaw had very little in common (besides both being great satirists). Shaw was also not, like Waugh, an enthusiastic admirer of Franco and his regime in Spain. Although Franco established a one-party authoritarian government that is often considered fascist, the truth is that it was not fascist but Catholic and traditionalist. As scholar of fascism Robert Paxton avers, "fascist dynamism fit badly with his [Franco's] reserved temperament."[15]

There is one contemporary of Shaw's we have not yet discussed who would seem to be especially relevant. W.B. Yeats, like Shaw, came from Irish Protestant stock that "was no longer a ruling class but still a superior caste, and thought of itself in this way."[16] I take the above quote from Conor Cruise O'Brien's essay "Passion and Cunning: An Essay on the Politics of W.B. Yeats." Cruise persuasively argues that Yeats' eccentricities have provided his admirers with a means of avoiding the truth of Yeats' troubling politics. Of course the same can be said of Shaw. It is also customary to say that Yeats quickly "became 'disillusioned with fascism.'" O'Brien claims that Yeats may have become disillusioned with fascism in Ireland, but that this was only after he realized that the Irish Blueshirts had failed and that "de Valera was no von Papen. O'Duffy, failing to devize anything effective in reply, revealed that he was no Hitler. The blue began to fade, and Yeats's interest in it faded proportionately." Yeats "was no lover of hopeless causes" and neither was Shaw, who as far as I can tell never even commented on Eoin O'Duffy and his Blueshirts. As far as the continental fascist movements that did go on to become governments are concerned, O'Brien contends that Yeats was quite aware of their brutality and indeed wanted to see "force...break the reign of the mob."[17] In politics Yeats was "either anti-English or—in Irish politics—aristocratic and, from the time Fascism had appeared, distinctly and exultantly pro-Fascist."[18] Like Shaw, Yeats feared the mob and looked to a strong government to impose order.

In 1894, Shaw and Yeats shared the stage in a double bill, Yeats' *The Land of Heart's Desire* preceding Shaw's *Arms and the Man*. In his autobiography Yeats recalls thinking that Shaw's play was "inorganic, logical straightness," although he "stood aghast before its energy." That night Yeats "had a nightmare that [he] was haunted by a sewing machine, that clicked and shone, but the incredible thing was that the machine smiled, smiled perpetually."[19] Interestingly, Shaw frequently referred to himself as a "writing machine." Yeats and Shaw both lived in the early decades of the machine age, Yeats more ambivalent about it than Shaw.

While both feared the rise of the masses, Shaw seemed to revel in the advances made by technology, fascinated by cars, cameras, and in the proliferation of technological inventions generally. In *Farfetched Fables* he imagines that in the far-off future humankind will reproduce itself in laboratories, and as early as *Misalliance* one of his characters cries, "Let the family be rooted out of civilization! Let the human race be brought up in institutions!" (vol. 4, 199). He wanted to control the environment and transcend the body. Omniscience and omnipotence is what he craved.

That craving continues in Faustian man. Bodiless immortality and the elimination of sexual reproduction, it is claimed, are within reach: "the problem of mortality," one former NASA scientist asserts, will be solved "by moving from our biological substrate." He goes on to say that evolution has brought us to the goal of our existence, the "Supreme Mind," which will "eventually reach immense power. It will be able to move all over the universe, to control and use its laws. It will become God, if the notion of God implies something that knows and does everything. In other words, Man will become God." This "transition to immortality" will at first only be affordable to the very wealthy, although in time the number of actual human beings will diminish until

> it gets to the minimum necessary for the zoos and small reservations. In all likelihood, the feelings that E-creatures may have towards humans as their ancestors, will be fading away, in proportion to the growing gap between the mental capacity of humans and electronic creatures, till they become comparable to our own attitude towards apes or even bugs.[20]

Shaw's prevision of the coming race could not have foreseen nanotechnology and the merging of man and machine, but the impulse for omnipotence is the same. Melville's Ahab sums up this drive for power best: "all my means are sane, my motive and my object mad."[21]

Notes

Introduction

1. From the editor's introduction of George Bernard Shaw, *The Rationalization of Russia*. Ed. Harry M. Geduld (Bloomington: Indiana University Press, 1964) 22–23.
2. All quotes from Shaw's plays and prefaces are from *Bernard Shaw: Complete Plays with Prefaces*, six volumes (New York: Dodd, Mead & Company, 1963) and will be cited within the text itself. Shaw's sometimes idiosyncratic spelling and grammar, particularly with apostrophes, has been retained. All other citations will be cited by an endnote number.
3. Quoted in Sally Peters, *Bernard Shaw: The Ascent of the Superman* (New Haven: Yale University Press, 1996) 16.
4. Karl Popper, *The Open Society and Its Enemies*, vol. 1: *The Spell of Plato* (Princeton: Princeton University Press, 1962). See especially chapter nine.
5. Bernard Shaw, "Sixty Years of Fabianism." *Fabian Essays: Jubilee Edition*. Ed. Bernard Shaw (London: George Allen & Unwin, 1948) 229.
6. This is a contested issue among Shaw scholars.
7. Popper 166.
8. George Orwell, *The Collected Essays, Journalism & Letters: As I Please*, vol. 3. Ed. Sonia Orwell and Ian Angus (Boston: Nonpareil Books, 2000) 222.
9. Robert Jay Lifton, *The Nazi Doctors: Medical Killing and the Psychology of Genocide* (New York: Basic Books, 2000) 377.
10. Maurice Valency, *The Cart and the Trumpet: The Plays of George Bernard Shaw* (New York: Oxford University Press, 1973) 429.
11. For instance Martin Meisel in his essay, "Shaw and Revolution: The Politics of the Plays." *Shaw: Seven Critical Essays*. Ed. Norman Rosenblood (Toronto: University of Toronto Press, 1971).
12. Beatrice Webb, *The Diary of Beatrice Webb*, vol. 4. Ed. Norman and Jeanne MacKenzie (London: Virago Press Limited, 1985) 132.
13. There are some signs that this reticence might be loosening. See Stanley Weintraub, "GBS and the Despots," a 22 August 2011 article in the *Times Literary Supplement*. http://www.the-tls.co.uk/tls/public/article707002.ece
14. C.E.M. Joad, *Shaw* (London: Victor Gollancz, 1949) 159–60.
15. Russell Jacoby, *Picture Imperfect: Utopian Thought for an Anti-Utopian Age* (New York: Columbia University Press, 2005).
16. Popper, chapter nine.
17. Edward Rothstein, "Utopia and Its Discontents." *Visions of Utopia* (Oxford: Oxford University Press, 2003) 5.
18. Hannah Arendt, *The Origins of Totalitarianism* (Orlando: Harcourt, 1968) 398.
19. Tzvetan Todorov, *Hope and Memory: Lessons from the Twentieth Century*. Trans. David Bellos (Princeton: Princeton University Press, 2003) 26–27.

20. Quoted in Alan Chappelow, *Shaw—"The Chucker-Out": A Biographical Exposition and Critique* (New York: AMS Press, 1969) 293, 294.
21. Chappelow 231–33.
22. Bernard Shaw, *The Perfect Wagnerite. Major Critical Essays* (London: Penguin Books, 1931) 242.
23. Quoted in Arnold Silver, *Bernard Shaw: The Darker Side* (Stanford: Stanford University Press 1982) 164.
24. I am thinking of Sally Peters, *Bernard Shaw: The Ascent of the Superman* (1996) and A.M. Gibbs, *Bernard Shaw: A Life*, (2005) as well as Michael Holroyd, *Bernard Shaw,* four volumes (1988, 1989, 1991, 1992).
25. Eric Bentley, *Bernard Shaw* (New York: New Directions Publishing, 1947, 1957).
26. Blanche Patch, *Thirty Years with G.B.S* (New York: Dodd, Mead & Company) 204–5.
27. We will examine some of these in the body of the book, especially in Chapter 3.
28. Margery M. Morgan, *The Shavian Playground: An Exploration of the Art of George Bernard Shaw* (London: Methuen, 1972) 286–302.
29. See Gabriel Marcel, *Man Against Mass Society.* Trans. G.S. Fraser (Chicago: Henry Regnery Company, 1965).
30. Preface to Sidney and Beatrice Webb's *English Local Government: English Prisons under Local Government* (1921). Reprinted as "Imprisonment (English Local Government by Sidney and Beatrice Webb" in *Prefaces by Bernard Shaw* (London: Constable and Company, 1934) 304.
31. Lifton 17.
32. Quoted in David Nathan's "Failure of an Elderly Gentleman: Shaw and the Jews." *SHAW: The Annual of Bernard Shaw Studies Volume Eleven: Shaw and Politics.* Ed. T.F. Evans (University Park: The Pennsylvania State University Press, 1991) 226–27.
33. Lifton 50–51.
34. Lifton 116.
35. Lifton 72.
36. Chappelow 403.
37. The speech can be found under the title, "The Unavoidable Subject," in *Platform and Pulpit.* Ed. Dan H. Laurence (New York: Hill and Wang, 1961) 286–92. Because of the war the speech was censored by the British authorities and never read.
38. Letter to Siegfried Trebitsch, 18 March 1938, printed in *Bernard Shaw Collected Letters,* vol. 4: 1926–1950. Ed. Dan H. Laurence (New York: Viking Penguin, 1988) 496.
39. *Collected Letters,* vol. 4, 336–37. This letter to Trebitsch is from May 1933.
40. Chappelow 334.
41. Lifton 479.
42. Shaw, "Imprisonment" 306.
43. Chappelow 314. Shaw wrote this in the July 1941 issue of *Labour Monthly.* The italics are Chappelow's.
44. Chappelow 252–53.
45. Stephen Koch, *Double Lives: Stalin, Willi Munzenberg, and the Seduction of the Intellectuals* (New York: Enigma Books, 1994, 1995, 2004) 7.

46. Koch 7.
47. Todorov 29.
48. Beatrice Webb, *The Diary of Beatrice Webb*, vol. 4. Ed. Norman and Jeanne MacKenzie (London: Virago Press, 1985) 135.
49. Todorov 33–39.
50. "When Shaw asks, therefore, how much trouble a troublesome person is worth, surely the answer is, infinite trouble." From Maurice Colbourne, *The Real Bernard Shaw* (New York: The Dodd, Mead & Company, 1940) 195. And as far as capitalists are concerned, Chappelow believes that Shaw would have reserved "only for the most obdurate the sanguinary demise of the firing squad." Chappelow 234.
51. Chappelow 184. This quote is taken from the *London Recorder*, December 1933.
52. Morgan 286.

1 Previsions of the Superman in the Coming Age of Will: *The Quintessence of Ibsenism*

1. From Chesterton's *Heretics*, quoted in Davis S. Thatcher, *Nietzsche in England: 1890–1914* (Toronto: University of Toronto Press, 1970) 210.
2. Charles A. Carpenter, *Bernard Shaw and the Art of Destroying Ideals* (Madison: University of Wisconsin Press, 1969) 13. Shaw's dramaturgical method, which developed after he wrote his book on Ibsen, was devoted to planting ideas in people's minds (what we now call memes); he believed that ideas were infectious, so he conveyed them amid levity and humor so that the audience, coming to be entertained, would leave with his ideas firmly ensconced in their brains.
3. A.M. Gibbs, *Bernard Shaw: A Life* (Gainseville: University Press of Florida, 2005) 236.
4. Shaw says in a footnote that

    > Schopenhauer's philosophy, like that of all pessimists, is really based on the old view of the will as original sin, and on the 1750–1850 view that the intellect is the divine grace that is to save us from it. It is as well to warn those who fancy that Schopenhauerism is one and indivisible, that acceptance of its metaphysics by no means involves indorsement of its philosophy.
    >
    > *Quintessence* 6.

5. Michael Holroyd, *Bernard Shaw*, vol 1, 1856–1898: *The Search for Love* (New York: Random House, 1988) 197–98.
6. Holroyd 201.
7. Albert Camus, *The Rebel: An Essay on Man in Revolt*. Trans. Anthony Bower (New York: Vintage, 1991) 65–66. Camus' seminal essay was originally published in 1951.
8. Camus 225.
9. Camus 135.
10. Compare Perry Ellis on Marshall Berman's treatment of Marx: "For all its exuberance, Berman's version of Marx, in its virtually exclusive emphasis on the release of the self, comes uncomfortably close—radical and decent

though its accents are—to the assumptions of the culture of narcissism." Perry Anderson, "Modernism and Revolution." *Marxism and the Interpretation of Culture.* Ed. Cary Nelson and Lawrence Grossberg (Urbana: University of Illinois Press, 1988) 331.
11. See also Carpenter 14, where he says that "Shaw regarded as silly and often treacherous delusions" such "ideals" as "Marriage and the Family, Goodness in morals, Propriety in business, Justice in the State."
12. Mathew Arnold, *Culture and Anarchy.* Ed. Samuel Lipman (New Haven: Yale University Press, 1994) 109.
13. Arnold 52.
14. Arnold 96–97.
15. James W. Hulse, *Revolutionists in London: A Study of Five Unorthodox Socialists* (Oxford: Clarendon Press, 1970) 119.
16. Bernard Shaw, *The Rationalization of Russia.* Ed. Harry M. Geduld (Bloomington: Indiana University Press, 1964) 108.
17. Robin Blick, *The Seeds of Evil: Lenin and the Origins of Bolshevik Elitism* (London: Steyne Publications, 1995) xi.
18. Blick 22.
19. Bernard Shaw, "Sixty Years of Fabianism." *Fabian Essays: Jubilee Edition.* Ed. Bernard Shaw (London: George Allen & Unwin, 1948) 229.
20. George Bernard Shaw, "The Illusions of Socialism." *Selected Non-Dramatic Writings of Bernard Shaw.* Ed. Dan H. Laurence (Boston: Houghton Mifflin Company, 1965) 407.
21. Shaw, "The Illusions of Socialism." 408–9.
22. Jose Ortega y Gasset, *The Revolt of the Masses.* Trans. Anonymous (New York: Norton, 1932) 50.
23. Michael Meyer, *Ibsen: A Biography* (Garden City: Doubleday & Company, 1971) 509.
24. Meyer 498.
25. Henrik Ibsen, *An Enemy of the People. Four Great Plays By Henrik Ibsen.* Trans. R. Farquharson Sharp (New York: Bantam Books, 1959) 195.
26. *An Enemy of the People* contains many characteristics that remind one of the later Shaw. In 1891 Shaw, as a Fabian, was still ostensibly committed to democracy—although the tone and overall message of *The Quintessence* is anti-democratic. (Eric Bentley has defended Shaw's democratic principles by saying that he espoused a democracy of aristocrats, which is to say that in the utopia Shaw longs for there will finally be a democracy he can believe in; when that occurs the realists will have supplanted the philistines and idealists—or perhaps it would be more precise to say that the philistines and idealists will have evolved into realists, while those who fail to evolve appropriately are eliminated, as they are in *Back to Methuselah*.) Later in life Shaw remarked that William Morris had been right to reject parliamentary government in the 1890s; and in his plays and other writings he repeatedly articulated his belief that only a strong leader unimpeded by parliamentary squabbling could get anything done (in other words, a dictator). This is Ibsen's view in *An Enemy of the People*, and Shaw is clearly in agreement. In *The Quintessence* he puts it this way:

> It is a scientific fact that the majority, however eager it may be for the reform of old abuses, is always wrong in its opinion of new developments, or rather is always unfit for them ... we shall never march a step

forward except at the heels of "the strongest man, he who is able to stand alone." (48)

It is the pioneers, the spiritual aristocracy, the intellectual elite that move society forward.
27. Ibsen 192–93.
28. Halib C. Malik, *Receiving Soren Kierkegaard: The Early Impact and Transmission of His Thought* (Washington DC.: The Catholic University of America Press, 1997) 155.
29. Meyer 358.
30. Meyer 365.
31. Meyer 380.
32. Meyer 632.
33. Ortega 134.
34. Ortega 134.

2 Utopia in Flames: Shaw and Wagner's *Ring*: *The Perfect Wagnerite*

1. *The Sanity of Art: An Exposure of the Current Nonsense About Artists Being Degenerate* was a revised version of an open letter to Max Nordau that Shaw originally wrote at the request of Benjamin Tucker, the American anarchist and editor of the magazine, *Liberty*. It appeared in the 27 July 1895 issue of that American magazine and was originally titled "A Degenerate's View of Nordau." Shaw revised it and issued it under the new title in 1908.
2. Although his legal father was Carl Friedrich Wagner, Richard had reason to believe that his biological father was his mother's lover, Ludwig Geyer; and Geyer was a notoriously Jewish name. As one of the most famous anti-Semites in Europe, this must certainly have been disconcerting. See Robert W. Gutman, *Richard Wagner: the Man, His Mind, and His Music* (New York: Harcourt, Brace & World, Inc.) 2–6.
3. Michael Meyer, *Ibsen: A Biography* (Garden City: Double Day & Company, 1971) 14.
4. Quoted in Joachim Kohler, *Wagner's Hitler: The Prophet and His Disciple*. Trans. Ronald Taylor (Cambridge: Polity Press, 2000) 202.
5. All quotes from *The Perfect Wagnerite* will be cited within the body of the essay and are from, Bernard Shaw, *The Perfect Wagnerite. Major Critical Essays* (London: Penguin Books, 1931). Additionally, all quotes from Shaw's plays and prefaces are from, *Bernard Shaw: Complete Plays with Prefaces,* six volumes (New York: Dodd, Mead & Company, 1963) and will also be cited within the body of the essay.
6. L.J. Rather, *The Dream of Self-Destruction: Wagner's Ring and the Modern World* (Baton Rouge: Louisiana State University Press, 1979) 56.
7. Quoted in David Nathan's "Failure of an Elderly Gentleman: Shaw and the Jews." *SHAW: The Annual of Bernard Shaw Studies Volume Eleven: Shaw and Politics*. Ed. T.F. Evans (University Park: The Pennsylvania State University Press, 1991) 226–27.

Notes   213

8. Martin Buber, *Tales of the Hasidim: Book One, the Early Masters* (New York: Schocken Books, 1947) 129–30.
9. Guttman 323.
10. Rather 99.
11. For instance Hitler remarked that, "For me Wagner is a god. His music is my religion. I go to his operas as others go to church." Quoted in Kohler 137.
12. [T]o both theologist and rationalist progress at last appears alarming, threatening, hideous, because it seems to tend toward chaos. The deists Voltaire and Tom Paine were, to the divines of their day, predestined devils, tempting mankind hellward. To deists and divines alike Ferdinand LaSalle, the godless self-worshipper and man-worshipper would have been a monster. Yet many who to-day echo LaSalle's demand that economic and political institutions should be adapted to the poor man's will to eat and drink his fill out of the product of his own labor, are revolted by Ibsen's acceptance of the impulse toward greater freedom as sufficient ground for the repudiation of any customary duty, however sacred, that conflicts with it. Society—were it even as free as LaSalle's Social-Democratic republic—*must*, it seems to them, go to pieces when conduct is no longer regulated by inviolable covenants.
Shaw, *Quintessence* 8.
13. Rather 118.
14. Andreas Huyssen, *After the Great Divide: Modernism, Mass Culture, Postmodernism* (Bloomington: Indiana University Press, 1986) 183.
15. Bernard Shaw, *The Adventures of the Black Girl in Her Search for God. The Portable Bernard Shaw*. Ed. Stanley Weintraub (New York: The Viking Press, 1977) 652.
16. An exception to this might seem to be Shaw's supposed love of actresses such as Mrs. Patrick Campbell; but these "love affairs" of his seem more play acting to me. See Sally Peters, *Bernard Shaw: The Ascent of the Superman* (New Haven: Yale University Press, 1996).
17. In 1927 Beatrice wrote in her diary that Shaw's "naïve faith in the Superman, before whose energy and genius all must bow down, is not a new feature in Shaw's mentality." Beatrice Webb, *The Diary of Beatrice Webb*, vol. 4. Ed. Norman and Jeanne MacKenzie (London: Virago Press, 1985) 132.
18. Shaw, *The Adventures of the Black Girl in Her Search for God*, 652.
19. Quoted in Nathan 225.
20. Zygmunt Bauman, *Modernity and the Holocaust* (Cambridge: Polity Press, 1989) 150, 149.
21. Bauman 165–66.
22. Daniel Dervin, *Bernard Shaw: A Psychological Study* (Cranbury: Associated University Presses, 1975) 72.
23. Friedrich Nietzsche, *Beyond Good and Evil: Prelude to a Philosophy of the Future*. Trans. R.J. Hollingdale (London: Penguin Books, 1973) 84.
24. See for instance the preface to *On the Rocks*, vol. 5, 496, where Shaw writes, "capital punishment has been abolished in Russia (liquidation by the Ogpu is not punishment: it is only 'weeding the garden')." He also uses the metaphor in *Back to Methuselah*, *The Rationalization of Russia*, and elsewhere.
25. Bauman 113.

214 Notes

26. Shakespeare also brilliantly dramatizes the process in *Macbeth*.
27. Paul Tillich, *The Eternal Now* (New York: Charles Scribner's Sons, 1963) 90.

3 From Hell to Heaven: Creative Evolution and the Drive toward the Military-Industrial-Religious Complex: *Man and Superman, John Bull's Other Island, Major Barbara*

1. As in the previous chapters, all quotes from Shaw's plays and prefaces are from *Bernard Shaw: Complete Plays with Prefaces*, six volumes (New York: Dodd, Mead & Company, 1963) and cited within the body of the essay.
2. It is usual for critics to refer to the three plays as a trilogy, and Shaw himself in a 1919 letter to Trebitsch referred to them as "the big three." In that same letter Shaw suggested the title *Comedies of Religion and Science* for a German edition of the plays. See Louis Crompton, *Shaw the Dramatist* (Lincoln: University of Nebraska Press, 1969) 75 and 237 note 1. My analysis of the trilogy owes a great deal to Alfred Turco Jr. See *Shaw's Moral Vision: The Self and Salvation* (Ithaca: Cornell University Press, 1976).
3. Roger Griffin, *Modernism and Fascism: The Sense of a Beginning under Mussolini and Hitler* (Basingstoke: Palgrave Macmillan, 2007) 224.
4. Griffin 39.
5. Griffin 385 note 85.
6. Quoted in Bernard Semmel, *Imperialism and Social Reform: English Social Imperial Thought, 1895–1914* (Cambridge: Harvard University Press, 1960) 72–73.
7. Semmel 76. Semmel is quoting from Wells' autobiography.
8. Michael Holroyd, *Bernard Shaw*, vol. 2, 1898–1918: *The Pursuit of Power* (New York: Random House, 1988) 71.
9. Holroyd 67.
10. Holroyd 67.
11. *Sociological Papers* 74–5. http://www.archive.org/stream/sociologicalpape01 sociiala#page/74/mode/2up.
12. Quoted in Griffin 148.
13. Sidney Webb, for instance, wanted to improve the sanitary conditions in England because he was concerned about "breeding an even moderately Imperial race...an efficient army—out of the stunted, anemic, demoralized denizens of the slum tenements of our great cities." Quoted in Semmel 73.
14. J.W. Burrow, *The Crisis of Reason: European Thought, 1848–1914* (New Haven: Yale University Press, 2000) 101.
15. "Thus were laid the foundations of my life-long hatred of poverty, and the devotion of all my public life to the task of exterminating the poor and rendering their resurrection for ever impossible." Quoted in Hesketh Pearson, *Bernard Shaw* (London: Macdonald and Jane's, 1975) 15.
16. Burrow 99–100.
17. Semmel 51 footnote 2. Pearson, professor of Applied Mathematics and Mechanics at University College London, was a fervent social Darwinist and "national socialist," a lifelong advocate of eugenics and a key source of inspiration in the rise of British Fascism.
18. Semmel 51.

19. Nickolas Pappas, *Plato and the Republic* (London: Routledge, 1995) 11.
20. Plato, *The Republic*. Trans. Benjamin Jowett (Mineola: Dover Publications, 2000) 176.
21. Plato 187.
22. Eric Bentley, *The Playwright as Thinker* (New York: Meridian Books, 1957) 125–26.
23. "Savonarola, not being witty, was burnt alive by those whom his bludgeon hurt. Shaw, on the other hand, confesses that his mother wit has many times saved him from the stake's modern equivalent."

    The heretic, the reformer, the prophet, the revolutionary must always march ahead of the times, never with them. That is their function. And if they are successful they will be duly stoned, burnt, hanged, imprisoned, or banned, according to the age and place they live in. Nor will they escape these fates unless they happen to possess, as Shaw possesses, in addition to disturbing visions and iconoclastic zeal, the specific artistic talent of the mountebank. Then they will be spared, as Shaw has been spared, because the mountebank's amusing antics divert the mob's attention from the reformer's dangerous preachings.

    Maurice Colbourne, *The Real Bernard Shaw* (New York: Dodd, Mead & Company, 1940) 134, 135–36.
24. And that is also why Shavian scholars who defend Shaw by stressing that he is "only joking" are so off base; they cannot have it both ways: if Shaw is the great comic dramatist of ideas, the Fabian playwright who uses humor to permeate society with ideas that otherwise would not get a hearing, then the joke that Shaw told for over forty years about liquidating society's incorrigible delinquents needs to be taken as seriously as his other jokes that center around the reformation of society.
25. R.F. Rattray, *Bernard Shaw: A Chronicle* (London: The Leagrave Press, 1951) 237. Curiously, this same quote is attributed to "one of his hostesses" in Pearson 149.
26. Quoted in the editor's introduction to Shaw's *The Rationalization of Russia*. Ed. Harry M. Geduld (Bloomington: Indiana University Press, 1964) 32.
27. Maurice Valency, *The Cart and the Trumpet: The Plays of George Bernard Shaw* (New York: Oxford University Press, 1973) 429.
28. For instance in Pearson 43. Interestingly, Pearson uses Tanner's words to describe Shaw's experience.
29. Warren Sylvester Smith, *Bishop of Everywhere: Bernard Shaw and the Life Force* (University Park: The Pennsylvania State University Press, 1982) 31.
30. Griffin 148, 149.
31. Quoted in Carl H. Mills, "Shaw's Superman: A Reexamination." *Critical Essays on George Bernard Shaw*. Ed. Elsie B. Adams (New York: G.K. Hall & Co., 1991) 134.
32. Friedrich Nietzsche, *Ecce Homo. Basic Writings of Nietzsche*. Trans. Walter Kaufmann (New York: Modern Library Edition, 2000) 784.
33. Griffin 184–85. The italics are Griffin's.
34. Dan Stone, *Breeding Superman: Nietzsche, Race, and Eugenics in Edwardian and Interwar Britain* (Liverpool: Liverpool University Press, 2002) 106.
35. Rattray 251.

36. Rattray 310.
37. Rattray 313.
38. Rattray 310. This callousness is especially puzzling because Shaw could on occasion excoriate insensitivity, brutality, and violence, as Rattray alludes. A good example of this is Shaw's powerful diatribe against the British massacre of Denshawai villagers in Egypt in the preface to *John Bull* (vol. 2, 480–96). In a section sub-headed "The Denshawai Horror" Shaw produces a brilliant polemic against colonial arrogance and violence that is likely to earn the applause of any person of humanitarian feeling. The problem is that Shaw was inclined to attack the British while he was more often reticent about similar crimes with nations engaged in political experiments, such as Italy under Mussolini, the Soviet Union under Lenin and Stalin, and Germany under Hitler. It is also hard to know what really bothers Shaw, the brutality or the sheer stupidity and political inefficacy of the violence and repression at Denshawai. From my study I have learned that what bothers Shaw most is stupidity and waste.
39. Denis Mack Smith, *Mussolini* (New York: Alfred A. Knopf, 1982) 173.
40. Smith 149, 140.
41. Colbourne 199.
42. I would suggest to directors of *Man and Superman* that they might want to consider prerecording the actor playing Tanner reading from the *Handbook* as the audience enters the theatre; or better yet, video record the actor giving a stump speech reading his text to any passerby who cares to listen.
43. It is interesting that *John Bull's Other Island* in a sense represents the partitioning of the complete human personality into three separate parts, each part represented by one of the three major characters of the play. Hell can be seen as their estrangement from one another just as heaven, or utopia, would result from their union. Although Freud had not yet formulated his division of the psyche into three parts at the time of the composition of *John Bull*, he had written his first great book, *The Interpretation of Dreams*, just five years earlier. Although Shaw did not have a lot to say about Freud over the course of his career, he did remark in the preface to *Farfetched Fables* that he thought Freud was "an extraordinarily indelicate adventurer" (vol. 6, 456). It would be interesting to know how Freud would interpret these three plays, with the dream sequence in *Man and Superman* and Keegan's longing for utopia interpreted by him as "the dream of a madman" (vol. 2, 611).
44. Shaw was not, of course, a Protestant Christian, although his family was Protestant. But all his life he identified with the great Protestant reformers or revolutionaries like Martin Luther and John Bunyan, who protested against a corrupt status quo and longed to create a new unified religious community.
45. The word "totalitarian" was not in use until the 1920s.
46. Shaw frequently remarked that "backward" nations needed to be civilized, by force if necessary. In the preface to *John Bull* he says: "Tribes must make themselves into nations before they can claim the rights of nations; and this they can only do by civilization" (vol. 2, 442). A nation like an individual must through arduous and painstaking self-assertion create itself.
47. Nicholas Grene, *Bernard Shaw: A Critical View* (Basingstoke: The Macmillan Press,1984) 83.
48. *Bernard Shaw: Collected Letters 1898–1910*: 566.

49. Grene 99.
50. J.L. Wisenthal, "The Underside of Undershaft: A Wagnerian Motif in *Major Barbara*." *The Shaw Review XV*, May 1972: 56–64.
51. It is somewhat unclear why Undershaft has earned the encomium of a "self-made man" or "self-made millionaire" since he was adopted by a millionaire arms dealer and has succeeded his stepfather as head of the business.
52. Grene 94–95.
53. *Bernard Shaw: Collected Letters 1898–1910*: 566.
54. *Bernard Shaw: Collected Letters 1898–1910*: 565.
55. Irving Howe, "Bernard Shaw's Anti-Capitalism." *New International*, Vol. 14 No. 1, January 1948. http://www.marxists.org/history/etol/writers/howe/1948/01/shaw.htm.
56. Compare this to Mussolini's very similar statement: "better one day as a lion than a hundred years as a sheep." Quoted in Smith 173.
57. The Dionysian theme is strong throughout, but especially at the close of the second act when Barbara, having lost her faith, remains desolately behind while Cusins and Undershaft march off the stage in a swelling of Bacchic musical ecstasy. Shaw was influenced by the translator of Euripides Gilbert Murray at this time, but this is also probably Shaw's most Nietzschean play. Blake's *Marriage of Heaven and Hell* is also a major source for the play, and so Barbara's new religion, no longer recognizing evil—"there is no wicked side: life is all one" (vol. 1, 444)—will involve a marriage of heaven and hell, Undershaft representing the hellish influence throughout. See Margery M. Morgan, *The Shavian Playground: An Exploration of the Art of George Bernard Shaw* (London: Methuen, 1972) 134–57.
58. Bernard Shaw, *The Perfect Wagnerite*. *Major Critical Essays* (London: Penguin Books, 1931) 249.
59. Grene 93.
60. Barbara Bellow Watson, "Sainthood for Millionaires." *Bernard Shaw's Plays*. Ed. Warren Sylvester Smith (New York: Norton, 1970) 359.
61. Bernard Shaw, "Sixty Years of Fabianism." *Fabian Essays: Jubilee Edition*. Ed. Bernard Shaw (London: George Allen & Unwin, 1948) 224–28.
62. Bernard Crick, "Shaw as Political Thinker, or the Dogs that did not Bark." *SHAW: The Annual of Bernard Shaw Studies Volume Eleven: Shaw and Politics*. Ed. T.F. Evans (University Park: The Pennsylvania State University Press, 1991) 27.
63. Crick 30.
64. "Shaw cherished a photograph of Djerjinski which is still on display at Shaw's Corner, Ayot St Lawrence." Bernard Shaw, *The Rationalization of Russia*. Ed. Harry M. Geduld (Bloomington: Indiana University Press, 1964) 132, editor's note 60.
65. In *The Rationalization of Russia*, and in the prefaces to *On the Rocks* and *The Simpleton of the Unexpected Isles*.
66. Not all critics are in denial about the radical nature of Shaw's solutions to certain social problems. In his discussion of *Caesar and Cleopatra* Louis Crompton admits and defends Shaw's view that unredeemable criminals, like dangerous wild animals, should be killed. See Louis Crompton, *Shaw the Dramatist* (Lincoln: University of Nebraska Press, 1969) 71–72. And in his book analyzing Shaw's political thought Garreth Griffith discusses Shaw's

218　*Notes*

wish to see a modern day "inquisition...to judge whether an individual was more a social asset than a social nuisance." Gareth Griffith, *Socialism and Superior Brains: The Political Thought of Bernard Shaw* (London: Routledge, 1993) 130. Maurice Valency sums up Shaw this way:

> But while love is dispensable, eugenic marriages, and the weeding out of inferior individuals, are in Shaw's opinion, absolutely requisite to the evolution of a superior society...The social organism must be made subject to rational control by those best qualified to rule it...as in the *Republic* of Plato.

Maurice Valency, *The Cart and the Trumpet: The Plays of George Bernard Shaw* (New York: Oxford University Press, 1973) 426. And in an excellent book on Shaw from 1940 in the chapter titled "Programme" Maurice Colbourne is quite good in his discussion of Shaw's desired liquidation program, and very articulate in his defense of Shaw, putting much emphasis on Shaw's patience:

> When Shaw asks, therefore, how much trouble a troublesome person is worth, surely the answer is, infinite trouble. For until society is willing to undergo root treatment, it is bound by honour, duty and conscience to make the best it can of its crop of criminals, and accept its responsibility for them.

Nevertheless, some will "eventually find themselves judged intolerable. For them the door will be opened to the lethal chamber." Colbourne 195, 194. For a more recent defense see Stuart E. Baker, *Bernard Shaw's Remarkable Religion: A Faith that Fits the Facts* (Gainesville: University Press of Florida, 2002).

67. Quoted in Stone 129–30.
68. Stone 130.
69. Stone 132.
70. See Grene 99.
71. Pearson says that Shaw's relationship with the Fabians was based on a "reciprocal usefulness" and a common political aim, and that it "taught him to handle all sorts of antipathetic people, making it impossible for those who disliked him intensely to quarrel with him; but it was no more native to him than to William Morris, who could not breathe in it...[it kept] his feet on the ground." Pearson 379.
72. Bernard Shaw, "The Transition to Social Democracy." *Fabian Essays: Jubilee Edition*. Ed. Bernard Shaw (London: George Allen & Unwin, 1948) 186–87.
73. Shaw writing to Henry James, January 1909, *Bernard Shaw: Collected Letters 1898–1910*. Ed. Dan H. Laurence (New York: Dodd, Mead & Company, 1972) 827–28.

4　Shaw's Modern Utopia: *Back to Methuselah*

1. D.H. Lawrence, *Fantasia of the Unconscious. Psychoanalysis and the Unconscious and Fantasia of the Unconscious*. Ed. Bruce Steele (Cambridge: Cambridge University Press, 2004) 141.

Notes 219

2. Martin Meisel, "Shaw and Revolution: The Politics of the Plays." *Shaw: Seven Critical Essays*. Ed. Norman Rosenblood (Toronto: University of Toronto Press, 1971) 113.
3. Meisel 117.
4. Meisel 123.
5. Stanley Weintraub, *Journey to Heartbreak: The Crucible Years of Bernard Shaw 1914–1918* (New York: Weybright and Talley, 1971), especially chapter 7; and the editors' introduction, "Shaw's Theatre of War," to Bernard Shaw, *What Shaw Really Wrote about the War*. Ed. J.L. Wisenthal and Daniel O'Leary (Gainesville: University Press of Florida, 2006). Weintraub quotes a letter Shaw wrote to the Webbs after experiencing a German bomber near his house at Ayot St. Lawrence: "I positively caught myself hoping next night there would be another raid" 181. Weisenthal and O'Leary quote from the same letter, at greater length: "What is hardly credible, but true, is that the sound of the Zepp's engines was so fine, and its voyage through the stars so enchanting, that I positively caught myself hoping next night there would be another raid" 7–8.
6. Shaw, *What Shaw Really Wrote about the War* 199.
7. Shaw, *What Shaw Really Wrote about the War* 204.
8. H.G. Wells, *A Modern Utopia* (Lincoln: University of Nebraska Press, 1967) 5.
9. Wells 5.
10. Frederic Jameson, *Archaeologies of the Future: The Desire Called Utopia and Other Science Fictions* (London: Verso, 2005).
11. Northrop Frye, "Varieties of Literary Utopia." Sir Thomas More's *Utopia: a Norton Critical Edition*. Trans. and Ed. Robert M. Adams (New York: Norton, 1992) 207. The italics are Frye's.
12. This lecture was never published, but the section of it that relates to the superior race of the future and Bulwer-Lytton's novel is quoted in Louis Crompton, *Shaw the Dramatist* (Lincoln: University of Nebraska Press, 1969) 182.
13. Edward Bulwer-Lytton, *The Coming Race* (Peterborough: Broadview Press, 2002) 201.
14. Crompton 182.
15. Hesketh Pearson, *Bernard Shaw* (London: Macdonald and Jane's, 1975) 114.
16. Pearson 14.
17. Pearson 114–15.
18. The debate between Cain and Eve is some of Shaw's finest dialectical writing, on a level with the Devil and Don Juan's debate in *Man and Superman* and the Chaplain, Cauchon, and Warwick's debate in scene four of *Saint Joan*. Like all great dialectical writing, whether in Plato, Stoppard, Weiss, or Shaw, the tendency is to agree with whoever has the floor. Later in his career Shaw lost this quality; his matches became one-sided and lost their edge.
19. Robert Brustein, *The Theatre of Revolt: Studies in Modern Drama from Ibsen to Genet* (Chicago: Ivan R. Dee, 1991). Existential revolt in this instance is not to be confused with the twentieth-century philosophical movement called existentialism.
20. Biologists have determined that there are a number of different branches of evolution, and the "unilinear conception of organic relationship" that Shaw appears to posit here would seem to be derived from the concept of the Great

Chain of Being that still exerted a strong influence even in the nineteenth and early twentieth centuries. See Loren Eiseley, *Darwin's Century: Evolution and the Men Who Discovered It* (New York: Barnes & Noble, 2009) 295–96 and elsewhere.

21. Life is a force which has made innumerable experiments in organizing itself; that the mammoth and the man, the mouse and the magatherium, the flies and the fleas and the Fathers of the Church, are all more or less successful attempts to build up that raw force into higher and higher individuals, the ideal individual being omnipotent, omniscient, infallible, and withal completely, unilludedly self-conscious: in short, a god.

(vol. 3, 626)

See also the previous chapter, 80.

22. But whenever I feel that I must have anything, I get it, sooner or later. I feel that way about Barbara. I don't like marriage: I feel intensely afraid of it; and I dont know what I shall do with Barbara or what she will do with me. But I feel that I and nobody else must marry her.

(vol. 1, 387)

Cusins obeys the promptings of the Life Force, which is beyond rational explication. He and Barbara are agents of Creative Evolution.

23. In fact, we learn from Zoo that she believes the short-livers are "[slaves] to images and metaphors" (vol. 2, 166). This would seem Platonic since Plato was very suspicious of images, such as those that danced on the wall of his hypothetical cave; but in fact Plato is not intrinsically negative regarding images. Some images are good and some are bad. Plato frequently has Socrates mention the importance of maintaining a positive image within the mind, such as the image of the ideal state: "We have lost sight of the image which we had before us" and "neither we nor our guardians, whom we have to educate, can ever become musical until we and they know the essential forms of temperance, courage, liberality, magnificence, and their kindred, as well as the contrary forms, in all their combinations, and can recognize them and their images wherever they are found." Plato, *The Republic*. Trans. Benjamin Jowett (Mineola: Dover, 2000) 47 and 74. Iris Murdoch concurs, saying that Plato felt that "images are valuable aids to thought; we study what is higher first 'in images.' But images must be kept within a fruitful hierarchy of spiritual endeavour." Iris Murdoch, *The Fire and the Sun: Why Plato Banished the Artists* (Clarendon: Oxford University Press, 1977) 41.
24. Like so much else in this play, their names are taken from Swift.
25. Quoted in Margery M. Morgan, *The Shavian Playground: An Exploration of the Art of George Bernard Shaw* (London: Methuen, 1972) 222–23.
26. Morgan 225.
27. Although Shaw was frequently vocal about his antipathy toward ritual, his secretary Blanche Patch perhaps provides a hint as to why The Maiden is so antagonistic to the idea of taking meals together at particular times during the day. Much to his annoyance, Shaw was frequently interrupted at his work when it was time for lunch. See Blanche Patch, *Thirty Years with G.B.S.* (New York: Dodd, Mead & Company) 275.

28. Roger Griffin, *Modernism and Fascism: The Sense of a Beginning under Mussolini and Hitler* (Basingstoke: Palgrave Macmillan, 2007) 224.
29. Jameson 328–44. Regarding the discouragement theme, it seems much more likely that Shaw got the idea from Francis Galton's *Inquiries into Human Faculty* (1883), which noted just such a malady in certain non-Western tribes coming into their first contact with White civilization. The theme is also present in *The Coming Race*, the engineer shocked into a state of discouragement by his contact with such superior beings. See Crompton 183–84.
30. Morgan 223.
31. George Bernard Shaw, *The Quintessence of Ibsenism* (New York: Dover, 1994) 10.
32. Morgan 222.
33. Brustein 195, 203.

5 Shaw's Totalitarian Drama of the Thirties; or, Shaw and the Dictators: *Geneva, The Millionairess, The Simpleton of the Unexpected Isles*

1. *Saint Joan* opened in London in March 1924 with Sybil Thorndike as the titular saint. The production and the play was an immediate success, and it was largely responsible for Shaw being awarded the Nobel Prize for literature in 1925.
2. Michael Holroyd, *Bernard Shaw*, Volume 3, 1918–1951: *The Lure of Fantasy* (New York: Random House, 1991) 417.
3. Holroyd 417
4. The other is *Everybody's Political What's What?* (1944).
5. It should be noted that not all scholars are in agreement about whether Mussolini's Fascist regime was "totalitarian." Hannah Arendt, for instance, claims that before 1938 "Mussolini's Fascism...was not totalitarian but just an ordinary nationalist dictatorship." For Arendt totalitarian movements such as the National Socialists and the Bolsheviks did not desire to simply seize the state machine, but to destroy the state altogether:

   > The true goal of Fascism was only to seize power and establish the Fascist "elite" as uncontested ruler over the country. Totalitarianism is never content to rule by external means, namely, through the state and a machinery of violence; thanks to its peculiar ideology and the role assigned to it in this apparatus of coercion, totalitarianism has discovered a means of dominating and terrorizing human beings from within.

   Hannah Arendt, *The Origins of Totalitarianism* (Orlando: Harcourt, 1968) 325, 257. Tzvetan Todorov also excludes Mussolini's Fascism from his discussion of totalitarianism. See Tzvetan Todorov, *Hope and Memory: Lessons from the Twentieth Century*. Trans. David Bellos (Princeton: Princeton University Press, 2003). Nonetheless the actual term totalitarian came into being to describe Mussolini's unique, as many thought, form of dictatorship.
6. Shaw himself appends the term to the subtitles of *The Apple Cart, Too True to Be Good* (1931), and *Geneva* (1938).

7. Alan Chappelow, *Shaw—"The Chucker-Out": A Biographical Exposition and Critique* (New York: AMS Press, 1969) 327.
8. This line of thinking continued to preoccupy Shaw for the remainder of his life, and in 1944 he wrote that we

   > must then make up our minds to persecution up to an uncertain point as being a necessary function of government. It is unhesitating when a country advanced in civilization has to govern a less advanced one... Our Liberal friends of India... sometimes talk as if our duty to India is to cease all persecution and establish freedom of thought, speech, worship and education there. In truth, the persecutions are our only excuse for being in India at all.

   Bernard Shaw, *Everybody's Political What's What?* (New York: Dodd, Mead & Company, 1944) 151. Society advances through the innovations of the unbridled spiritual aristocracy, whom no law or code of ethics can be allowed to impose on. The dull idealists and lazy philistines who cannot be counted on to cooperate in evolution's advance are subject, however, to the full rigor of the law; and may even be executed at the whim of one of these elites if he feels the recalcitrant citizen is a drag on the advance of civilization.
9. Irving Howe, "Bernard Shaw's Anti-Capitalism." *New International*, vol. 14 no. 1, January 1948. http://www.marxists.org/history/etol/writers/howe/1948/01/shaw.htm.
10. *Bernard Shaw and Fascism* (Kensington: The Favil Press, 1928) 20. Everything summarized above, and much more, can be found in the first twenty-two pages of the text. This old volume from 1928 is a collection of letters on Mussolini by and to Shaw. The debate on Mussolini actually began with a series of letters between Shaw and the socialist politician Friedrich Adler. Adler initially wrote Shaw after reading an article by Shaw in the *Daily News* that went under the title "Bernard Shaw and Mussolini: A Defense." Shaw's 2 October letter to Adler is included in the collection of correspondence, but most of the short anthology is letters between Salvemini and Shaw. No editor is listed on the text and so it is not known who decided to collect the letters and publish them, although Salvemini himself later published his correspondence with Shaw in a volume titled *G. B. Shaw e il Fascismo* (1955).
11. George Bernard Shaw, *Cashel Byron's Profession* (Carbondale: Southern Illinois University Press, 1968) 86–8.
12. *Bernard Shaw and Fascism* 7.
13. *Bernard Shaw and Fascism* 4–5.
14. *Bernard Shaw and Fascism* 10.
15. *Bernard Shaw and Fascism* 18.
16. Letter to Augustin Hamon, 20 January 1936, printed in *Bernard Shaw Collected Letters, vol. 4: 1926–1950*. Ed. Dan H. Laurence (New York: Viking Penguin, 1988) 424. The letter says that

    > in the conflict between Danakil savage and civilized Italian you must, as a civilized man, be on the Italian side. Otherwise you find yourself in a position which is fundamentally indefensible... You must not fall back on the old notion that I stand for Italy merely to epater le bourgeois. I have been compelled to think the matter out very carefully by the fact that my wife

is furiously pro-Abyssinian. Nothing but the strongest conviction could induce me to write letters to *The Times* which distress her. But in the face of the scalp hunting North American Indian, the head hunting Dyak, the cannibal Maori, and the testicle hunting Danakil, European civilization must stand solid.

This was written not long after the invasion commenced and while it was still under way. In the preface to *Geneva*, written in 1945, Shaw writes that

> When Mussolini invaded Abyssinia and made it possible for a stranger to travel there without being killed by the native Danakils he was rendering the same service to the world as we had in rendering by the same methods (including poison gas) in the north west provinces of India, and had already completed in Australia, New Zealand, and the Scottish Highlands.
>
> (vol. 5, 642)

17. C.E.M. Joad, *Shaw* (London: Victor Gollancz, 1949) 232.
18. Preface to Sidney and Beatrice Webb's *English Local Government: English Prisons under Local Government* (1921). Reprinted as "Imprisonment (English Local Government by Sidney and Beatrice Webb" in *Prefaces by Bernard Shaw* (London: Constable and Company, 1934) 306.
19. To Friedrich Adler, 14 October 1927 and to Ramsay McDonald, 21 October 1927. In *Bernard Shaw Collected Letters, vol. 4: 1926–1950*. Ed. Dan H. Laurence (New York: Viking Penguin, 1988) 74, 75.
20. Quoted in *Bernard Shaw Collected Letters, vol. 4*: 510.
21. Quoted in *Bernard Shaw Collected Letters, vol. 4*: 510–11.
22. Shaw continually revised the text of *Geneva* to keep pace with dramatic changes in world affairs, thus the allusion to the US incarceration of Japanese-Americans in concentration camps, which of course occurred only after the attack on Pearl Harbor in 1941.
23. One thinks of Victor Klemperer, the German Jewish French professor and memoirist, who was "convinced that German Jews were Germans first and Jews second." Richard J. Evans, *The Third Reich in Power, 1933–1939* (New York: The Penguin Press, 2005) 602.
24. *Bernard Shaw Collected Letters, vol. 4: 1926–1950*: 336.
25. Quoted in *Bernard Shaw Collected Letters, vol. 4*: 643.
26. Quoted in *Bernard Shaw Collected Letters, vol. 4*: 650.
27. Gerard Anthony Pilecki, *Shaw's* Geneva: *A Critical Study of the Evolution of the Text in Relation to Shaw's Political Thought and Dramatic Practice* (London: Moulton & Co., 1965) 131.
28. This is the true joy of life, the being used for a purpose recognized by yourself as a mighty one; the being thoroughly worn out before you are thrown on the scrap heap; the being a force of Nature instead of a feverish selfish little clod of ailments and grievances complaining that the world will not devote itself to making you happy.

    (vol. 3, 510–11)
29. Shaw describes Siegfried as knowing "no law but his own humor" and possessing a "joyous, fearless, conscienceless heroism." Bernard Shaw, *The Perfect*

Wagnerite. Major Critical Essays (London: Penguin Books, 1931) 245, 227. See Chapter 2 for a detailed discussion.
30. Marshall Berman, *All That Is Solid Melts into Air: The Experience of Modernity* (New York: Simon & Schuster, 1982).
31. Richard J. Evans, *The Third Reich in Power, 1933–1939* (New York: The Penguin Press, 2005) 323.
32. Evans 372.
33. Robert Conquest tells how Stalin valued children informing on their parents but privately he was contemptuous of such children. See Robert Conquest, *Stalin: Breaker of Nations* (New York: Penguin Books, 1991) 11.
34. *Bernard Shaw Collected Letters, vol. 4*: 458.
35. Robert Conquest, *The Great Terror: A Reassessment* (New York: Oxford University Press, 1990) 38.
36. For Shaw the greatest sin was waste, not inhumanity. His well-known vegetarianism and opposition to vivisection were matters of hygiene and, especially, an aversion to waste, according to his secretary Blanche Patch:

> While...his objection to carnivorous diet was partly aesthetic and partly hygienic, it was mainly because it involved "an unnecessary waste of the labour of masses of mankind in the nurture and slaughter of cattle, poultry and fish for human food"; or, as he told an earlier disciple, the mischief lay in the waste of human energy in breeding and rearing and slaughtering millions of animals daily, a process which involved an appalling slavery of men to these creatures. Far from showing any sympathy for "these creatures", he almost blamed them for the trouble they gave in being slaughtered. Shaw was not sentimental about animals. His loathing for vivisection was a hygienic loathing.

Blanche Patch, *Thirty Years with G.B.S.* (New York: Dodd, Mead & Company, 1951) 268.
37. Hannah Arendt, *Eichmann in Jerusalem: A Report on the Banality of Evil* (New York: Penguin Books, 1963) 106.
38. Arendt, *Eichmann in Jerusalem* 105.
39. Geoffrey G. Field, *Evangelist of Race: The Germanic Vision of Houston Stewart Chamberlain* (New York: Columbia University Press, 1981) 464.
40. Field 464.
41. Shaw, *Fabian News* 1911, quoted in Field 464.
42. Field 464.
43. Field 464.
44. Ronald Bryden, "The Sorrows of Superwoman: An Essay on *The Millionairess*." *Shaw and His Contemporaries: Four Plays.* Ed. Denis Johnston (Oakville: Mosaic Press, 2001) 78.
45. Bryden 78.
46. *Bernard Shaw Collected Letters, vol. 4*: 602.
47. Bernard Shaw, "The Lysenko Muddle." Originally published January 1949 in the *Labour Monthly.* http://www.marxists.org/reference/archive/shaw/works/lysenko.
48. Shaw, "The Lysenko Muddle."
49. *Bernard Shaw Collected Letters, vol. 4*: 271.
50. *Bernard Shaw Collected Letters, vol. 4*: 273.

51. *Bernard Shaw Collected Letters, vol. 4*: 294. Shaw goes on to say why Marx, in his opinion, was wrong about Russia not being right for a communist revolution. He writes approvingly of Lenin's slaughtering syndicalist factory workers who were unable to operate the factories after they seized them. Shaw remarks that Lenin had instructed the peasants to take the land from the landlords, killing them if necessary, and this was successful; but it did not work in the factories, and after Lenin had the syndicalists shot he brought back the old bosses, provisionally, until Communist organization was ready to take over.
52. *Bernard Shaw Collected Letters, vol. 4*: 269. The emphasis is Shaw's. We might also note here that Bukharin had also said of Stalin that he "changes his theories according to the need he has of getting rid of somebody at such-and-such a moment." Quoted in Conquest, *The Great Terror* 17.
53. Quoted in Robert Conquest, *Stalin: Breaker of Nations* 165.
54. Patch 91.
55. Their names would seem to suggest Russian terms; Pra inevitably calling to mind *pravda* (meaning "truth," but also the name of the chief Soviet propaganda organ) and Prola calling to mind proletarian (but also prolific).
56. Arnold Silver, *Bernard Shaw: The Darker Side* (Stanford: Stanford University Press,1982) 27–51.
57. Patch 230.
58. Paul A. Hummert, *Bernard Shaw's Marxian Romance* (Lincoln: University of Nebraska Press, 1973) 177.
59. Conquest, *The Great Terror* 466.

6 George Bernard Shaw 1856–1950, Utopian to the End: *Farfetched Fables*

1. See Blanche Patch, *Thirty Years with G.B.S.* (New York: Dodd, Mead & Company, 1951) 260–61.
2. Patch 245.
3. From *The Times*, 5 December 1947. Quoted in Alan Chappelow, *Shaw—"The Chucker-Out": A Biographical Exposition and Critique* (New York: AMS Press, 1969) 19. The italics are mine.
4. Chappelow 19.
5. Chappelow 18. Shaw had many of these postcards printed in advance with prepared answers on a great many topics that he was likely to receive multiple inquiries. Obviously Shaw did not have time to answer all his letters, and this was a polite way of dealing with the massive amount of letters he received.
6. Also from the 1947 letter to *The Times* and quoted in Chappelow 21.
7. In fact Shaw had a printed postcard designed for inquiries about his vegetarianism, stating that his "objection to carnivorous diet is partly aesthetic, partly hygienic, mainly as involving an unnecessary waste of the labor of masses of mankind in the nurture and slaughter of cattle, poultry, and fish for human food." Quoted in Chappelow 15–16.
8. George Bernard Shaw, "Are We Bolshevists?" *Labour Leader*, 24 April 1919. Quoted in Chappelow 235. For some reason Chappelow does not put

226 Notes

quotation marks around Shaw's words, but I have verified the quote and the words are indeed Shaw's own.
9. Chappelow 169–70.
10. For a very interesting analysis of Plato as playwright and father of the modern drama of ideas, see the recent book by Martin Puchner, *The Drama of Ideas: Platonic Provocations in Theatre and Philosophy* (New York: Oxford University Press, 2010).
11. Quoted in Chappelow 395. The italics are mine.
12. Karl Popper, *The Open Society and Its Enemies*, vol. 1: *The Spell of Plato* (Princeton: Princeton University Press, 1962) 155.
13. Popper 200.
14. Bernard Shaw, "Sixty Years of Fabianism." *Fabian Essays: Jubilee Edition*. Ed. Bernard Shaw (London: George Allen & Unwin, 1948) 230.
15. From an unpublished draft article now in the British Museum, entitled "Advanced Socialism for Intelligent People"; quoted in Chappelow 343.
16. Shaw, "Sixty Years of Fabianism" 229. This quote is actually a reference to the Fabian elite, but can clearly be applied to the Soviet elite as well. For how Shaw calculated that the director class, the upper ten percent of the population, should get exactly eleven percent more income than everyone else, see Chappelow 279.
17. From the July 1941 issue of *Labour Monthly*, quoted in Chappelow 314. The italics are Chappelow's.
18. Chappelow 338. On the same page Chappelow says that in 1933 in *Nash's Magazine* Shaw wrote that "for many years he had said that what democracy needed was a trustworthy anthropometric machine for the selection of qualified rulers." And in 1918 Shaw had written in the Workers' Educational Association Education Year Book that

> We seem far from the day when persons classed by natural capacity as distinguished from acquirements will be disqualified or conscripted for public work according to their degree; when Class A1 will be compelled on incorruptible evidence to select representative peers to undertake the highest duties of the State, and Class Z17, however self-assertive and noisily popular, will be absolutely debarred from voting at elections, contesting Parliamentary seats, or running newspapers.
> Quoted in Chappelow 339.

19. G.K. Chesterton and Bernard Shaw, *Do We Agree? A Debate between G.K. Chesterton & Bernard Shaw with Hillaire Belloc in the Chair* (Oxford: Kempt Hall Press, 1928) 25.
20. Michael Holroyd, *Bernard Shaw*, Volume 3, *The Lure of Fantasy 1918–1951* (New York: Random House, 1991) 483.
21. For an interesting take on Shaw's possible Hegelianism see Robert Whitman, *Shaw and the Play of Ideas* (Ithaca: Cornell University Press, 1977). Whitman contends that Shaw was a Hegelian whose understanding of Hegel's philosophy came either through his own reading (although Shaw never mentions reading Hegel) or his friendship with the Hegel scholar Belfort Bax (or both).

Epilogue

1. Gary Saul Morson, "*Uncle Vanya* as Prosaic Metadrama." *Modern Critical Views: Anton Chekhov*. Ed. Harold Bloom (Philadelphia: Chelsea House Publishers, 1999) 221.
2. Stephen Koch, *Double Lives: Stalin, Willi Munzenberg, and the Seduction of the Intellectuals* (New York: Enigma Books, 1994, 1995, 2004) 164.
3. Koch 166.
4. Koch 28, 30.
5. Tzvetan Todorov, *Hope and Memory: Lessons from the Twentieth Century*. Trans. David Bellos (Princeton: Princeton University Press, 2003) 148.
6. Todorov 148.
7. Todorov 149.
8. Lawrence Switzky, "Shaw among the Modernists." *SHAW: The Annual of Bernard Shaw Studies Volume Thirty-One*. Ed. Michel Pharand (University Park: The Pennsylvania State University Press, 2011) 135.
9. Switzky 140, 143.
10. Roger Griffin, *Modernism and Fascism: The Sense of a Beginning under Mussolini and Hitler* (Basingstoke: Palgrave Macmillan, 2007) 4.
11. Andreas Huyssen, *After the Great Divide: Modernism, Mass Culture, Postmodernism* (Bloomington: Indiana University Press, 1986) 4.
12. Modris Eksteins, *Rites of Spring: The Great War and the Birth of the Modern Age* (Boston: Mariner Books, 2000) 300–31.
13. Martin Puchner, *Poetry of the Revolution: Marx, Manifestos, and the Avant-Gardes* (Princeton: Princeton University Press, 2006) 110.
14. Quoted in Alastair Hamilton, *The Appeal of Fascism: A Study of Intellectuals and Fascism 1919–1945* (New York: The Macmillan Company, 1971) footnote 2, 284.
15. Robert O. Paxton, *The Anatomy of Fascism* (New York: Vintage Books, 2004) 149.
16. Conor Cruise O'Brien, "Passion and Cunning." *Passion and Cunning and Other Essays* (London: Weidenfeld and Nicolson, 1988) 11.
17. O'Brien 40–41.
18. O'Brien 45.
19. W.B. Yeats, *Autobiographies* (London: The Macmillan Company, 1973) 283.
20. The words are former NASA scientist Alexander Bolonkin, quoted in Derrick Jensen and George Draffan, *Welcome to the Machine: Science, Surveillance, and the Culture of Control* (White River Junction: Chelsea Green Publishing, 2004) 63–69.
21. Herman Melville, *Moby Dick; or, the Whale* (Chicago: Encyclopedia Britannica, Inc., 1952) 137.

Bibliography

Anderson, Perry. "Modernism and Revolution." *Marxism and the Interpretation of Culture*. Ed. Cary Nelson and Lawrence Grossberg. Urbana: University of Illinois Press, 1988.
Arendt, Hannah. *Eichmann in Jerusalem: A Report on the Banality of Evil*. New York: Penguin Books, 1963.
———. *The Origins of Totalitarianism*. Orlando: Harcourt, Inc., 1968.
Arnold, Matthew. *Culture and Anarchy*. Ed. Samuel Lipman. New Haven: Yale University Press, 1994.
Baker, Stuart E. *Bernard Shaw's Remarkable Religion: A Faith that Fits the Facts*. Gainesville: University Press of Florida, 2002.
Barzun, Jacques. *Darwin, Marx, Wagner: Critique of a Heritage*. Garden City: Doubleday Anchor Books, 1941.
Bauman, Zygmunt. *Modernity and the Holocaust*. Cambridge: Polity Press, 1989.
Bellamy, Edward. *Looking Backward: 2000–1887*. New York: Signet Classics of the New American Library, 1960.
Bentley, Eric. *Bernard Shaw*. New York: New Directions Publishing Corporation, 1947, 1957.
———. *The Cult of the Superman: A Study of the Idea of Heroism in Carlyle and Nietzsche, with Notes on Other Hero-Worshippers of Modern Times*. London: Robert Hale Limited, 1947.
———. *The Playwright as Thinker: A Study of Drama in Modern Times*. Cleveland: The World Publishing Company, 1955.
Berman, Marshall. *All That Is Solid Melts into Air: The Experience of Modernity*. New York: Simon & Schuster, 1982.
Biddiss, Michael D. *The Age of the Masses: Ideas and Society in Europe since 1870*. New York: Harper Colophon Books, 1977.
Blick, Robin. *The Seeds of Evil: Lenin and the Origins of Bolshevik Elitism*. London: Steyne Publications, 1995.
Brustein, Robert. *The Theatre of Revolt: Studies in Modern Drama from Ibsen to Genet*. Chicago: Ivan R. Dee, Inc., 1991.
Bryden, Ronald. "The Sorrows of Superwoman: An Essay on *The Millionairess*." *Shaw and His Contemporaries: Four Plays*. Ed. Denis Johnston. Oakville: Mosaic Press, 2001.
Buber, Martin. *Tales of the Hasidim: Book One, the Early Masters*. New York: Schocken Books, 1947.
Bulwer-Lytton, Edward. *The Coming Race*. Peterborough: Broadview Press, 2002.
Burrow, J.W. *The Crisis of Reason: European Thought, 1848–1914*. New Haven: Yale University Press, 2000.
Butler, Samuel. *Erewhon*. London: Penguin Classics, 1970.
Camus, Albert. *The Rebel: An Essay on Man in Revolt*. Trans. Anthony Bower. New York: Vintage, 1991.

Carlyle, Thomas. *On Heroes, Hero-Worship, and the Heroic in History*. London: Oxford University Press, 1904.
Carpenter, Charles A. *Bernard Shaw and the Art of Destroying Ideals: The Early Plays*. Madison: The University of Wisconsin Press, 1969.
Chappelow, Alan. *Shaw—"The Chucker-Out": A Biographical Exposition and Critique*. New York: AMS Press, 1969.
Chekhov, Anton. "The House with the Mezzanine." *The Image of Chekhov*. Trans. Robert Payne. New York: Alfred A. Knopf, 1967.
Chesterton, G.K. *George Bernard Shaw*. New York: Hill and Wang, 1956.
———. *Heretics*. London: The Bodley Head, 1960.
Chesterton, G.K and Bernard Shaw. *Do We Agree? A Debate between G.K. Chesterton & Bernard Shaw with Hillaire Belloc in the Chair*. Oxford: Kempt Hall Press, 1928.
Cohn, Norman. *The Pursuit of the Millennium: Revolutionary Millenarians and Mystical Anarchists of the Middle Ages*. New York: Barnes and Noble, 2009.
Colbourne, Maurice. *The Real Bernard Shaw*. New York: The Dodd, Mead & Company, 1940.
Conquest, Robert. *The Great Terror: A Reassessment*. New York: Oxford University Press, 1990.
———. *Stalin: Breaker of Nations*. New York: Penguin Books, 1991.
Crick, Bernard. "Shaw as Political Thinker, or the Dogs that did not Bark." *SHAW: The Annual of Bernard Shaw Studies Volume Eleven: Shaw and Politics*. Ed. T.F. Evans. University Park: The Pennsylvania State University Press, 1991.
Crompton, Louis. *Shaw the Dramatist*. Lincoln: University of Nebraska Press, 1969.
Davis, Tracy C. *George Bernard Shaw and the Socialist Theatre*. Westport: Greenwood Press, 1994.
Dervin, Daniel. *Bernard Shaw: A Psychological Study*. Cranbury and London: Associated University Presses, 1975.
Djilas, Milovan. *Fall of the New Class*. Trans. John Loud. New York: Alfred A. Knopf, 1998.
Dostoyevsky, Fyodor. *Crime and Punishment*. Trans. David McDuff. London: Penguin Classics, 1996.
Eagleton, Terry. *On Evil*. New Haven: Yale University Press, 2010.
———. *Reason, Faith, and Revolution: Reflections on the God Debate*. New Haven: Yale University Press, 2009.
Eksteins, Modris. *Rites of Spring: The Great War and the Birth of the Modern Age*. Boston: Mariner Books, 2000.
Eiseley, Loren. *Darwin's Century: Evolution and the Men Who Discovered It*. New York: Barnes & Noble, 2009.
Evans, Richard J. *The Third Reich in Power, 1933–1939*. New York: The Penguin Press, 2005.
Evans, T.E. (Editor). *Shaw: The Critical Heritage*. London: Routledge & Kegan Paul, 1976.
Field, Geoffrey G. *Evangelist of Race: The Germanic Vision of Houston Stewart Chamberlain*. New York: Columbia University Press, 1981.
Frye, Northrop. "Varieties of Literary Utopia." Sir Thomas More, *Utopia: A Norton Critical Edition*. Trans. and Ed. Robert M. Adams. New York: Norton, 1992.

Gassner, John "Bernard Shaw and the Making of the Modern Mind." *Bernard Shaw's Plays.* Ed. Warren Sylvester Smith. New York: Norton, 1970.
Gatch, Katherine Haynes. "The Last Plays of Bernard Shaw: Dialectic and Despair." *English Stage Comedy.* Ed. W.K. Wimsatt, Jr. New York: AMS Press, 1964.
Gibbs, A.M. *The Art and Mind of Shaw: Essays in Criticism.* Basingstoke: Palgrave Macmillan, 1983.
———. *Bernard Shaw: A Life.* Gainesville: University Press of Florida, 2005.
Greenleaf, W.H. *The British Political Tradition, Volume Two: The Ideological Heritage.* London: Methuen, 1983.
Grene, Nicholas. *Bernard Shaw: A Critical View.* Basingstoke: The Macmillan Press, 1984.
Griffin, Roger. *Modernism and Fascism: The Sense of a Beginning under Mussolini and Hitler.* Basingstoke: Palgrave Macmillan, 2007.
Griffith, Gareth. *Socialism and Superior Brains: The Political Thought of Bernard Shaw.* London: Routledge, 1993.
Gutman, Robert W. *Richard Wagner: The Man, His Mind, and His Music.* New York: Harcourt Brace Jovanovich, 1974.
Hamilton, Alastair. *The Appeal of Fascism: A Study of Intellectuals and Fascism 1919–1945.* New York: The Macmillan Company, 1971.
Hedges, Chris. *When Atheism Becomes Religion: America's New Fundamentalists.* New York: Free Press, 2008.
Hobsbawm, Eric. *The Age of Empire 1875–1914.* New York: Vintage Books, 1989.
———. *The Age of Extremes 1914–1989.* New York: Vintage Books, 1994.
Holroyd, Michael. *Bernard Shaw,* four volumes. New York: Random House, 1988, 1989, 1991, 1992.
Howe, Irving. "Bernard Shaw's Anti-Capitalism." *New International,* vol. 14 no. 1, January 1948. http://www.marxists.org/history/etol/writers/howe/1948/01/shaw.htm.
Hulse, James W. *Revolutionists in London: A Study of Five Unorthodox Socialists.* Oxford: Clarendon Press, 1970.
Hummert, Paul A. *Bernard Shaw's Marxian Romance.* Lincoln: University of Nebraska Press, 1973.
Huyssen, Andreas. *After the Great Divide: Modernism, Mass Culture, Postmodernism.* Bloomington: Indiana University Press, 1986.
Ibsen, Henrik. *An Enemy of the People. Four Great Plays By Henrik Ibsen.* Trans. R. Farquharson Sharp. New York: Bantam Books, 1959.
———. *Emperor and Galilean. The Plays of Ibsen.* Trans. Michael Meyer. New York: Washington Square Press, 1986.
Innes, Christopher. "Utopian Apocalypses: Shaw, War, and H.G. Wells." *SHAW: The Annual of Bernard Shaw Studies Volume Twenty-Three.* Ed. Gale K. Larson and Maryann K. Crawford. University Park: The Pennsylvania State University Press, 2003.
Irvine, William. *The Universe of G.B.S.* New York: McGraw-Hill, 1949.
Jacoby, Russell. *Picture Imperfect: Utopian Thought for an Anti-Utopian Age.* New York: Columbia University Press, 2005.
Jameson, Frederic. *Archaeologies of the Future: The Desire Called Utopia and Other Science Fictions.* London: Verso, 2005.

Jensen, Derrick and George Draffan. *Welcome to the Machine: Science, Surveillance, and the Culture of Control.* White River Junction: Chelsea Green Publishing, 2004.

Joad, C.E.M. *Shaw.* London: Victor Gollancz, 1949.

Kaye, Julian B. *Bernard Shaw and the Nineteenth-Century Tradition.* Norman: University of Oklahoma Press, 1958.

Klaic, Dragan. *The Plot of the Future: Utopia and Dystopia in Modern Drama.* Ann Arbor: The University of Michigan Press, 1991.

Koch, Stephen. *Double Lives: Stalin, Willi Munzenberg, and the Seduction of the Intellectuals.* New York: Enigma Books, 1994, 1995, 2004.

Lawrence, D.H. *Psychoanalysis and the Unconscious and Fantasia of the Unconscious.* Ed. Bruce Steele. Cambridge: Cambridge University Press, 2004.

Lifton, Robert Jay. *The Nazi Doctors: Medical Killing and the Psychology of Genocide.* New York: Basic Books, 2000.

Linehan, Thomas. *British Fascism 1918-39: Parties, Ideology and Culture.* Manchester: Manchester University Press, 2000.

———. "The British Union of Fascists as a Totalitarian Movement and Political Religion." *Fascism, Totalitarianism and Political Religion.* Ed. Roger Griffin. London: Routledge, 2005.

MacCarthy, Desmond. *The Court Theatre 1904-1907: A Commentary and Criticism.* London: A.H. Bullen, 1907.

MacKenzie, Norman and Jeanne. *The Fabians.* New York: Simon and Schuster, 1977.

Malik, Halib C. *Receiving Soren Kierkegaard: The Early Impact and Transmission of His Thought.* Washington D.C.: The Catholic University of America Press, 1997.

Marcel, Gabriel. *Man Against Mass Society.* Trans. G.S. Fraser. Chicago: Henry Regnery Company, 1965.

Marcuse, Herbert. "The End of Utopia." *Five Lectures: Psychoanalysis, Politics, and Utopia.* Trans. Jeremy J. Shapiro and Shierry M. Weber. Boston: Beacon Press, 1970.

Meisel, Martin. *Shaw and the Nineteenth Century Theater.* Princeton: Princeton University Press, 1963.

———. "Shaw and Revolution: The Politics of the Plays." *Shaw: Seven Critical Essays.* Ed. Norman Rosenblood. Toronto: University of Toronto Press, 1971.

Melville, Herman. *Moby Dick; or, the Whale.* Chicago: Encyclopedia Britannica, Inc., 1952.

Meyer, Michael. *Ibsen: A Biography.* Garden City: Doubleday & Company, 1971.

Mills, Carl H. "Shaw's Superman: A Reexamination." *Critical Essays on George Bernard Shaw.* Ed. Elsie B. Adams. New York: G.K. Hall & Co., 1991.

Morgan, Margery M. *The Shavian Playground: An Exploration of the Art of George Bernard Shaw.* London: Methuen, 1972.

Morris, William. *News from Nowhere. News from Nowhere and Other Writings.* London: Penguin Books, 1993.

Morson, Gary Saul. "*Uncle Vanya* as Prosaic Metadrama." *Modern Critical Views: Anton Chekhov.* Ed. Harold Bloom. Philadelphia: Chelsea House Publishers, 1999.

Mosse, George L. *Toward the Final Solution: A History of European Racism.* New York: Howard Fertig, 1978.

Mumford, Lewis. *The Story of Utopias*. New York: The Viking Press, 1962.
Murdoch, Iris. *The Fire and the Sun: Why Plato Banished the Artists*. Clarendon-Oxford: Oxford University Press, 1977.
Nathan, David. "Failure of an Elderly Gentleman: Shaw and the Jews." *SHAW: The Annual of Bernard Shaw Studies Volume Eleven: Shaw and Politics*. Ed. T.F. Evans. University Park: The Pennsylvania State University Press, 1991.
Nethercot, Arthur H. *Men and Supermen: The Shavian Portrait Gallery*. Cambridge: Harvard University Press, 1954.
Nietzsche, Friedrich. *Beyond Good and Evil: Prelude to a Philosophy of the Future*. Trans. R.J. Hollingdale. London: Penguin Books, 1973.
———. *Ecce Homo. Basic Writings of Nietzsche*. Trans. Walter Kaufmann. New York: Modern Library Edition, 2000.
———. *Thus Spoke Zarathustra*. Trans. R.J. Hollingdale. Middlesex: Penguin Books, 1961.
———. *The Will to Power*. Trans. Walter Kaufman and R.J. Hollingdale. New York: Vintage Books, 1968.
O'Brien, Conor Cruise. "Passion and Cunning." *Passion and Cunning and Other Essays*. London: Weidenfeld and Nicolson, 1988.
Ortega y Gasset, Jose. *The Revolt of the Masses*. Trans. Anonymous. New York: Norton, 1932.
Orwell, George. *The Collected Essays, Journalism & Letters: As I Please, Vol. 3*. Ed. Sonia Orwell and Ian Angus. Boston: Nonpareil Books, 2000.
Pappas, Nickolas. *Plato and the Republic*. London: Routledge, 1995.
Patch, Blanche. *Thirty Years with G.B.S.* New York: Dodd, Mead & Company, 1951.
Paxton, Robert O. *The Anatomy of Fascism*. New York: Vintage Books, 2004.
Pearson, Hesketh. *Bernard Shaw*. London: Macdonald and Jane's, 1975.
Pearson, Karl. *The Life, Letters and Labours of Francis Galton, Volume III: Correlation, Personal Identification and Eugenics*. London: Cambridge University Press, 1930.
Peters, Sally. *Bernard Shaw: The Ascent of the Superman*. New Haven: Yale University Press, 1996.
Pfaff, William. *The Bullet's Song: Romantic Violence and Utopia*. New York: Simon and Schuster, 2004.
Pilecki, Gerard Anthony. *Shaw's Geneva: A Critical Study of the Evolution of the Text in Relation to Shaw's Political Thought and Dramatic Practice*. London: Moulton & Co., 1965.
Plato. *The Republic*. Trans. Benjamin Jowett. Mineola: Dover Publications, Inc., 2000.
Popper, Karl. *The Open Society and Its Enemies, vol. 1: The Spell of Plato*. Princeton: Princeton University Press, 1962.
———. *The Open Society and Its Enemies, vol. 2: The High Tide of Prophesy: Hegel, Marx, and the Aftermath*. Princeton: Princeton University Press, 1962.
Postlewait, Thomas. *Prophet of the New Drama: William Archer and the Ibsen Campaign*. Westport: Greenwood Press, 1986.
Puchner, Martin. *The Drama of Ideas: Platonic Provocations in Theater and Philosophy*. New York: Oxford University Press, 2010.
———. *Poetry of the Revolution: Marx, Manifestos, and the Avant-Gardes*. Princeton: Princeton University Press, 2006.

Rather, L.J. *The Dream of Self-Destruction: Wagner's Ring and the Modern World.* Baton Rouge: Louisiana State University Press, 1979.

Rattray, R.F. *Bernard Shaw: A Chronicle.* London: The Leagrave Press, 1951.

Rothstein, Edward. "Utopia and It's Discontents." *Visions of Utopia.* Oxford: Oxford University Press, 2003.

Reich, Wilhelm. *The Mass Psychology of Fascism.* New York: Farrar, Straus, and Giroux, 1970.

Ryan, Vanessa L. "Shaw and the Death of the Intellectual." *SHAW: The Annual of Bernard Shaw Studies, Volume Twenty-Seven.* University Park: The Pennsylvania State University Press, 2007.

Sage, Steven F. *Ibsen and Hitler: The Playwright, the Plagiarist, and the Plot for the Third Reich.* New York: Carroll and Graff Publishers, 2006.

Salvemini, Gaetano and Bernard Shaw. *Bernard Shaw and Fascism.* Kensington: The Favil Press, 1928.

Segal, Erich. *The Death of Comedy.* Cambridge: Harvard University Press, 2001.

Semmel, Bernard. *Imperialism and Social Reform: English Social-Imperial Thought, 1895–1914.* Cambridge: Harvard University Press, 1960.

Shaw, George Bernard. *The Adventures of the Black Girl in Her Search for God. The Portable Bernard Shaw.* Ed. Stanley Weintraub. New York: The Viking Press, 1977.

———. *Bernard Shaw Collected Letters: 1898–1910.* Ed. Dan H. Laurence. New York: Dodd, Mead & Company, 1972.

———. *Bernard Shaw Collected Letters, vol. 4: 1926–1950.* Ed. Dan H. Laurence. New York: Viking Penguin, 1988.

———. *Bernard Shaw: Complete Plays with Prefaces*, six volumes. New York: Dodd, Mead & Company, 1963.

———. *Cashel Byron's Profession.* Carbondale: Southern Illinois University Press, 1968.

———. *Everybody's Political What's What?* New York: Dodd, Mead & Company, 1944.

———. "The Illusions of Socialism." *Selected Non-Dramatic Writings of Bernard Shaw.* Ed. Dan H. Laurence. Boston: Houghton Mifflin Company, 1965.

———. *The Intelligent Woman's Guide to Socialism, Capitalism, Sovietism and Fascism.* New York: Random House, 1955.

———. "Imprisonment (English Local Government by Sidney and Beatrice Webb." *Prefaces by Bernard Shaw.* London: Constable and Company, 1934.

———. "Killing for Sport." *Prefaces by Bernard Shaw.* London: Constable and Company, 1934.

———. *The Perfect Wagnerite. Major Critical Essays.* London: Penguin Books, 1931.

———. *Platform and Pulpit.* Ed. Dan H. Laurence. New York: Hill and Wang, 1961.

———. *The Quintessence of Ibsenism.* New York: Dover, 1994.

———. *The Rationalization of Russia.* Ed. Harry M. Geduld. Bloomington: Indiana University Press, 1964.

———. "Sixty Years of Fabianism." *Fabian Essays: Jubilee Edition.* Ed. Bernard Shaw. London: George Allen & Unwin, 1948.

———. "The Transition to Social Democracy." *Fabian Essays: Jubilee Edition.* Ed. Bernard Shaw. London: George Allen & Unwin, 1948.

———. *What Shaw Really Wrote about the War.* Ed. J.L. Wisenthal and Daniel O'Leary. Gainesville: University Press of Florida, 2006.

Silver, Arnold. *Bernard Shaw: The Darker Side.* Stanford: Stanford University Press 1982.
Smith, Denis Mack. *Mussolini.* New York: Alfred A. Knopf, 1982.
Smith, Warren Sylvester. *Bishop of Everywhere: Bernard Shaw and the Life Force.* University Park: The Pennsylvania State University Press, 1982.
———. *The London Heretics: 1870–1914.* New York: Dodd, Mead & Company, 1968.
Solzhenitsyn, Alexander. *The Gulag Archipelago: An Experiment in Literary Investigation, Volume One.* Trans. Thomas P. Whitney. New York: Harper Perennial Modern Classics, 2007.
Stone, Dan. *Breeding Superman: Nietzsche, Race and Eugenics in Edwardian and Interwar Britain.* Liverpool: Liverpool University Press, 2002.
Switzky, Lawrence. "Shaw among the Modernists." *SHAW: The Annual of Bernard Shaw Studies Volume Thirty-One.* Ed. Michel Pharand. University Park: The Pennsylvania State University Press, 2011.
Tillich, Paul. *The Eternal Now.* New York: Charles Scribner's Sons, 1963.
Thatcher, David S. *Nietzsche in England: 1890–1914.* Toronto: University of Toronto Press, 1970.
Todorov, Tzvetan. *Hope and Memory: Lessons from the Twentieth Century.* Trans. David Bellos. Princeton: Princeton University Press, 2003.
Tunney, Jay R. *The Prizefighter and the Playwright: Gene Tunney and Bernard Shaw.* Richmond Hill: Firefly Books, 2010.
Turco Jr., Alfred. *Shaw's Moral Vision: The Self and Salvation.* Ithaca: Cornell University Press, 1976.
Valency, Maurice. *The Cart and the Trumpet: The Plays of George Bernard Shaw.* New York: Oxford University Press, 1973.
Webb, Beatrice. *The Diary of Beatrice Webb,* four volumes. Ed. Norman and Jeanne MacKenzie. London: Virago Press, 1985.
Weintraub, Rodelle. "Bernard Shaw's Fantasy Island: *Simpleton of the Unexpected Isles.*"*SHAW: The Annual of Bernard Shaw Studies Volume Seventeen: Shaw and Science Fiction.* Ed. Milton T. Wolf. University Park: The Pennsylvania State University Press, 1997.
Weintraub, Stanley. "GBS and the Despots." *Times Literary Supplement,* 22 August 2011. http://www.the-tls.co.uk/tls/public/article707002.ece.
———. *Journey to Heartbreak: The Crucible Years of Bernard Shaw 1914–1918.* New York: Weybright and Talley, 1971.
Wells, H.G. *A Modern Utopia.* Lincoln: University of Nebraska Press, 1967.
West, Alick. *George Bernard Shaw: "A Good Man Fallen Among Fabians."* London: Lawrence & Wishart, 1950.
Whitman, Robert F. *Shaw and the Play of Ideas.* Ithaca: Cornell University Press, 1977.
Wilson, Edmond. "Bernard Shaw at Eighty." *The Triple Thinkers: Ten Essays on Literature.* New York: Harcourt, Brace and Company, 1938.
Winsten, Stephen. *Jesting Apostle: The Life of Bernard Shaw.* Boston: EP Dutton, 1957.
———. *Salt and His Circle.* London: Hutchinson, 1951.
Wisenthal, J.L. *The Marriage of Contraries: Bernard Shaw's Middle Plays.* Cambridge: Harvard University Press, 1974.

―――. "Shaw and Ibsen." *Shaw and Ibsen: Bernard Shaw's* The Quintessence of Ibsenism *and Other Related Writings*. Toronto: The University of Toronto Press, 1979.

―――. "Shaw's Utopias." *SHAW: The Annual of Bernard Shaw Studies Volume Seventeen: Shaw and Science Fiction*. Ed. Milton T. Wolf. University Park: The Pennsylvania State University Press, 1997.

―――. "The Underside of Undershaft: A Wagnerian Motif in *Major Barbara*." *The Shaw Review XV*, May 1972.

Wolfe, Willard. *From Radicalism to Socialism: Men and Ideas in the Formation of Fabian Socialist Doctrines, 1881–1889*. New Haven: Yale University Press, 1975.

Yeats, W.B. *Autobiographies*. London: The Macmillan Company, 1973.

Index

Adler, Friedrich, 145, 147, 150
The Adventures of the Black Girl in Her Search for God (1933), 61
age of faith, 27, 30
age of reason, 27, 30, 56
All That is Solid Melts into Air: The Experience of Modernity (Berman), 160
Anderson, Perry, 210
Androcles and the Lion (1912), 17, 111, 113, 154
Annajanska, the Bolshevik Empress (1917), 60
anthropometric device, Shaw's idea, 187, 199
Antoine, Andre, 46
The Apple Cart (1929), 60, 143–4, 221
Archaeologies of the Future: The Desire Called Utopia and Other Science Fictions (Jameson), 8, 114
Archer, William, 46, 71
Arendt, Hannah, 9, 20, 164–5, 208, 221, 224
Arms and the Man (Shaw), 206
Arnold, Matthew, 35–6, 211
artificial selection, 72, 74
Astor, Nancy Witcher Langhorne Astor, Viscountess, 1, 151
Astor, Waldorf Astor, Viscount, 1
atheism, Shaw's profession of, 29
Auschwitz, gas used at, 14
avant-garde movement, British, 204–5

Back to Methuselah (1921), 5, 8, 14–15, 63, 67, 80, 111
   "As Far as Thought can Reach," 132–8
   central idea, 116
   chief difference between *Man and Superman* and, 117
   contents, 114
   extension of human life in, 117
   "The Gospel of the Brothers Barnabas," 122–4
   "In the Beginning," 118–22
   omission from surveys of utopian literature, 114
   OUP publication, 139
   as part of the new Bible, 116
   preface, 112, 116–17, 193
   purpose, 115
   religious intent, 114
   subtitle, 116
   tension between hope and despair in, 117
   "The Thing Happens," 124–6
   "Tragedy of an Elderly Gentleman," 126–31
   world view, 117–18
Bacon, Francis, 114
Baker, Stuart E., 218
barbarians (Arnold), 36
Bauman, Zygmunt, 61–2, 64, 213
Beckett, Samuel, 68
Beerbohm, Max, 71
Beethoven, 141, 194
Bellamy, Edward, 8, 115, 197
Belloc, Hilaire, 17
Bentham, Jeremy, 27
Bentley, Eric, 11–12, 76, 105, 209, 211, 215
Bergson, Henri-Louis, 6, 168
Berman, Marshall, 160, 210, 224
Bernard Shaw (Bentley), 11–12
Bernard Shaw: A Chronicle (Rattray), 83
Bernard Shaw: The Darker Side (Silver), 4
biocracy, 14
Blake, William, 72, 76
Blick, Robin, 37, 211
Bloom, Harold, 8
blueprint utopias, 7, 195, 198
Boer War, 69

Book of Genesis, Shaw's attempt to write a new, 67
Brand (Ibsen), 42–3
Brandt, Karl, 14–15, 17
Breeding Superman (Stone), 83
British Socialist Revival, 2
British Union of Fascists (BUF), 43
Brustein, Robert, 121, 141–2, 219, 221
Bryden, Ronald, 166, 224
Buber, Martin, 19, 53, 213
Buber-Neumann, Margarette, 150
Buchenwald, 202
Budberg, Moura, 202
buffoon, Shaw's presentation of himself as, 71, 76–7
Bulwer-Lytton, Edward, 115, 116, 191, 219
Bunyan, John, 76, 194, 216
Buoyant Billions (1948), analysis, 198–200
Burrow, J.W., 73, 214
Butler, Samuel, 6, 28, 115, 168

Caesar and Cleopatra (1898), 60, 63–4
Campanella, Tommaso, 114
Camus, Albert, 30–1, 34, 210
Candida (1895), 67
Candide (Voltaire), 181
capitalism, 8–9, 28, 57, 109, 115, 146–7
Captain Brassbound's Conversion (1899), 66
career path, Shaw's, 26, 46, 66, 75
Carlyle, Thomas, 6, 81
Carpenter, Charles A., 27, 210, 211
Cashel Byron's Profession (1883), 146
castor oil, torturing of dissidents with, 145
catastrophism, in Shaw's writing, 112–13
celibacy, Shaw's, 80
Chamberlain, Houston Stewart, 165
chaos
 influence of the threat of on Shaw, 115
 Shaw's fear of, 81
Chappelow, Alan, 6, 10, 12, 15, 22, 209, 210, 222, 225, 226
Cheka, 172

Chekhov, Anton, 201, 202
Chesterton, Cecil, 120
Chesterton, G.K., 25, 226
childhood, Shaw's, 2–3
Christianity, 16, 36, 41–2, 81–2, 104, 154
City of the Sun (Campanella), 114
class, Shaw and Arnold's delineations, 36
The Cloud of Unknowing (anon), 196
the Coefficients, 70, 86, 91
Colbourne, Maurice, 6, 22, 210, 215, 216, 218
The Coming Race (Bulwer-Lytton), 115, 116
"Common Sense about the War" (1914), 113
communism
 Hulse on, 37
 Soviet Communism, 7, 9, 43, 167–8, 203
communist anarchism, 37
The Communist Manifesto (Marx/Engels), 160, 205
Comte, Auguste, 3
concentration camps
 Holroyd on Shaw's attitude to Hitler and the, 199
 in post-war French literature, 202–3
 Shaw's rationalization, 164
Conquest, Robert, 224, 225
creation, as theme in Shaw's plays, 151
creative destruction, 76–7, 82, 98, 103, 121, 150, 190
 Nietzsche's rhetoric, 82
Creative Evolution, 4, 6–9, 13, 17, 66–7, 69, 71, 73, 75, 77, 79, 81, 83, 85, 87, 89, 91, 93, 95, 97, 99, 101–3, 105, 107, 109, 114, 116, 121, 123–5, 138–9, 148, 157, 166, 182–3, 185, 189–90, 193, 199
 as expressed in *Back to Methuselah* and *Farfetched Fables*, 193
 Shaw's advocacy, 9
 Shaw's attempt to work out a synthesis of his religion of with his political socialism, 67–8

238 *Index*

Creative Evolution – *continued*
  Shaw's contention, 4
  as twentieth-century religion, 116
Crick, Bernard, 105, 217
Crime and Punishment (Dostoyevsky), 65
Crompton, Louis, 214, 217, 219
cultural segregation, 38
Culture and Anarchy (Arnold), 35

Daily Telegraph, 27
Darwin, Charles, 73, 116
Das Kapital (Marx), 153
Das Rheingold (Wagner), 49
death penalty, Stalin's extension to children, 172
death, Shaw's, 185
Der Ring des Nibelungen (Wagner), 47, 52
  banning of, 55
  interpreting the end of, 59–60
  moral perspective, 54
  outline, 48–9
  sexual element, 57–8
  Shaw's analysis, 50, 54–6
  Wagner's message in, 60
Der Untergang (Downfall) (Hirschbiegel), 85
Dervin, Daniel, 62, 213
despots, Shaw's identification with, 151
The Devil's Disciple (1897), 66
dialectical drama, Platonic beginnings, 75
dialectical materialism, 168
Dickens, Charles, 76
Die Walküre (Wagner), 49
Dietrichson, Lorentz, 40
discussion drama, 67, 95, 111, 123
disorder, 80, 95, 98, 110, 114, 146, 199
The Doctor's Dilemma (1906), 111
A Doll's House (Ibsen), 46
domination, Shaw's desire for, 48
Don Juan in Hell
  analysis, 74–86
  Court Theatre performance, 71
  description of Shaw's psychological transformation in, 78–9
  origins, 67

  setting, 74
  as Shavio-Socratic dialogue, 75–6
Dostoyevsky, Fyodor Mikhailovich, 65
Downfall (Hirschbiegel), 85
Draffan, George, 227
Dresden uprising, 47
duty
  repudiation of, 34
  Shaw on the evolution of the conception, 33–4
dystopia, 7, 43, 110, 118, 178
Dzerzhinsky, Felix, 17, 106, 164, 181, 217

Ecce Homo (Nietzsche), 82
Eckhart, Meister, 196
economics, Shaw's preoccupation with, 26
Eichmann in Jerusalem: A Report on the Banality of Evil (Arendt), 164
Einstein, Albert, 164
Eiseley, Loren, 220
Eksteins, Modris, 8, 205
Eliot, T.S., 201
Emperor and Galilean (Ibsen), 10, 40–2, 47
end of history, 34
An Enemy of the People (Ibsen), 40–2, 51, 63
epiphanic modernists, 68–9
equal incomes doctrine, 196–7
Erewhon (Butler), 115
Ervine, St. John, 119–20
Ethiopia, Shaw's support of Mussolini's invasion, 147
eugenics
  basis of Shaw's advocacy, 3
  class and, 73–4
  and equal incomes doctrine, 197
  etymology, 73
  European vogue for, 41
  as form of social modernism, 81
  in Ibsen, 41
  Shaw's *Sociological Papers* entry, 73
  Shaw's vision, 50–1; *see also* Shaw's eugenic utopianism
  in *The Simpleton*, 174–5
  and social Darwinism, 51
  as theme of *Man and Superman*, 72

Europe, Ortega y Gasset's observation on the population of, 39
the European dictators, Shaw's admiration, 17, 43, 60, 82, 154
euthanasia, 13–14, 17, 131
  Shaw's recommendations, 12
  see also extermination
Evans, Edith, 166
Evans, Richard J., 161, 170, 223, 224
Evans, T.E., 209, 212, 217
Everybody's Political What's What? (1944), 60
evil, Shaw's view, 28
extermination, 3, 6, 11, 14, 31–2, 39, 52, 84, 105, 116, 118, 131, 140, 142, 155, 169–70, 176, 181–3, 196–7
  of the unfit or recalcitrant, 6, 10, 31–2, 39, 52, 84, 105, 116, 118, 140, 155, 170, 182, 196–7

Fabian model state, Stalin's Russia as near facsimile, 203
Fabian News, 165
Fabian Society, 26–7, 39, 69, 107
  crisis within, 69
  reasons for existence, 38
  Shaw joins, 26
Fabianism
  Shaw's disillusionment with, 38
  in Shaw's first plays, 5
Fabianism and the Empire (1900), 69
Fanny's First Play (1911), 111
Farfetched Fables (1950), 5, 7, 14–15, 80, 154, 185, 188, 192–3, 198, 207
  analysis, 185, 194
  Back to Methuselah comparison, 186
  preface, 192–3
  themes, 185–6
fascism
  part of the attraction of, 85
  Pilecki on Shaw's advocation of, 155
fascist dictum, 85
fascist leanings, of Shaw's contemporaries, 201, 203
Faust (Goethe), 159, 160
Field, Geoffrey G., 165, 224
Final Solution, comparison with Shaw's eugenic utopianism, 13–15

First World War, 6–7, 16, 83–4, 89, 99, 111, 113, 144, 148, 152, 201
forced labour camps, 150
forsytism, 31
Foundations of the Nineteenth Century (Chamberlain), 165
France, post-war atmosphere among the intelligentsia, 202
Freud, Sigmund, 57
Frye, Northrop, 115, 219
future society, *Quintessence*'s concerns with, 27

Galton, Francis, 73–4, 81
garden, Shaw's fondness for the metaphor of society as, 64
gas chambers, 10, 15, 52, 107
Geneva (1938), 60
  analysis, 148–56
  characters, 147
  continual revisions, 184
  hint of disapproval toward Soviet Communism, 167
  preface, 61, 154, 158, 164
  racist joke in, 152
  on social control, 16
  Soviet Communism in, 168, 183
George, Henry, 75
Getting Married (1908), 111, 174
Ghosts (Ibsen), 46
Gibbs, A.M., 209, 210
Gide, Andre, 202
Gobineau, Arthur, Comte de, 54
The God that Failed (ed. Crossman), 202
Goethe, Johann Wolfgang von, 23, 141, 159, 160, 194
golden rule, 43, 45
Gotterdammerung (Wagner), 50
gradualism, Shaw's acceptance of over catastrophism, 112
Granville-Barker, Harley, 67
Great Purge, 172
Grein, Jacob, 5, 46
Grene, Nicholas, 94, 95, 97, 105, 216, 217, 218
Griffin, Roger, 68–9, 81–2, 138, 160, 204, 215, 221
Griffith, Gareth, 217, 218

Gulag system, 186, 202
Gulliver's Travels (Swift), 115
Gutman, Robert W., 54, 212

Hamon, Augustin, 169–70
Hamsun, Knut, 203
Harris, Frank, 78
Heartbreak House (1919), 60, 89, 111–13, 142, 166, 182
Heartbreak House, Great Catherine and Playlets of the War (1919), 113
Hedda Gabler (Ibsen), 44
Himmler, Heinrich, 14, 164–5
Hippolytus (Euripides), 67
Hirschbiegel, Oliver, 85
Hitler, Adolf
    Holroyd on Shaw's attitude to, 199
    Ibsen's influence, 41–3
    Mackenzie King on, 143
    Shaw's admiration and approval, 15, 61, 138, 153
    Shaw's support for, 62
    Stalin's admiration for, 202
Hitler (Lewis), 203
The Hitler Cult (Lewis), 203
Hogarth, William, 76
the Holocaust, 30, 61, 186
Holroyd, Michael, 71, 143, 199, 209, 210, 214, 221, 226
Horton, R.F., 83
"The House with the Mezzanine" (Chekhov), 201
Howe, Irving, 101, 145, 217, 222
Hulse, James W., 37, 211
human conscience, as impediment to a new world order, 60
human rights, 7, 172
human society, tripartite model, 37
human suffering, Pilecki on Shaw's lack of concern for, 155
humanitarianism, Shaw as symbol of, 195
humanity, Wagner's depiction of the lower orders of, 50
Hummert, Paul A., 183, 225
Huyssen, Andreas, 57, 204, 213
hypnotism, Ibsen's interest, 44

Ibsen, Henrik
    Brand, 42–3
    A Doll's House, 46
    Emperor and Galilean, 10, 40–2, 47
    An Enemy of the People, 40–2, 51, 63
    eugenics in the works of, 41
    Ghosts, 46
    Hedda Gabler, 44
    impact on Shaw's career, 46
    influence on Hitler, 41–3
    influence on Shaw's utopian thinking, 40
    interest in hypnotism, 44
    legitimacy doubts, 47
    The Master Builder, 42, 44
    message of plays, 27
    Peer Gynt, 43
    press treatment, 26–7
    Shaw on the prophetic message of, 27
    Shaw's opinion, 26
    takes London by storm, 25
    use of the term idealist, 34
    The Wild Duck, 31
    see also *The Quintessence of Ibsenism* (1891)
Ibsen and Hitler: The Playwright, the Plagiarist, and the Plot for the Third Reich (Sage), 41
ideal city, Plato's, 3, 77, 132
ideal society, Shaw's, 3
idealist, Ibsen's use of the term, 34
idealists, 29, 34, 36–7, 48, 50, 55, 64, 118, 126, 140
idleness, Shaw's belief, 10
Il Duce, 146
    see also Mussolini, Benito
immortality, 15, 118–19, 123, 137–8
In Good King Charles's Golden Days (1939), 60
Independent Theatre Society, 46
individual will, Shaw's glorification, 28
Inge, William Ralph, 169
the Inquisition, 171–2
insensitiveness, Shaw's streak of, 83–5
instrumental rationality, Shaw's approval, 52

The Intelligent Woman's Guide to Socialism and Capitalism (1928), 60, 143
intelligentsia, 47, 201–2
intolerance, possible explanation for Shaw's, 145

Jacoby, Russell, 7, 208
James, Henry, 109
Jameson, Frederic, 8, 114, 138–9, 219, 221
Jews, Shaw on Hitler's treatment of, 152–3, 164
Joad, C.E.M., 6, 149, 208, 223
John Bull's Other Island (1904), 67, 125, 182
  analysis, 86–95
  Keegan's great line from, 77
  setting, 68
Journey to Heartbreak (Weintraub), 113
"Joy Riding at the Front" (1917), 113–14
Joyce, James, 64
Judaism, 16
Judeophobia, Shaw speculates on the derivation of Hitler's, 165
judicial liquidation, 187
  see also extermination
Junkerism, Shaw's assignation of blame for the war to, 113

Kantsaywhere (Galton), 81
Kierkegaard, Søren, 42
King, William Lyon Mackenzie, 143
Kirov, Sergei, 172
Koch, Stephen, 17, 209, 210
Koestler, Arthur, 202
Koselleck, Reinhart, 81
Koudachova, Maria Pavlova, 202
Krynin, Dmitry, 1, 171
kulaks, 171

Labour Monthly, 168
Lamarck, Jean-Baptiste, 168
The Land of Heart's Desire (Yeats), 206
Langner, Lawrence, 152
LaSalle, Ferdinand, 33, 193
Lawrence, D.H., 111, 118, 218
Lee, George Vandeleur, 47

legitimacy, doubts about Shaw's, 47
Lenin, Vladimir Ilyich, 17, 82, 112
  Shaw's admiration for, 37
Les Jours de notre mort (Rousset), 202
Les Jours de notre vie (Sartre/Merleau-Ponty), 203
the lethal chamber, 10–12, 106–7, 109, 125
Lewis, Wyndham, 201, 203
Life Force
  in *Buoyant Billions*, 198
  depiction of in *Saint Joan*, 143
  development, 29
  in *Major Barbara*, 72
  in *Man and Superman*, 72
  origins, 28
  Shaw's belief, 148
  Shaw's faith in, 199
  transcendent nature, 31
  Warren Sylvester Smith on Shaw and the, 80
Lifton, Robert Jay, 4, 14, 208, 209
liquidation, 91, 121, 140, 167, 170, 196
  see also extermination
Litvinov, Maxim, 1
Looking Backward (Bellamy), 8, 115, 197
Louis XVI, Camus on the killing of, 30
love, Shaw's view, 57–9
Luck or Cunning? (Butler), 28
"The Lysenko Muddle" (1949), 168
Lysenko, Trofim, 168

MacDonald, Ramsay, 69, 182
MacKenzie, Norman and Jeanne, 208, 210, 213
magnum opus, Shaw's, 8, 114
Major Barbara (1905), 57, 60, 82, 84, 87–8, 113, 125–6, 147, 156–8, 180, 197
  analysis, 95–110
  and equal incomes doctrine, 197
  preface, 106, 110
  setting, 68
  Vedrenne-Barker production, 67
Malik, Halib C., 42, 212

Man and Superman (1903), 28–9, 45, 51, 82
  analysis of act three, 74–86; see also *Don Juan in Hell*
  background, 69
  Beerbohm's reaction, 71
  Butler's influence, 28
  characterizations, 69–71
  Platonic aspects, 71
  preface, 66, 69, 72, 76, 158
  Shaw's expectations for the performance of, 67
  subtitle, 71
  theme, 72
  Vedrenne-Barker production, 67
Man of Destiny (1895), 60
Manchester Guardian, 145
Mann, Thomas, 57
Mansfield, Richard, 66
Marat/Sade (Weiss), 75
Marcel, Gabriel, 13, 209
Marcuse, Herbert, 158
Marinetti, F.T., 205
marriage, 34, 36, 46, 66, 71, 111, 176, 197
  disquisition on the institution of, 111
  Shaw's, 63, 66
Marriage of Heaven and Hell (Blake), 72
The Master Builder (Ibsen), 42, 44
masters of reality, 77
Matteoti, Giacomo, 145
"Maxims for Revolutionists," 45, 66, 84, 94, 187, 200
McDonald, Ramsay, 150
megalomania, Valency on Shaw's, 78
Mein Kampf (Hitler), Shaw's letters praising, 153–4
Meisel, Martin, 112–13, 208, 219
Melville, Herman, 207, 227
Merleau-Ponty, Maurice, 203
Meyer, Michael, 40
Michelangelo, 141
Mill, John Stuart, 24
millenarianism, in Shaw's writing, 10

The Millionairess (1935), 60
  analysis, 156–66
  as fascist allegory, 157, 162, 166
  preface, 165
Mills, Carl H., 215
Misalliance (1910), 111, 113, 207
A Modern Utopia (Wells), 8
Modernism and Fascism: The Sense of a Beginning under Mussolini and Hitler (Griffin), 68, 160
A Modest Proposal (Swift), 12
monogamy, 34
More, Thomas, 7–8, 114, 115
"More Common Sense about the War" (1915), 113
Morgan, Margery M., 12, 24, 134, 139, 140, 210, 217, 220, 221
Morris, William, 8, 197, 198, 211, 218
Morson, Gary Saul, 201
Mosley, Oswald, 17, 43
Mozart, 141, 194
Murdoch, Iris, 220
Murray, Gilbert, 67, 95, 99, 100, 217
Mussolini, Benito, 17, 85
  background, 146
  resemblance to Andrew Undershaft, 147
  Shaw's admiration for, 138
  Shaw's idealised picture of, 147
  Shaw's mania for, 60
  Shaw/Salvemini debate on, *see* Shaw/Salvemini debate on Mussolini
  Shaw's support for, 6
  takes power in Italy, 144
mystics, 13, 29, 83, 87, 189, 196

Nathan, David, 209, 212, 213
National Ideals and Race Regeneration (Horton), 83
National Socialism/Socialists, 7, 9, 15–16, 43, 85, 161
Nazi genocide, Shaw's refusal to believe in the, 61
Nazis/Nazism, 13–14, 16–17, 28, 52, 82, 107, 150, 161, 185, 202, 205
New Atlantis (Bacon), 114

New Economic Policy, Lenin's switch
  to, 112
the New Protestantism, 55
New Statesman, 113
News from Nowhere (Morris), 8
Nietzsche, Friedrich, 125, 154
  confirmation of Shaw's worldview,
    5–6
  creative destruction rhetoric, 82
  fear of the future, 29–30
  feelings on socialism, 81
  on he who fights with monsters, 64
  influence on Shaw, 81
Nietzschean superman, 98, 121
Night of the Long Knives, 163

O'Brien, Conor Cruise, 206
O'Duffy, Eoin, 206
O'Leary, Daniel, 113
omnipotence, Shaw's craving for, 4, 207
On the Rocks (1933), 52, 60, 144
  logical progression to *The Simpleton*, 182
  preface, 11, 32, 41, 182
  subject, 182
optimism, Shaw's, 57
The Origin of Species (Darwin), 74
Ortega y Gasset, Jose, 39, 44, 211, 212
Orwell, George, 4, 84, 140, 208
The Other Kingdom (Rousset), 202
outsider, Shaw views himself as an, 47

Paine, Tom, 33
Pall Mall Gazette, 26, 28
Pankhurst, Emmeline, 69
Pappas, Nickolas, 215
parasites, extermination of, *see* extermination
party of national efficiency, Webb's intentions to form, 70
"Passion and Cunning: An Essay on the Politics of W.B. Yeats" (O'Brien), 206
Passos, John Dos, 202
Patch, Blanche, 6, 12, 172, 179, 188, 209, 220, 224, 225
Paxton, Robert O., 206, 227

Payne-Townsend, Charlotte, 63, 66
  see also Shaw, Charlotte
Pearson, Hesketh, 6, 12, 120, 214, 219
Pearson, Karl, 74
peasants, Soviet extermination, 39, 171
Peer Gynt (Ibsen), 43
The Perfect Wagnerite (1898), 5, 51, 63, 65, 82, 84
  desire for power in, 15
  eugenicism in, 52
  first edition, 11
  later addition, 57
  pivotal nature of composition year
    in Shaw's life, 63
  relationship to *The Quintessence*, 46–7
  seeds for Shaw's ends justifying the
    means policy, 170
  "Siegfried as Protestant" chapter, 56
  similarities with *Quintessence*, 59
pessimistic plays, 86, 89, 113, 157, 182
Peters, Sally, 208, 209, 213
philistines, 29, 34–7, 39, 48, 50–2, 62–4, 89, 118, 126
philosopher kings, 36, 77, 99–100, 181, 195
philosophical vitalism, 51
phonetic alphabet, 185
Pilecki, Gerard Anthony, 155, 223
Pilgrim's Progress (Bunyan), 44, 115
Plato
  anecdote about, 75
  and dialectical drama's beginnings, 75
  influence on Shaw, 195
  model of a properly ordered society, 64
  Popper's critique, 4, 195
  and Shaw's understanding of "realist," 36
Platonic dialogue, key to a successful, 76
Plato's ideal city, 3, 77, 132
Plato's *Republic*, 7–8, 36, 62–3, 68, 75, 100, 115, 118, 120
Plays for Puritans (1900), 66
Plays Unpleasant (1898), 46

political treatises, Shaw's, 60
Popper, Karl, 3–4, 7–8, 195, 208, 226
Popular Front, 202
Pound, Ezra, 201, 203
"Preface on Bosses," 156, 163, 166–7
programmatic modernism/modernists, 68–9, 82, 138
progressivism, convergence of conservativism and, 206
Prometheus Unbound (Shelley), 58
Protestant spirit, Shaw's admiration, 44
Puchner, Martin, 205, 226, 227
Pygmalion (1913), 21–3, 111, 113, 134

The Quintessence of Ibsenism (1891), 5
  as address to the Fabian Society, 39
  Chapter 1 – The Two Pioneers, 33–4
  Chapter 2 – Ideals and Idealists, 34, 36–7
  Chapter 4 – The Plays, 40–3
  chapters, 33
  concerns with future society, 27
  desire for power in, 15
  first publication, 25
  humble beginnings, 25
  as indicator of Shaw's thinking, 26
  intimation of the dawning of a new era, 28
  preface remarks, 25
  religious intention in, 29
  seeds for Shaw's ends justifying the means policy, 170
  Shaw's anticipation of the totalitarian age in, 9
  Shaw's description of the quintessence of Ibsenism, 45
  Sidney Webb's concerns, 28

Rather, L.J., 51, 57, 212
The Rationalization of Russia (1964), 11, 31, 37, 84, 169–70
Rattray, R.F., 6, 78, 83, 215, 216
realist, Platonic perspective, 36
The Rebel (Camus), 30
recalcitrant, extermination of, *see* extermination
regicide, Camus' view, 30

Reich, Wilhelm, 158
Reinhardt, Max, 143
religion, Shaw's view, 16, 29
Religion of Humanity, Comte's, 3
religious belief, decline of, 29
The Republic, 7–8, 36, 62–3, 68, 75, 100, 115, 118, 120
The Revolt of the Masses (Ortega y Gasset), 39
revolutionary outlook, Shaw's, 30–1
revolutionary violence, Meisel on, 113
revolutionary writer, Shaw's view of himself as a, 2, 47
The Revolutionist's Handbook (1903), 66, 70–1, 80, 86, 103, 134, 187, 205
Revolutionists in London (Hulse), 37
Ring cycle, Wagner's, see *Der Ring des Nibelungen* (Wagner)
Rolland, Romain, 202
Rothstein, Edward, 8
Rousset, David, 202–3
rulers/ruling, Shaw's obsession with, 60
Russell, Bertrand, 70
Russia, Shaw on, 31–2

sadism, Shaw's streak of, 4, 84
Sage, Steven F., 8, 41–2
"Sainthood for Millionaires" (Watson), 105
Saint Joan (1924), 60, 143–5
Saint Simon, Henri de, 204
Salvemini, Gaetano, 145, 146, 147, 158, 163, 222
  see also Shaw/Salvemini debate on Mussolini
The Sanity of Art (1908), 47
Sardoodledom, 75
Sartre, Jean-Paul, 203
Schopenhauer, Arthur, 52, 57, 59
scientism, Shaw's, 10
Second World War, 85, 186, 191
  Shaw's prediction, 113
secular justice, 30
Seeds of Evil: Lenin and the Origin of Bolshevik Elitism (Blick), 37
self-selecting elite, 37
self-worship, 33–4

Semmel, Bernard, 214
Shakespeare, William, 76
The Shavian Playground (Morgan), 12
Shaw, Charlotte, 17, 63, 147
 see also Payne-Townsend, Charlotte
Shaw, George Bernard (GBS), 71
 admiration for Lenin, Mussolini, Hitler, and Stalin, 17, 43, 60, 82, 154
 career path, 26, 46, 66, 75
 death, 185
 early years, 2
 first three plays, 46
 ideal society, 3
 influences, 28
 instant fame, 67
 legitimacy doubts, 47
 lifestyle, 80
 marriage, 63, 66
 need to manage other people's affairs, 78
 optimism, 57
 phases in playwriting period, 144
 series of physical misfortunes, 63
 support for Britain's Boer War involvement, 69
 teenage psychological experience, 78–9
 upbringing, 80
 utopian thinking, *see* Shaw's utopian thinking
 view of himself, 2, 47
"Shaw and Revolution: The Politics of the Plays" (Meisel), 112
Shaw on Stalin and the USSR, 167–82
 The Simpleton of the Unexpected Isles, 173–82
Shaw/Salvemini debate on Mussolini, 145–66
Shaw's eugenic utopianism, comparison with Germany's Final Solution, 13–15
Shaw's utopian thinking
 Ibsen and, 40
 impact of the war, 112
 influence of Plato's *Republic* on, 115
 persistence, 84, 185
 resemblance to Plato or Comte, 3
 timespan of utopia, 114

Shaw—"The Chucker-Out" (Chappelow), 11
Shelley, Percy Bysshe, 26, 58
The Shewing-up of Blanco Posnet (1909), 111
shirkers, extermination of, 196
 see also extermination
Short Stories, Scraps, and Shavings (1932), 114
Siegfried (Wagner), 49
Silver, Arnold, 4, 84, 140, 176, 178, 209, 225
The Simpleton of the Unexpected Isles (1934)
 analysis, 173–82
 characters, 174, 176
 disappearances, 180
 final lines, 181
 logical progression from *On the Rocks* to, 182
 Margery Morgan's analysis, 12
 preface, 11, 32, 171
 presentation of Shaw's enthusiasm for the Russian experiment, 170
 raison d'etre for the creation of, 172
 setting and theme, 170
 Silver's reading, 176, 178
 structure and outline, 173
 themes, 171, 175
"Sixty Years of Fabianism," 38
Smith, Denis Mack, 216
Smith, Warren Sylvester, 80, 215, 217
social Darwinism, 51, 54, 96, 117, 129
socialism
 Mussolini and, 146
 need for the state to convert to, 36
 Nietzsche's feelings on, 81
 Shaw's view, 2, 10
society, Shaw's impatience with the entire structure of, 36
society as a garden, Shaw's fondness for the metaphor, 64
Socrates, 75–7, 86, 107, 194–5
Solzhenitsyn, Alexander, 150
South Africa, 169
Soviet Communism, 7, 9, 43, 167–8, 203
Soviet-German Non-aggression Pact, 202

Soviet Politburo, 52, 196
Soviet Union
  Bellamy's vision of the American future looking like an ideological glorification of the, 8
  extermination of peasants, 39, 171
  Shaw's faith in the, 84
  Shaw's trip, 1, 167
Stalin, Joseph
  admiration for Hitler, 202
  criticisms of, 202
  First Five Year Plan, 1
  liquidation policies, 12
  pact with Hitler, 15
  purges, 30, 163
  Shaw's admiration for, 15, 138
  Shaw's meeting with, 167
  Shaw's support for, 37, 62, 105, 145, 201
  the state, Shaw and Arnold's belief in the importance of, 36
state regulation, Shaw on, 16
Steffens, Lincoln, 202
Stewart, Donald Ogden, 202
Stone, Dan, 83, 107, 215, 218
Stoppard, Tom, 75
Strindberg, August, 44
superman
  appeal to Shaw of Siegfried as, 50
  Beatrice Webb on Shaw's faith in the, 6
  resemblance of Shaw's idealised Mussolini to, 147
  source of Shaw's ideal of the, 81
  theory development, 38
Swift, Jonathan, 105, 115, 134, 154
Switzky, Lawrence, 204, 205

Tales of the Hasidim (Buber), 53
Thatcher, David S., 210
Theatre Libre, 46
The Theatre of Revolt (Brustein), 141
Thus Spoke Zarathustra (Nietzsche), 81
Tillich, Paul, 65, 214
The Times, 187
Todorov, Tzvetan, 10, 19, 208, 210, 221
Todt, Fritz, 161
Too True to Be Good (1931), 144, 167
totalitarian ideology, Todorov on the birth of, 10
totalitarian movements, Arendt on, 9
Travesties (Stoppard), 75
Trebitsch, Siegfried, 15–16, 61, 81, 153
trickle-down theory, 65
tripartite model, Shaw's, 27, 35, 37, 48
Turati, Augusto, 85
Turco, Alfred, Jr., 38, 214
Turner, Reginald, 76

unfit, extermination of, *see* extermination
unity, Shaw's preoccupation with, 76, 83, 87, 90, 178
An Unsocial Socialist, 26
the unworthy, Shaw's typology, 13–14
upbringing, Shaw's, 80
utopia(s)
  blueprint vs iconoclastic, 7; *see also* blueprint utopias
  Frye's description, 115
  H.G. Wells' description, 114
  late-nineteenth century resurgence, 115
  Shaw's tendency to follow up pessimistic plays with, 182
  Shaw's vision, 8–9; *see also* Shaw's eugenic utopianism
Utopia (More), 8, 114–15
utopian literature
  Back to Methuselah's omission from surveys of, 114
  historical perspective, 7–8
utopian plays, 5, 7, 10, 14, 119–20, 170, 186
utopian political structures, Shaw's support for, 7
utopian social engineering, Popper's argument, 7
utopian thinking, Shaw's, *see* Shaw's utopian thinking

utopian works, late-nineteenth century prevalence, 115
utopian writers, Shaw's omission from the canon, 8

Valency, Maurice, 78, 90, 208, 215, 218
Vedrenne, John, 67
Vedrenne-Barker productions, 67
vegetarianism, Shaw's, 80
Vorticists, 204

Wagner, Richard, 45, 46–7
Das Rheingold, 49
Die Walküre, 49
Ring cycle, see *Der Ring des Nibelungen* (Wagner)
Siegfried, 49
"The Work of Art of the Future," 51
see also *The Perfect Wagnerite* (1898)
Walters, Ensor, 169
war, Shaw's simultaneous hatred of and fascination with, 113
war reparations, exacted on Germany, 113
Watson, Barbara Bellow, 105, 217
Waugh, Evelyn, 206
Webb, Beatrice, 6, 14, 15, 17, 18, 28, 29, 44, 52, 60, 61, 69, 70, 72, 91, 106, 107, 110, 154, 171, 185, 208, 209, 210, 213, 214, 219, 223

Webb, Sidney, 28–9, 44, 69–70, 91, 107, 171, 185
Weintraub, Stanley, 113, 208, 213, 219
Weiss, Peter, 75
Welfare State, 185
Wells, H.G., 8, 70, 114, 167, 181, 194, 202, 214, 219
Western intellectuals, Comintern's level of control over, 202
What Shaw Really Wrote About the War (Wisenthal/O'Leary), 113
Whitman, Robert F., 226
Widowers' Houses (1892), 5, 26, 46
The Wild Duck (Ibsen), 31
will to justice, 30
will to power, 30, 44, 104, 148
Wilson, Edmond, 111, 184
Winter, Ella, 202
Wisenthal, J.L., 113, 217, 219
Wordsworth, William, 141
"The Work of Art of the Future" (Wagner), 51
The World as Will and Representation (Schopenhauer), 28
world-bettering, Shaw's passion for, 27, 198
world's will, 9, 16, 28–9, 35, 52, 148, 199

Yeats, W.B., 67, 201, 206, 227

Printed and bound in the United States of America